NUTTALL

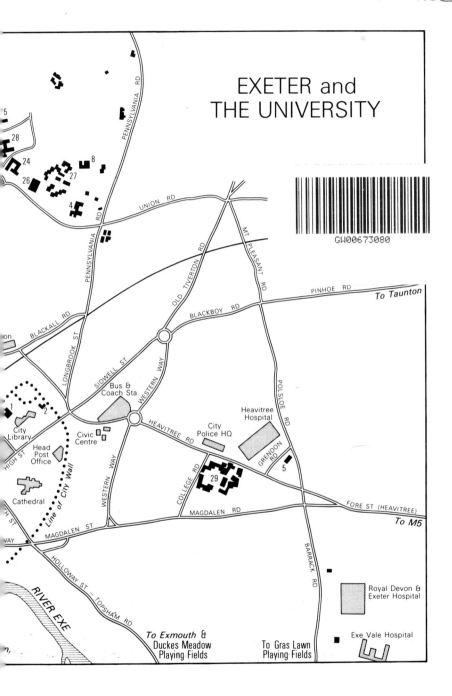

EXETER and
THE UNIVERSITY

GW00673080

THE UNIVERSITY OF EXETER:
A HISTORY

Frontispiece *Reed Hall*

THE UNIVERSITY OF EXETER:
A HISTORY

by

B. W. Clapp

THE UNIVERSITY OF EXETER

1982

First published 1982 by the University of Exeter

© 1982 B. W. Clapp

ISBN 0 85989 133 X

Printed in Devon by ⊕ Underhill (Plymouth) Ltd.

FOREWORD

BY THE VICE-CHANCELLOR

'There has been a crisis of some sort almost every year I have been here and we have emerged safely from them all so far' (1900) — A. W. Clayden, Principal, University College of the South West. (see page 33).

When, in this momentous year for all British universities, I came across the above remark from Principal Clayden, I looked across my lawn to the end of the garden where I see the roofs of the practice rooms of the Department of Music. The house is named 'Clayden'. I shall look towards it with even greater affection in the future. Here, from 1900, is a timely reminder that universities are likely to outlive the aberrations of their Governments, even today; though 'slings and arrows' are too often in the air, wise institutions learn to live with them.

Brian Clapp's *History* is not only timely but fills a very definite gap in our records as I can testify from personal experience. When I was appointed Vice-Chancellor, I naturally wished to read the early history of the Albert Memorial College and the University. It did not prove to be easy. Materials were often sketchy and the different authors varied in their aims and coverage of events. Behind the bare outline one sensed there was probably a mirror-like reflection of the nineteenth century's attitude to education; the zeal and energy of a few far-sighted citizens trying to fire the indifference of the majority. Mr Clapp has certainly given life to this early period of Art School and University College and I am immensely grateful to him for the scholarly acumen with which he has revealed so much about our beginnings.

We now have a fascinating educational record that adds another piece to the national jigsaw of nineteenth and early-twentieth century development, but for those of us with a particular interest in this University, it throws light both on our past and on our present. As with other universities that developed from university colleges, our past is an anchor point. The new university did not feel that it had to 'strive officiously' to create a unique image for itself, for as a college it had already existed for many years and had traditions which it followed and respected. Its primary aim was not to make an individual statement

v

about higher education but to ensure that standards—that sacred word in universities—were maintained. Thus development was within the mould, not outside it. It is, of course, both the strength and the weakness of this kind of university. The detached commentator observes that, though the emerging university follows the tradition of British universities, its individuality is expressed in a combination of many features, few of which are necessarily unique to Exeter, but which together make up a distinctive contribution with its own unmistakable personality. Perhaps in a long-distance race such as creating a university, one lesson is not to set off too quickly—time gives strength.

Again, the University that did evolve after a century of Art School and University College was firmly established in its region with a tradition of support from local residents. This has continued, notably in the work of the Council of the University where lay members have been outstanding in their services. Inevitably the main burden has fallen on our Officers, particularly in the 1970s on the Pro-Chancellor, Mr Kenneth Rowe, and on the Treasurer, the late Mr R. W. Turner, who held office from 1955 to 1979. But so many others have chaired committees and given generously of their time and wisdom that I welcome this opportunity of recording my appreciation of their support and of saying how important it is to the University that it should sustain these ties with its region. Universities are international institutions and this was only too evident when Exeter was host to the Commonwealth Executive Heads Conference in 1973. Some 300 Vice-Chancellors from universities in New Zealand and Australia, Pakistan and India, Africa and Canada enjoyed their residence on our site. The local flavour of the University, particularly as it emerges in the services of our support staff who are local residents, is always appreciated by our visitors, however far they may have travelled.

Town and Gown will always have a lively relationship. They represent different interests and have different outlooks upon life, but both can contribute to each other's well-being. At a time when social life is changing fast, which is one way of saying the future will be different from the present, it is essential for a university to maintain its links with its community. This is especially so for this University, where our geographical position almost requires it of us; our nearest university is eighty miles to the north and our nearest polytechnic is Plymouth, over forty miles to the South West. As national institutions make an increasing contribution to their regions, as I believe is probable, our established local connections will become of greater significance and, pertinently enough for Exeter, will fulfil many of the aspirations of our founding fathers.

Scanning the whole history of the College and University, there is one delightful anomaly on which I like to reflect. The little College on its one acre site in the middle of the City of Exeter was the inspiration of a few eminent Victorians, trying to rouse the enthusiasm and sense of responsibility of their kinsfolk. Often they dragged along with them some reluctant city fathers and always they were short of money and resources. But out of their efforts emerged the gift of the Streatham estate to provide Exeter with one of the outstanding sites of any university in Britain. Its significance cannot be exaggerated. It transformed both the scale and the amenities, giving the University grounds that are characteristic of the abundant arboreal beauty of Devon and doing so without isolating it on a remote hillside. There was even space enough to meet the unforeseen scale of expansion in the post-1945 period on a site where the fringes still touched the City at several points.

It is always a pleasure to observe the sensitivity and professional skill with which the site has been developed, notably by its first architect, Vincent Harris, and then, to a radically modified plan, by Lord Holford. It is not the distinction of any one building but the manner in which they harmonize with their natural surroundings that is such a feature of our estate. The Barbara Hepworth sculpture, *Mother and Child*, is one of her outstanding works but it gains immeasurably from its setting, where it rests beside our buildings though surrounded by undulating lawn and mature trees. It is my dream that one day, I suppose in a distant future, someone standing in the natural architectural beauty of these grounds and looking across the valley to the twin towers of the Cathedral will appreciate that what is now required is an act of imagination of the same order as that which inspired the founders of the Cathedral. I like to think that in the uniqueness of our estate there will arise one architectural jewel, one building of pure poetry, not large in size but rare in quality, that will be an inspiration to all who work here, to all who live in the region, and especially to the artists and craftsmen, the musicians and writers who work in the South West. The School of Art of 1855 — with its much wider connotations than its title would imply today — will then have come home.

I was reminded recently that it would be in keeping with an early tradition of the University if certain reports were dated 26 December. This Foreword may have been started, but was certainly not completed on that day — but so be it.

26 December 1981   *HARRY KAY*

PREFACE

The outlines of the origins and history of the University of Exeter are well known. A detailed account, except for the important period 1920–1924, is for the first time attempted here. It must always be a delicate task to trace the history of a living institution especially when the historian is himself a member of it. He has to temper mercy with candour and if possible to be inoffensively truthful. It is for the reader to judge whether in the present case the author has succeeded in preserving a just balance between potentially competing loyalties.

If he has failed to do this he has only himself to blame. Over the years a good many colleagues have contributed in conversation, sometimes unwittingly, to the store of anecdotes and impressions on which the work is partly based. Preliminary drafts of the text have been widely read, corrected, and subjected to good-tempered but sometimes trenchant criticism. In particular the Vice-Chancellor, Dr Harry Kay, and successive chairmen of Publications Committee, Mr Malcolm Shaw and Professor Ivan Roots, have shrewdly and firmly pointed out many possible improvements. If not all these suggestions have found their way into the final version the fault lies at the door of an obstinate author. For the remaining errors, omissions or lapses of taste he alone is responsible.

Thanks are due to Council and Senate, who kindly granted the author a year's study leave to enable him to complete the manuscript. The Vice-Chancellor, amidst a press of more urgent business, readily agreed to write a foreword. The Deputy Registrar, Mr R. A. Erskine, has discussed the work with the author on several occasions and has read a preliminary draft. His services do not end there. But for him many of the early records of the University might have been lost or destroyed. He has not only arranged for their preservation, but has acted as an informal, but far from amateurish, archivist. Anyone who uses the University's now copious records owes him a substantial debt of gratitude. Mrs B. V. Mennell prepared the text for the printer and saw it through the press with her customary efficiency and enthusiasm. Mr D. F. Batty put his wide knowledge of the university's photographic archives at the author's disposal. Mr F. J. Saunders took some splendid photographs specially for the book and artfully improved some old ones to make them good enough for publication. Mr R. E. J. Fry drew the maps. Several secretaries played a part in deciphering a perplexing manuscript. In particular, Miss J. C. Peters produced a clean copy fit for a printer's eyes. Archivists and librarians from outside as well as inside the University of Exeter have given willing assistance: Mrs M. Rowe and the staff of Devon Record Office; Mrs D. Owen, archivist to the University of Cambridge, and her staff; the staff of the Public Records Office, Kew. The author is grateful to all these colleagues, academic, administrative, technical and secretarial, for their help, forbearance and encouragement.

B. W. Clapp

January 1982   Exeter

CONTENTS

LIST OF PLATES

PART I

FROM ART SCHOOL TO UNIVERSITY COLLEGE

I

ART, SCIENCE AND THE
ALBERT MEMORIAL

The known history of higher education in Exeter begins with the
enthronement of the first Bishop of Exeter in 1050. Bishop Leofric was a
lover of books and at his death in 1072 bequeathed 66 manuscripts or
books to the cathedral chapter as a library for the use of his successors.
Small as the number may sound to an age accustomed to the mass-
production of books, it represented in Leofric's day a substantial
benefaction. His good example inspired others to add to the library and
by the early fourteenth century the Cathedral Library contained some
300 volumes. Like many other book collectors Leofric knew that books
tend to wander from their proper home, and took what precautions he
could. In his copy of the Latin poet Prudentius, for example, he wrote
'Leofric . . . gives this book to his cathedral church, for the relief of his
soul and the use of his successors. If however anyone shall take it away
from thence, let him lie under perpetual malediction.' This particular
book has, in fact, long been in the Bodleian Library, Oxford and many
other medieval books from Exeter have similarly migrated[1] in bland
disregard of Leofric's curse. Despite the periodic loss of books the
Cathedral Library continued to exist and to contribute to the education
of the clergy of the diocese. For the twelfth century there remains only
scattered and tantalising evidence of educational effort in Exeter. It is
probable that the Cathedral had a theological school attached to it by
1160, and possibly much earlier, and at a lower level there is evidence of
a song school (a first school for clerks and choristers) by 1175, and of a
grammar school, probably by 1150 and definitely by 1225. In 1283 it was
laid down that the Chancellor of the Cathedral should lecture in
theology, and this rule was observed for the next half century and in all

1

likelihood until the Reformation. From the fourteenth century there is continuous evidence for schooling in Exeter at various levels of attainment.[2] But the early promise of university education hinted at in the school of theology did not materialise. Though a cathedral city and the seat of county government, frequented by clergy and lawyers, Exeter remained until the fifteenth century a small town, apparently too remote to challenge the claims of equally small but more central places of learning like Oxford and Cambridge. The opportunity had passed. When Oliver Cromwell founded a third English university in 1657, he established it at Durham, not Exeter.*

In early modern times Exeter became a prosperous manufacturing town and port. Its population grew to about 12,000 in 1660[3] and to 17,000 by 1801. It was well-endowed with grammar schools and like all towns of any size attracted enterprising, sometimes desperate, men who set up private schools as a modest way to make a living. Other indications of cultural interests in the population of Exeter were a theatre and from 1807 a Public Select Library. This was a subscription and circulating library which claimed to have the most extensive and valuable collection of books in the West of England. For the 'very moderate charges' of 2s. 6d. or 5s. (12½p or 25p) a year, subscribers gained access to this library, which came to number some 7,000 books.[4] Further evidence of organised intellectual activity in Exeter is furnished by the establishment in 1813 of the Devon and Exeter Institution, whose objects were the promotion of science literature and the arts. The Institution soon came to possess more and, indeed, more valuable books than the Public Select Library. Its promoters hoped to found a museum as well as a library and did make a start, but were frustrated by lack of space. Eventually the Institution settled down as a select reading room and lending library for the clergy, gentry and professional classes of Devon and Exeter. Richard Ford, the writer of a celebrated *Handbook of Spain*, has been perhaps its most famous member. If it never had the scientific distinction of the Literary and Philosophical Society of Manchester or of the Lunar Society of Birmingham, it did at least testify to intellectual awareness among the upper classes in and near Exeter.[5] The Exeter Literary Society, founded a generation later in 1842, did with more modest resources for the citizens of Exeter what the Institution did for the clergy and gentry: it provided a library for its members and a forum

---

*Cromwell's foundation was short-lived. It died with the restoration of the monarchy in 1660.

for the discussion of a wide variety of topics from literature to natural history.

Similar institutions—calling themselves natural history societies, mechanics institutes, literary and philosophical societies, the Athenaeum —were springing up in the early nineteenth century in all towns with any pretension to wealth or culture. Parliament gave one aspect of the movement its blessing in the Free Libraries Act of 1850. This unassuming measure allowed town councils to spend the proceeds of a halfpenny rate on the purchase or rent of land and buildings for library purposes. The legislators appeared to take it for granted that private benefactors would give the books, maps and specimens of art and science with which to fill the libraries. A further act of 1855 raised the limit of expenditure to a penny rate.[6] These Acts of Parliament like the people of the time did not distinguish between library, museum and art gallery; all might co-exist in the one building, as indeed they did and still do in the British Museum. In similar fashion they did not distinguish too nicely in science between theory and technology, or in art between beauty and utility: the same school might provide a course in fine arts as well as in industrial design. Exeter's Albert Memorial Museum and its schools of art and science were in this respect typical of their age.

Government first provided a grant in aid of schools of design (or schools of art as they came to be called) in 1837. The first school opened in Somerset House in that year and others soon followed in the major industrial towns.[7] The young Stafford Northcote, Devon landowner, civil servant, Conservative Member of Parliament and ultimately Chancellor of the Exchequer, had a hand in the administration of the government's grant to schools of design. In 1850 in an address to Exeter Literary Society he urged the necessity for bodies like the Society to be connected with a museum, an art gallery, with schools of art, with drawing classes and music classes and with a really good library.

> We must seriously apply ourselves to remedy the defect which we have noticed in English education, to cultivate the study of the fine arts not as an end in itself, but as an important auxiliary to other branches of learning and never to rest until we have wiped away the reproach which will most justly attach to us if with our materials and our advantages we come behind the other countries of the world, or any country whatsoever, in the article of National Taste.[8]

The first Free Libraries Act had just been passed, and a public meeting in Exeter by a large majority endorsed a proposal that Exeter should adopt the act. When opponents of the scheme demanded a poll of the ratepayers the proposal was rejected overwhelmingly—only one-seventh of the votes cast being in favour of a public library. The ratepayers feared for their pockets more than they feared the devils of drink, socialism and pauperism, which (they were assured) a library would help to exorcise.[9]

For the time being the public library movement in Exeter was dead, but there was encouragement for a school of art. The success of the Great Exhibition of 1851 drew renewed attention to the importance of industrial design and in 1852 a Department of Science and Art was set up in the Board of Trade to promote good design and scientific education, by grant, inspection and a system of examinations. In 1857 the Department of Science and Art was transferred to the care of the Committee of Education of the Privy Council and thence in 1900 to the Board of Education, now known as the Department of Education and Science. The decision to establish a school of art in Exeter was taken in 1854. Sir Stafford Northcote was among the founders and became first President of the School. Unlike a public library a school of art made no call on the ratepayers. It relied on subscriptions from patrons and sympathisers, on the fees paid by pupils and on whatever grant it could earn from the Department of Science and Art. Grants depended on satisfactory attendance by pupils and on examination successes. The School of Art, distant ancestor of the University of Exeter, opened its doors on New Year's Day 1855. It had premises over the Lower Market in Milk Street. Both day and evening tuition was offered, organised in six classes lettered from A to F. The subjects taught ranged from freehand drawing, and practical geometry and perspective, to building construction and machine-drawing. The classes for ladies, mostly the young daughters of well-to-do families living in and around Exeter, were held in the daytime. Substantial fees of a guinea or a guinea and a half were charged since government grants were made only when tuition was afforded to the 'industrial classes'. The latter could attend only in the evening after working hours, and paid 2s a month for tuition in class C, which was the recognised artisans' class.* Class D for students, E for beginners and F for teachers completed the range of classes offered.[10]

The artisans' class attracted young men from a wide range of

---

*2s. (or 10p) a month was a substantial sum c. 1860. An equivalent fee in 1980 would perhaps amount to £6 a month for a skilled worker.

occupations. The building and furniture trades were particularly well represented with carpenters, masons, cabinet-makers and the occasional architect figuring among the members. Patternmakers, engineers and smiths represented the metal-working trades. Other occupations included clerk, letter-carrier (postman), engraver, photographer and trunk maker. The largest single group of members was none of these but schoolboys and other lads under 15 years old. One little boy of nine described himself as a grocer. In every surviving list of occupations, boys under 15 account for over 40 per cent of the total number, chiefly schoolchildren. Most of the others were aged under 20 and no artisan over the age of 40 was either ambitious or prosperous enough to enrol in the School of Art. A somewhat different clientèle attended the students' class (D), which presumably offered more advanced tuition. From the fragmentary information that survives it seems that the class was well suited to architects and their articled pupils, and to teachers. There were fewer young boys under 15, a sprinkling of men in their twenties and thirties; well over half the class were aged 15 to 19.[11]

The School of Art quickly established itself as a flourishing institution. It had adequate financial support from local well-wishers, some of whom made once-for-all donations while others promised a regular subscription. The expenses were moderate, consisting of rent, fuel and light and the purchase of some equipment. The headmaster* received no fixed salary but rather like a Scottish professor took half the fees paid by his students together with the grant earned from the Department of Science and Art. At its most prosperous in the 1870s the school afforded the headmaster, J. B. Birkmyer, a handsome income of some £350 a year with fluctuations that might take it as high as £400 or as low as £320.[12] Numbers attending the classes naturally varied somewhat from week to week, but none of the classes ever suffered the fate not uncommon among evening classes today of cancellation for lack of support. The most popular of the classes was that for artisans with up to 80 enrolments. In all, the school in an average year had about 250 pupils, most of whom would attend twice a week, usually in the evening. In addition the School of Art offered teaching in local schools and in the Diocesan Training College, already better known as Saint Luke's. Through these connections it greatly increased its range of influence, since several hundred pupils a year received tuition in

*The first headmaster was Montague Wigzell. He was succeeded in 1861 by J. B. Birkmyer.

freehand-drawing and geometry from the headmaster and his assistants.* The success of the art school encouraged Sir Stafford Northcote and his associates to found a parallel school of science. A meeting held in the rooms of the Literary Society at the Athenaeum in Bedford Circus on 17 April 1863 decided on this step. It was a slightly speculative decision since at the time there was not one certificated teacher of science in Devon, and the Department of Science and Art would give grants only when classes were conducted by qualified teachers. The difficulty was soon overcome when W. S. M. D'Urban, later the first curator of the Albert Memorial Museum, was awarded his first-grade teacher's certificate in vegetable physiology. William Sheppard of London University was recruited to teach elementary mathematics, and F. P. Perkins, later also librarian at the Albert Memorial, began his long career in the School of Science, teaching inorganic chemistry, geology, and animal physiology.[13] Science, unlike art, had no great reputation as an accomplishment for young ladies. The Science School therefore lacked the day classes and the useful income that accrued to the School of Art from the daughters of the wealthier inhabitants of Exeter. Nor was it as popular among the young workmen of Exeter as some of the more practical tuition offered in the School of Art. After five years working, the Science School could make no stronger boast than that

> Upwards of 100 individuals have received more or less instruction in the various classes since their formation and between 30 and 40 have obtained Queen's and other prizes [for passing examinations in elementary science]. When the classes meet in the Albert Memorial Building there is every reason to hope that there will be a large accession of pupils.[14]

Sir Stafford Northcote in his address to the Literary Society in 1850 had sketched a design for a cultural centre in Exeter that would include a museum, art gallery, library and school of art.† The rebuff administered by the ratepayers to the project for a library scotched any hope of a major public building to house these institutions for a considerable time to come. But at the end of 1861 Sir Stafford returned to the 'threadbare theme' (his own words) at the annual meeting of the School of Art. 'Nothing' he argued, 'could be more advantageous to a school of art than a museum in which there would naturally be a picture gallery and a

---

*In 1864 the following schools took part in the scheme: St John's Hospital; Hele's; National; Central; Mint Wesleyan; Episcopal Charity.

†Sir Stafford did not mention a school of science in 1850 because such institutions had not yet appeared in the provinces. It was the Great Exhibition and the establishment of the Department of Science and Art in 1852 that first gave an impetus to schools of science.

collection of specimens of natural history. Exeter ought in order to keep up its character to have such an institution as this.' It is likely that some preliminary soundings had been taken privately before this suggestion was made, because a committee was quickly formed and a substantial sum of money promised. Albert the Prince Consort had died some three weeks before the museum project had been raised again, and when a memorial to the Prince was mooted the Northcote group readily agreed to put their funds into the common pool.[15] R. S. Gard, one of the members for Exeter, generously gave a rectangular piece of land with frontages of 140 feet to Queen Street and 70 feet to Upper Paul Street and the organising committee brought further land behind. With the limited funds available it was not possible to build on the whole site. The old properties of Upper Paul Street provided some income to the trustees and the land at the northern or railway end of the plot therefore became the site of the first part of the Museum to be completed. Building began in 1865 to the Gothic designs of a local architect, J. Hayward. A part of the Museum opened in 1868 and the first stage was finished in 1870. By then about half the site had been built on, and little by little over the next thirty years further rooms and galleries were added until the Museum reached the shape and extent that is familiar to the citizens of Exeter today.* When the Devon and Exeter Albert Memorial Museum opened in 1868, the Schools of Art and Science moved into it from their respective premises in Milk Street and Bedford Circus. They now had new rent-free accommodation, and in 1870 with the completion of stage I a small room became available as a laboratory for the School of Science. But the amount of space allotted to the schools did not allow for extravagance: the trustees of the Albert Memorial had also to find room for museum exhibits, for a reference library, a newspaper room, the lending library and a picture gallery. They had financial worries, too. The generosity of the people of Devon and Exeter had provided money for the building of a museum, but hardly any was left over for its endowment with an income to cover running costs. It must have been with some relief that the trustees learned that Exeter City Council was at last going to adopt the Free Libraries Act. In April 1870 the trustees transferred the Albert Memorial to the City, which agreed to provide an income of £600 a year (rather less than the proceeds of a penny rate). Control of the institution was vested in a committee some of whose members were city councillors, others well-known figures in the life of

*Extensions were opened in 1884, 1891, 1895 and 1899.

Exeter and east Devon. At their first meeting they appointed sub-committees for finance, the library and the museum, and a joint committee for the schools of art and science.[16] The schools were henceforth to work, seemingly, within an assured institutional framework and with the backing of the local authority. For the committee, though in practice given a free hand, were technically exercising powers delegated to them by the city council. The City Council received their minutes and carefully preserved them in the city's archives.

The new status of the schools of art and science made little immediate difference to their method of working or to their contribution to education in Exeter. For the time being some of the members of the old committees that had run the schools lost their seats, but they were soon invited back. The Mayor, *ex-officio* chairman of the schools' joint committee, ceased to attend after 1874 and the schools found it convenient to resume their separate identity with distinct committees. The museum and the library spent the whole of the tiny income that accrued to the Albert Memorial, and the School of Science continued as before to struggle with a chronic shortage of money. The School of Art, which normally had a small surplus at the end of the year, paid it into the general funds of the Albert Memorial until after 1877 in the gradual reversion to old ways it once more retained the balances for its own use.[17] In the short run the schools of art and science gained the substantial but sole advantage of comfortable quarters in an impressive new building. It was only twenty years later when public money was made available for technical education that the true importance of the move into the Albert Memorial became apparent. Meanwhile the School of Art pursued its prosperous course. It continued to attract upwards of 250 pupils and in some years, like 1877 and 1881, nearly 300 were enrolled. The intervening years caused a little anxiety: 'For the past three years the School of Art has felt the effects of the depression of trade and the number of students decreased considerably. The returns for the year ending in December 1880, however, show that the School is recovering itself,' with a substantial increase in attendance at the classes for artisans. Compared with other towns whose population fell within the range 40,000 to 200,000 Exeter could feel well satisfied with the size of its School of Art. With one of the smallest populations in the range, Exeter had the fifth largest school out of 41. Average attendances naturally fell some way short of enrolments, but at 65 or 70 per cent were not to be despised. Examinations though did not appeal so strongly; the young ladies seeking accomplishments had no incentive to submit to examinations whose standards were steadily rising; of the artisans, articled pupils and teachers who stood to gain from passing the Department's grades many evidently felt that they could not prepare for a paper every year. For these reasons only a third or a half of the students sat for examinations in any given year and by no means all of them passed. When the school was criticised for not entering many candidates for advanced work the headmaster justly pointed out that economic conditions in Exeter did not encourage advanced work. Wages were low and the most ambitious workmen left for other towns.[18]

Numbers enrolling for art courses fell off in the 1880s and by the end of the decade scarcely exceeded 200. After 1885 local schools stopped relying on the art school for instructors. Over the years the supply of qualified art teachers in Devon should have risen considerably thanks to the work of the art school, thus allowing local schools to appoint their own art teachers. As a result the income of the school declined and with it the income of its ageing headmaster, J. B. Birkmyer. His half of the fee income, for example, fell from £153 in 1885 to only £116 in 1892. By the early 1890s the school was for the first time running at a loss.[19] For the School of Science losses were no novelty. There had never been a large body of subscribers to supplement the income from fees and government grant. Sir Stafford Northcote died in 1887, the last of the subscribers who had launched the school a generation earlier. He had hoped 'to make this City, for which I believe it has natural and acquired advantages, a Centre of Education for the West'.[20] The hope was as far from realisation in 1887 as when the school opened. All through the 1870s and 1880s the number of students fluctuated at a little below 100. In 1888 enrolments fell as low as 80, which was not as bad as it sounded because students often took more than one course. For its small size the school offered a generous range of subjects in mathematics and elementary natural science.

Subject	No of Students[21] 1871–2	1889–90
Mathematics	17	14
Theoretical mechanics	13	8
Inorganic chemistry	43	20
Geology	18	4
Vegetable physiology	21	—
Systematic and economic botany	22	15
Physical geography	9	17
Machine construction and drawing	5	8
Building construction	12	19
	160	105

The last two subjects—machine construction and drawing and building construction—though classified as scientific by the Department of Science and Art were taught in Exeter in the art school. In 1889, in addition to the classes listed above, a course in magnetism and electricity was also being offered; vegetable physiology had disappeared as a separate subject and presumably was part of the botany course by that time. The life sciences gave their teachers some little embarrassment in a prudish age. The teacher of animal physiology reported in 1876 that the enrolment of a lady in the class had been 'a hindrance rather than otherwise as many explanations could not be made owing to her presence; her attendance and attention has however been excellent and she has thus shown a good example to the younger students'. In the early 1880s the teacher of botany felt obliged to run separate classes for men and women. It is not clear from the surviving records when the school steeled itself to an unblushing acceptance of mixed classes in such a dangerous field.[22] Unlike the School of Art the Science School mostly attracted students who needed qualifications in order to get better jobs. The committee that ran the school often appealed to employers to encourage attendance at the classes:

> It is in these classes that young men receive regular and systematic instruction in elementary science and by this means improve their education, and everything that improves education confers not only an additional blessing, but a national power which leads to national success.[23]

Few employers in the city heeded these appeals but it was in the interests of the young men who did attend the classes to sit the examinations. At first the Department of Science and Art was the only examining body, but the City and Guilds of London Institute, founded in 1878, later supplemented the Department's work by examining the more technical and less theoretical subjects. In 1888 the Institute appointed the science school committee as its local committee for examination purposes. The pass rate in scientific and technical examinations fluctuated round the 80 per cent level. In the vintage year 1878 all candidates passed and one outstanding student W. H. Tozer passed in eight subjects and was awarded a Whitworth Scholarship tenable at Manchester for three years. It was unusual for part-time students to attempt so many subjects at one time: most took one or two papers only. By national standards the Exeter science school was doing well, since over the country as a whole the Department passed about 70 per cent of the candidates.[24]

Success must have been due to the quality of the teaching and the diligence and ability of the students. It certainly owed little to the laboratory and its equipment. The room allotted was unheated and in a cold winter frost broke much of the more delicate apparatus. By 1880 the laboratory had removed from the Albert Memorial to an old house in Upper Paul Street. The City Surveyor reported in 1886 that the house was unsafe, and the chemistry lecturer complained that he and his pupils had to work in their overcoats because

> ice-cold air rushes in through the brown paper with which the pane is mended and through the rotten sashes.

Waste pipes leaked and the atmosphere was so damp that labels would not stick to bottles. If the chemistry lecturer lacked comforts at least his apparatus satisfied the regulations of the Department of Science and Art. Other science lecturers were not so lucky. The lecturer in mechanics had no air pump, no pulleys, and no working model of an inclined plane. The lecturer in geology even lacked a geological map of England and Wales! It would have cost £17 to remedy the deficiencies in equipment, of which the Department was willing to pay half. But since the Science School was quite without funds to pay its half of the bill, a crisis threatened. The Department threatened to cut off its regular grants to the School unless the laboratories reached the minimum standards laid down.[25]

An appeal to the general committee of the Albert Memorial followed. A little research in the minutes revealed that constitutionally the Science School was an offspring, neglected and forgotten perhaps, but legitimate and deserving, of the Albert Memorial. The general committee handsomely recognised their parental responsibility and voted whatever was necessary to equip the laboratories to the proper standard. An important corollary of this decision was that the City Council assumed ultimate responsibility for the school.[26] All this happened some two years before Parliament laid on boroughs and county councils a duty to promote technical education in their area. The logical consequences of the city's rescue of the Albert Memorial in 1870 were about to be worked out.

Notes

1 Frank Barlow and others, *Leofric of Exeter* (University of Exeter 1972), pp.32, 40, 44.
2 Nicholas Orme, *Education in the West of England, 1066–1548* (University of Exeter 1976), pp.23, 42–53.

3 W. G. Hoskins, *Exeter in the Seventeenth Century: tax and rate assessments 1602–1699* (Devon and Cornwall Record Society, new series, Vol.2, Torquay 1957), p.xvi.

4 *West of England and Trewman's Exeter Pocket Journal*, 1862 [Devon and Exeter Institution]; Albert Memorial [hereafter AM] Finance Committee, 3 May 1871 (Devon Record Office [hereafter DRO]).

5 Robert Newton, *Victorian Exeter* (Leicester 1968), p.14.

6 13 and 14 Vict. c.65; 18 and 19 Vict. c.70.

7 M. Argles, *South Kensington to Robbins: an account of English technical and scientific education since 1851* (Longmans 1964).

8 Sir Stafford Northcote, 'On Taste' in *Lectures and Essays* (1887), pp.68, 79.

9 *Woolmer's Exeter and Plymouth Gazette*, 25 January, 15 and 29 March 1851 [Devon and Exeter Institution].

10 This paragraph is based on the attendance registers and annual reports of the School of Art, in the archives of the University of Exeter.

11 Attendance registers, School of Art, for 1859, 1866, 1877 and 1879.

12 Treasurer's cash book, 1854–94 [University of Exeter archives].

13 G. T. Donisthorpe, *An Account of the Origins and Progress of the Devon and Exeter Albert Memorial Museum* (Exeter 1868), pp.30–1; Anon., *History and Description of the Devon and Exeter Albert Memorial* (Exeter 1879) [Westcountry Studies Library, Exeter].

14 Donisthorpe, *An Account . . .*, p.31.

15 *Exeter Flying Post*, 1 January and 12 February 1862; Donisthorpe, *An Account*, pp.9–11.

16 AM, general committee, 28 April 1870 [DRO].

17 AM, 14 and 19 November 1887; annual report for 1887–8; Art School, treasurer's account book 1854–94 [DRO].

18 Albert Memorial Museum, *Annual reports* 1871ff [University of Exeter archives]; AM, School of Art committee, 14 November 1872; letterbook 1888–99, Dallas to Shorto, February 1891 [University archives].

19 AM, committee for Schools of Science and Art 1889–94; *Exeter Flying Post*, 1 January 1862; *Annual reports*, 1891 and 1892.

20 Sir Stafford Northcote's address to the first annual meeting of the School of Science, quoted in *Annual report*, 1887.

21 AM *Annual Reports 1868–84* [volume in Westcountry Studies Library, Exeter]; *Annual report* for 1891.

22 *Annual report* for 1876; Science School committee, March 1881.

23 Ibid.

24 *Annual reports*

25 Science School committee, 15 March 1873; *Annual Report*, 1880; AM, general committee, 13 December 1886; Science School committee, 14 February and 3 November 1887.

26 AM, general committee, 14 and 19 November, 12 December 1887.

II

UNIVERSITY EXTENSION AND
TECHNICAL EDUCATION

In Victorian England university education was the privilege of a tiny
minority. At mid-century neither Oxford nor Cambridge had as many as
2000 students; the London colleges—King's and University—were less
than thirty years old; Durham founded in 1832 confined itself largely to
theology, and Owens College, Manchester, which opened in 1851, led for
twenty years a precarious existence. No further university colleges were
founded until the 1870s. There were those who felt uneasy that higher
education was the preserve of so few. Their unease was characteristic of
an age in which some men were beginning to question their own right to
privilege. The rich and the great had always acknowledged obligations to
lesser men. Beowulf symbolised for the Anglo-Saxon thegn the spirit of
generosity that lords were expected to display. Rich medieval merchants
made wills founding almshouses and schools. Aristocratic landowners
before and after the French Revolution took it for granted that rank
imposed some obligations: old and faithful retainers had their pensions;
the poor were given blankets and soup in a hard winter; the fabric of the
parish church might be restored with the aid of a timely gift. But it was in
no such spirit of lordly condescension that the founders of the university
extension movement went about their business. Unlike Beowulf, Sir
Thomas Gresham, or the Seventh Earl of Shaftesbury, they felt
somewhat guilty at their own good fortune and resolved to share their
learning, or some of it, with others less fortunate than themselves. A
similar frame of mind inspired the university settlements that began to
spring up in London and elsewhere in the 1880s. Toynbee Hall and its
imitators were the English equivalent of Tsarist Russia's 'going to the
people'. Wronsky and Levin are the Russian counterparts of Robert

Elsmere, Tolstoy of T. H. Green and Mrs Humphrey Ward. At a more mundane and cruder level Joseph Chamberlain a successful businessman himself expressed the same anxieties when he asked: 'What ransom will property pay for the security which it enjoys?'

It was in Oxford that the idea of extra-mural work was first mooted in 1850. Nothing came of the suggestion at the time and the initiative then passed to Cambridge and in particular to a young fellow of Trinity College, James Stuart. In 1867 he gave a series of lectures on astronomical subjects to working men in Crewe and Rochdale. They were so popular that further lectures were arranged at Derby, Nottingham and Sheffield. In 1872 Stuart* persuaded the University of Cambridge to assume responsibility for what had hitherto been a private venture. A Board of Extra-Mural Studies was set up, lecturers appointed, local committees called into existence. In 1886 Cambridge devised an affiliation scheme. Students who had successfully completed a three-year tutorial course, and passed certain examinations, were excused from one year's residence on proceeding to Cambridge to take a degree. London in 1876 and Oxford in 1885 also began extra-mural work.[1]

Exeter was slow to take advantage of these opportunities. Not until 1886 did the city approach the University of Cambridge for a course of lectures. The initiative was taken after a meeting held in the Albert Memorial on Saturday 10 July 1886. Among those present were the Bishop of Exeter, the Mayor, the Sheriff, the Dean, and R. G. Moulton one of the most popular lecturers on the Cambridge panel. A large committee was formed that consisted of those present (about fifty in number) together with the members of the Cambridge Local Examinations Committee. The Bishop was elected patron, the Mayor President, W. Cotton Treasurer (he was also Treasurer of the science and art schools) and J. A. Hobson Secretary.[2] Hobson was then a young classics master at Exeter School. He later became famous as an original economist and as the author of many books among them *Imperialism, The Evolution of Modern Capitalism*, and the *Physiology of Industry*. Not many universities have among their founding fathers a writer who influenced men as diverse as Lenin, Keynes and R. H. Tawney. The Committee set enthusiastically to work. It raised a guarantee fund to

*In 1886 Stuart established the department of mechanical engineering at Cambridge and was elected first holder of the chair. He resigned in 1891 on marrying a daughter of J. J. Colman of Colman's Mustard, Norwich. He became a partner in the business, entered Parliament as a Liberal and published his entertaining *Reminiscences* (1911).

which the Local Examinations Committee contributed. It fixed 7s. 6d. as the fee for each course, with a reduced rate of 1s. for workingmen on tickets obtainable from employers. The first course of lectures was delivered in the autumn of 1886 in the Athenaeum, Bedford Circus, at 8 p.m. on Friday evenings. Workmen came in by a separate entrance and sat apart from those who paid the full fee. The lecturer, G. H. Leonard, took as his subject 'The Growth of English Commerce'. (For many years economic history was a popular choice by extra-mural classes all over the country.) Attendance at this first course of lectures averaged 168 and as many as 62 stayed behind for the discussion classes. But only 15 entered for the examination. A second course of lectures given in the New Year 1887 was even more popular. R. G. Moulton lectured on 'Four Thinkers on Life' to an audience averaging 212* of whom one half also came to the discussion classes. But again only a handful of students submitted themselves to ordeal by examination. In the autumn of 1887 a third course of lectures given by Ernest Radford on 'Studies in the History of Art' attracted audiences numbering more than 100. Financially the first three courses were a success. After a modest capital investment in 100 chairs, a magic lantern stand and blinds for the Art Gallery where Radford lectured, there still remained a balance of £5 in hand.

Despite this encouraging start the movement languished. Hobson resigned as secretary on leaving the district in 1887 and was succeeded by H. Macan, who taught science at Exeter School. Cambridge offered to provide lectures in physiology or physical geography for early 1888, but these were thought unattractive by the committee which found itself without any lectures at all. It was at this low point in the extension movement's history that Miss J. D. Montgomery joined the committee. She had attended Ernest Radford's lectures the previous autumn and was one of the few (all women) who had entered for the examination† using the nom de plume of *Deutsch-gesinnt*, meaning German-minded, or Germanophile. She also entered for the examination after a course of lectures given in Exeter on behalf of the extra-mural department of the University of Oxford and on that occasion won a prize.[3] Jessie Montgomery was the daughter of the minor poet Robert Montgomery, who had had the misfortune to be savagely reviewed by the young Macaulay.[4] After her father's death she lived with an uncle who was a

*In larger towns, Moulton could attract an audience of 700. He once gave a course of lectures on English grammar to an audience of 300.
†In 1895 she was awarded the Vice-Chancellor's certificate after successfully completing six courses of Cambridge lectures and the accompanying examinations.

canon of Exeter Cathedral. She soon became joint secretary of the Exeter university extension committee and breathed new life into it. In the early months of 1889 two courses were run, one by Moulton, the other by H. J. Mackinder, the celebrated geographer. Other young lecturers who would later make a mark in the world and who gave extra-mural courses in Exeter in the 1890s included the historians J. Holland Rose, J. H. Clapham and A. J. Grant, and the statistician A. L. Bowley.

After the first course of lectures in the Athenaeum, Bedford Circus, it became the practice to hold them in the Museum. Several members of the extension committee were also on the committee of the Albert Memorial and the extension chairman C. T. K. Roberts, who had been Mayor in 1887–88, was prominent in all the affairs of the Albert Memorial. Undoubtedly the overlapping membership helped the association between the new body and the older one. At Miss Montgomery's suggestion the rules of the extension committee were amended to provide that its membership should be fully representative of the local community: the Mayor was invited to be *ex-officio* president; the Bishop one of the vice-presidents: the County Council, the Exeter School Board, the Literary Society, the Chamber of Commerce and the Workingmen's Society were all entitled to representation on the committee; ex-officio members of the committee were to include the chairman of the city's technical education committee and the headmasters and headmistresses of the principal schools. The wide representation of city and county interests stood the movement in good stead during the reorganisation of technical and higher education that took place in 1893.[5]

Not everybody was pleased with the intrusion of university extension into the routine of educational work in the Albert Memorial. The headmaster of the art school found himself distracted by a long crocodile of extension students wending its way through his classroom en route to their evening lecture. The curator of the museum, James Dallas, also resented the intrusion of the newcomers. In 1891 he asked Sir Philip Cunliffe Owen of the Department of Science and Art to come down to Exeter on the occasion of the opening of the new laboratories in the Albert Memorial:

> Our schools [of art and science] are in some danger just at present in consequence of an attempt which is being made to depreciate their work as compared with the new fad of University Extension, and it is thought very desirable that something should be done in their support.[6]

Sir Philip came and made a speech before a large audience in favour

Plate 1 *Jessie Montgomery,*
Secretary of the University
Extension Committee,
1888–1918

Plate 2 *Sir Henry Lopes, Deputy*
President 1922–1936;
President 1936–1938

Plate 3 *Sir James Owen,*
Treasurer, 1922–1924

Plate 4 *W. H. Moberly, Principal,*
1925–1926

Plate 6   *H. J. W. Hetherington, Principal, 1920–1924*

Plate 5   *A. W. Clayden, Principal, 1893–1920*

of technical education, but naturally failed to check the progress of 'the new fad'.

James Dallas was being unduly pessimistic about the future of technical education in Exeter. It may well have been the case that young ladies of leisure preferred lantern slides on the history of art to classes in freehand drawing and solid geometry. But classes on building construction or theoretical mechanics stood in no danger from the new movement. On the contrary ample funds were for the first time being put at the disposal of 'technical education', as that term was understood by Parliament. In 1889 the Technical Instruction Act empowered local authorities to spend the proceeds of a penny rate on technical or manual instruction. Manual instruction was defined as 'instruction in the use of tools, processes of agriculture and modelling in clay, wood or other material'. Technical instruction was defined as 'instruction in the principles of science and art applicable to industries'. Inconsistently, not to say absurdly, neither form of instruction was to include 'teaching the practice of any trade or employment'. Any subject already receiving or that might in future receive assistance from the Department of Science and Art might be regarded as technical instruction, and in this connection modern languages and commercial and agricultural subjects were specifically mentioned.[7] Of even more practical importance were two further acts passed in 1890. One placed additional duties on beer and spirits, the revenue from which was allotted by the other to local authorities to spend on technical instruction.[8] This was the famous 'whisky money', distilling genius out of gin and brewing brains out of beer, in the words of a contemporary wag. Whisky money provided much larger funds for technical education than councils were prepared to raise from the rates.

Exeter City Council made a cautious start in the exercise of its new powers. The proceeds of a penny rate amounted to about £900. The grant of £50 made in 1890 to the art school was therefore little more than a gesture.[9] More immediately promising seemed to be a scheme for co-operating with Devon County Council. Its Technical Education sub-committee wished to secure art training for elementary school teachers in Devon and was willing to spend £250 if the Exeter School of Art would provide the necessary teachers. Unluckily the scheme got off to a bad start: of 17 teachers who attended an art class put on for them at Axminster, only three passed the examination that concluded the course. It is not surprising that Devon's money was not available for a second experiment in the following year.[10] Piecemeal co-operation with Devon was resumed a few years later, but the county did not put its full weight behind the Albert Memorial and its various educational enterprises until after the First World War. Exeter could not so easily escape. Early in 1893 it substantially increased its grant to the schools of art and science — to £250— as a foretaste of the more generous supplies that whisky money would make possible.[11] The problem that faced the city fathers in 1893 was not a shortage of cash but embarrassing riches. The schools of art and science had limited aims and had not recently been showing much vitality. If Exeter was to make full use of the whisky money a daring initiative was needed. It was at this point that Miss Jessie Montgomery made her decisive contribution to the development of higher education in Exeter.

In 1890, the year when whisky money was first voted, Miss Montgomery was already sketching plans for an amalgamation of university extension and technical education in Exeter. It is likely that she was developing a suggestion thrown out by Halford Mackinder and Michael Sadler in a little book that they had recently published, *University Extension: has it a future?* They argued that whisky money should be channelled along university extension streams, and that beside the public library there should be established a centre of stimulus and guidance:

> It must combine some of the functions of the higher forms in the Public School [sc. the elementary school], of the University classroom and of the Royal Institution . . . However incomplete, however tentative, University Extension is the one great agency in the field which seeks to fulfil this ideal.

Miss Montgomery submitted her ideas to the Rev. G. F. Browne, secretary to the Local Examinations and Lectures Syndicate of the University of Cambridge. He encouraged her to proceed[12] but it was not until February 1893 that she formally put a scheme to the city's Museum and Technical Education Committee.* She envisaged three complementary departments, working under a principal who should be a university graduate. The first department was to be a university extension college teaching history, literature and a more advanced brand of science to which the science school teaching would be a suitable introduction. Occasional courses in Latin, modern languages, the

---

*This was the new name for the governing body of the Albert Memorial, which was entrusted with responsibility for technical education in Exeter under the terms of the Technical Instruction Act of 1889.

principles of art, commercial geography, economics and the science of teaching were also suggested. If like the schools of art and science the university extension committee had a permanent rent-free home in the Museum 'it could aim at greater continuity of study, which is difficult where popular support supplies the sinews of war'. Secondly, Miss Montgomery proposed the establishment of technical schools which would embrace but at the same time greatly extend the work done by the existing schools of science and art. To them she proposed to add a commercial section teaching modern languages, geography, commercial correspondence, book-keeping and typing.* A technological section would work for the City and Guilds examinations in sanitary engineering and plumbing, in carpentry, and in *slojd* (a Swedish scheme for artistic woodwork). Finally, manual instruction, not only in *slojd* but in such womanly subjects as cookery, dressmaking, and domestic economy completed the scheme for the proposed technical schools. Thirdly Miss Montgomery hoped to establish a teachers' department that would provide courses of instruction for assistant and pupil teachers.

These elaborate proposals cannot have been sprung on the committee without warning, though they appear rather abruptly in the records. As precedent was and remains all important in the conduct of affairs in England, it was useful that Miss Montgomery could point to the University Extension College at Reading as a model for the institution she had in mind. The college at Reading, ancestor of the modern university, had come into existence in the previous year with the generous support of Christ Church, Oxford. Michael Sadler, secretary to the Oxford Delegacy for University Extension, wrote (no doubt at Miss Montgomery's invitation) to commend her scheme:

> That the future of such a college at Exeter would be bright and useful, I have no doubt whatever. Every year would show its value to the intellectual and therefore to the social and general well-being of the City.

Even more weightily the Department of Science and Art gave cordial support in general terms. This did not exhaust the number of external backers that Miss Montgomery enlisted. The University of Cambridge through its board of extra-mural studies went beyond the expression of good wishes to the offer of practical help. If the City would pay the Principal a salary of £200, Cambridge would find him work and add

---

*It is ironic that none of the records extant in the University's archives was typewritten until 1904, when the college bought its first typewritter.

£150 to his salary for each of the next three years. In return Cambridge would require the services of the Principal two evenings a week for university extension lectures. The Principal was to be appointed by the City from a panel of candidates submitted by the University of Cambridge.[13] The City accepted this generous offer and on 15 April 1893 appointed Arthur W. Clayden as Principal of Exeter Technical and University Extension College. He took up his post on 1 June 1893.[14]

Arthur Clayden was born at Boston in Lincolnshire in 1855, the son of P. W. Clayden, a Unitarian minister, who later became a journalist and eventually night editor of the *Daily News*.* Clayden was educated at University College School and read the natural science tripos at Christ's College, Cambridge. He took his degree in 1876 and taught science at Bath College, Jersey, from 1878 to 1887. He then began to lecture for the Cambridge Board of Extra-Mural Studies, and published papers in geology and in meteorological photography. In 1889 he made a model of the world's ocean currents which is said to have facilitated the building of the Panama Canal. In 1890 he served as secretary to the meteorological photography committee of the British Association for the Advancement of Science. After appointment as Principal, Clayden continued to publish. *The History of Devonshire Scenery* appeared in 1906; it embodied some work that Clayden had done himself, but with a well-established subject like geology there was little scope for originality in a general review of a much-studied county. *Cloud Studies*, published in 1905, was one of relatively few works so far devoted to that branch of meteorology. It earned Clayden some reputation, and it was a great satisfaction to him that the airship R34 carried a copy of his manual when it crossed the Atlantic in 1919. A second edition was published in 1925. His books made solid, sober reading.† There are conflicting accounts of his abilities as a teacher. An HMI who knew him in his later years found his lectures uninspiring and his students ill-informed.[15] On the other hand, Sir Ernest Kennaway, the distinguished pathologist, who had as a young man attended Clayden's geology lectures described him 'as a born teacher'.[16] To the post of Principal he brought two important qualities--academic distinction and vision. But he lacked interest in routine and had too little force and energy to make a first-rate administrator.[17]

*In 1930 the *Daily News* absorbed the *Daily Chronicle* and took the name *News Chronicle*. The *News Chronicle* ceased publication in 1960.
†Clayden had some skill with the brush as well as the camera and the pen. A seascape of his was presented to the Museum in 1916 by Sir E. Chaning-Wills (now lost).

Clayden's first weeks as Principal of the College must have tested his powers of diplomacy. Two of the leading figures in the educational work of the Albert Memorial were not well pleased with the turn of events. James Dallas, curator of the Museum and local examinations secretary for the science and art schools, had made his position clear when the university extension movement first began to encroach on his preserves. J. B. Birkmyer, headmaster of the School of Art, now found himself a subordinate in the enlarged institution. He retained the title of headmaster but there is some evidence that he felt disappointed at being passed over for the principalship.[18] Clayden soon won Dallas over. By the end of 1893 they were on excellent terms and Dallas was writing more cordially to the Principal than to men whom he had known much longer.[19] As it turned out, Birkmyer had nothing to fear from the new régime. The School of Art proceeded much as before. There was little overlap between its work and that of the university extension department. The school was left to its own devices and though lodged in the same building tended to drift away on its own separate course. Complete separation occurred in 1922 and academic collaboration did not resume for a further forty years. By then the School of Art had developed into a college which had a high reputation and which was doing much advanced work. As it stood in the 1890s the school was out of place in an institution that aspired to university status, and its subsequent history has little bearing on the development of university education in Exeter.*

The establishment of a technical and university extension college marked a great step forward. One small sign of the higher status of the college was that the Principal attended meetings of the controlling bodies, the Museum and Technical Education committee and the Technical Education sub-committee. Birkmyer had never had that privilege: the decisions of the Art School Committee reached him only after the event by letter from Dallas. The Principal was not a member of the committees, but attended *ex-officio*. With his Cambridge degree and scientific reputation he was in a strong position to forward the interests of the college. Money, too, was more plentiful than it had ever been before. Whisky money and funds from the rates amounted to £1,000, a large sum in comparison with the past budgets of the schools of art and

---

*Birkmyer remained headmaster until his death in 1899. He exhibited at the Royal Academy on several occasions between 1869 and 1898. The Museum has one of his oils, a view of Maer Rocks, Exmouth.

science. In addition there was income from fees and the grants that could be earned from the Department of Science and Art. Of this large prospective growth of income (perhaps £1,500 in all) £200 was earmarked for the Principal's salary and £100 for the university extension committee. The balance was large enough for the college to pay salaries rather than leave its teachers to earn what they could from fees and grants. On the side of technical education two full-time appointments were made, one in mathematics* the other in physiology, commercial geography and history. The teaching of physics was shared between Clayden and John Trott, a long-serving teacher in the science school. Trott's post was part-time, as were appointments to teach modern languages, book-keeping, sanitary engineering, telegraphy, and botany. Clayden's qualifications were so high by the standards to which the Department of Science and Art was accustomed that he was licensed to teach 'Practical plane and solid Geometry, Mathematics (stages 1 and 2), Theoretical Mechanics, Sound Light and Heat, Magnetism and Electricity, Theoretical and Practical Inorganic and Organic Chemistry, Geology, Human Physiology, General Biology, Zoology, Botany and Physiography'.[20] Modestly he confined himself to some chemistry (F. P. Perkins of the science school having resigned) some physics and a little geology. By 1895 the college had 27 teaching staff, the great majority part-timers. Twelve of them were university-educated including two women from Newham College, Cambridge;[21] but the women had no letters to put after their names, because Cambridge did not award degrees to women until 1947.

Formally, the university extension department was separate from the technical department and the art school. Miss Montgomery acted as secretary for university extension, Dallas for the technical department and the art school until 1894 when the Town Clerk, G. R. Shorto, undertook the duties. Clayden provided a measure of unity since he was head of both departments. But the chief unifying force was the students, many of whom received instruction in all departments of the college. In meeting their needs the arbitrary division between university extension and technical department soon broke down. The plans for the new college included the education of pupil teachers, girls and boys aged between fourteen and eighteen who gave lessons for part of the week, and received lessons themselves in the evening and on Saturdays. If at the

---

*J. F. Young. He resigned in 1894 to work in educational administration. He later became Secretary (Director) of Education for Devon County Council.

age of eighteen they passed their examinations they could proceed to training college and after two years become certificated (fully qualified) teachers. The university extension department provided pupil teachers with classes in music, history, geography and English; classes in mathematics were available in the science school. A sense of rivalry between the departments came to seem misplaced, and the eventual fusion of university extension and science school was prepared.[22]

As an institution of further education, the college was anxious to avoid treading on the preserves of the local schools. It therefore fixed a lower age limit of eighteen for its students. To this limit it allowed many exceptions: pupil teachers; students attending elementary schools aged sixteen and desiring technical training; students at work in the day; students from outside the city; students of the School of Art.[23] A rule so freely disregarded can have had little impact. The only students under the age of eighteen likely to have been hampered by it were those intending to take courses in the university extension department. For all practical purposes the college was functioning as a secondary school of the comprehensive kind now known as a sixth-form college. In this capacity it had considerable success. One good measure of its achievements was the average grant earned from the Department of Science and Art per examination paper worked: nationally in 1895 the sum earned was 14s. 10½d. (74½p); in training colleges £1. 2s. 6½d. (112½p); Exeter students did better still by earning £1. 5s. 7½d. (128p). Between 1893 and 1898 the grant doubled, reflecting a higher ratio of examination passes, rather than an increased number of students.[24]

In 1895 the college took an important step forward when it began to provide day classes. Miss Montgomery believed that there would be a strong demand for these classes. The local secondary schools did not, in her opinion, offer education appropriate to children seeking careers in the civil service or in commerce. Modern languages, history, geography, Latin and the 'right' kind of mathematics were the subjects needed and these the college could provide.

> We have the necessary buildings, sufficient 'plant' and a thoroughly efficient principal; but we have not the funds to increase our teaching staff.

because government grants were not being made available for secondary education.[25] Like many other education authorities, Exeter did not observe the nice distinction between secondary and technical education; the teaching at the college from the beginning included obviously non-technical subjects like geography and history. Miss Montgomery's fears were therefore much exaggerated. The problem was, rather, a general lack of funds to finance day classes and the full-time salaries that they would entail. When established, the day classes did not attract the students that Miss Montgomery had hoped for. Pupil teachers came, but few prospective clerks, whether in commerce or government. Students seeking advanced tuition leading to the external degrees of London University had to be turned away. In 1898 the college tried to solve this problem by allowing private tutors to use college premises for advanced teaching at fees to be fixed by the college.[26] This makeshift arrangement did not work well. At the end of the decade the college had about 900 students, each of whom on average took 2.2 courses. Their ages ranged from thirteen years upwards, most of them being between sixteen and thirty. Teachers and pupil teachers made up a considerable proportion of the whole, but a still larger part was supplied from the ranks of the artisans. The decade had witnessed considerable additions to the buildings of the Albert Memorial—a chemistry laboratory in 1891, and further additions in 1895 and 1899 completely filled the site. The college had the smaller rooms, which were scattered inconveniently around the building. The Museum and Public Library occupied the larger rooms. The Museum did not open to the public until 10 a.m.; when lectures were scheduled for an earlier hour students and staff had to enter through the stokehole.[27]

In 1889 Parliament voted a small sum for distribution by the Treasury to universities and university colleges; thirty years later in 1919 the administration of this grant was entrusted to a new body, the University Grants Committee [UGC]. Despite the miscellaneous nature of the teaching and the lack of endowments and proper buildings of its own, the Exeter college applied in 1894 for a share of the money available. This and a further application in 1896 were turned down. But evidently the Treasury did not consider the applications impudent for it invited the college to try again in 1902.

> Surely [Clayden asked] the means will soon be found to secure the appoint-
> ment of the small number of resident Professors necessary to change the
> verdict.[28]

The Treasury, it turned out, was not to be so easily impressed. The staff did need strengthening but what was equally important was to offer advanced teaching. Most of the work done by the college in the 1890s simply continued the traditions of the science and art schools. Some of the classes put on by the university extension department were of higher calibre, but most were aimed at pupil teachers who had previously been educated at elementary schools. The response to the offer of private tutors for advanced work had been disappointing, and it was clear that there was only a small demand for such courses. Anxious to preserve the broader educational base established in 1893, Cambridge University went on paying its subvention to the Principal's salary until 1900, though the original agreement had been for three years only: 'Had the [University of Cambridge] not taken part in this movement at Exeter there would have been founded merely a Technical Institute on narrow lines.'[29] If the college was to raise its standards and maintain its broad appeal it had to attract large numbers of well-qualified students. What profession recruited as heavily as teaching? What better field for advanced work than the training of teachers?[30]

Notes

1 R. D. Roberts, *Eighteen years of university extension* (Cambridge 1891), pp.1-2, 85ff.
2 This and the following paragraphs are based on a University Extension Minute Book 1886-88 [University of Exeter archives].
3 *The Evening Post*, 5 May 1888 [Devon and Exeter Institution].
4 *The works of Lord Macaulay* (1913 ed.) VII, 503-27; G. O. Trevelyan, *Life and Letters of Lord Macaulay* (1909 ed.), pp.538, 599.
5 H. J. Mackinder and M. E. Sadler, *University Extension: Past Present and Future* (3rd ed. 1891), pp.51-2.
6 Dallas to Department of Science and Art, 19 January 1891; to G. R. Shorto, January 1891 [Letter Book, 1889-99 — University of Exeter].
7 52 and 53 Vict. c.76.
8 53 Vict. c.8 and 60.
9 *Annual Report* 1890; letterbook 1888-99, Dallas to Shorto, 22 September and 4 November 1890.
10 Letterbook 1889-99, Dallas to Devon County Council, 5 and 14 January, to Department of Science and Art, 19 January, and 16 March 1892, to W. H. B. Catford (Axminster), 20 September 1892.
11 *Annual report*, 1893.
12 H. J. Mackinder and M. E. Sadler, *University Extension: Has it a Future?* (Oxford 1890), pp.1-2, 5; Cambridge University Archives, BEMS 12/2 [Cambridge University Library].
13 AM, Museum and technical education committee, 22 February and 6 March 1893; technical education sub-committee, 27 February 1893; Cambridge University Archives, Local examinations and lectures syndicate, 18 February, 10 March and 6 May 1893 [LES 1/3, Cambridge University Library].
14 AM, technical education sub-committee, 8 and 15 April 1893.

15 Royal Albert Memorial College, [hereafter RAMC] *Students Magazine*, IV, no.1 (March 1908); Principals' Papers box G [hereafter PPG] file 2 being memories of Clayden by W. J. Harte and F. T. Howard who had both known him well and by F. H. Newman, physicist and W. S. Lewis, geographer, who were familiar with his research.

16 J. W. Cook (Vice-Chancellor) — Presidential address — 'Potpourri: higher education and research in Devon' (*Transactions of the Devonshire Association*, vol.93, 1961, pp.21-33). Cook had worked with Kennaway in London and had this information from Kennaway himself.

17 Sir Hector Hetherington, *The University College at Exeter 1920-1925* (University of Exeter 1963), p.23.

18 Letterbook 1889-99, Dallas to Birkmyer, 3 and 5 June 1893.

19 Ibid., Dallas to Clayden, 16 December 1893.

20 Ibid., Dallas to Department of Science and Art, 11 July and to the Editor, *Daily Western Times*, 15 July 1893; technical education sub-committee, 11 September 1893.

21 *Calendar, 1893-94*; *Annual report*, 1895 [University of Exeter archives].

22 *Calendar, 1893-94*; *Annual report*, 1896 in Museum and Technical Education committee, 28 July 1896.

23 Museum and Technical Education committee, 24 July 1893.

24 Ibid., 3 August 1897; *Annual report*, 1895.

25 Royal commission on secondary education 1895, Memoranda, vol.5, letter from Miss J. D. Montgomery, 17 May 1894; *Annual report*, 1896 (Museum and Technical Education committee, 28 July 1896).

26 AM, college committee, 23 May and 10 October 1898.

27 *Annual report*, 1900; W. J. Harte, 'The development of the University College of the South West of England' (Exeter University College Club, *Bulletin*, March 1948).

28 Museum and Technical Education committee, 12 March 1894 and 9 March 1896; A. W. Clayden and others, *The Albert Memorial: College Museum Library* (Exeter City Council 1899), p.18 [University of Exeter archives].

29 Cambridge University Archives 'Report on the position of Exeter Technical and University Extension College with special regard to the Principalship'; note of decisions taken by the local lectures syndicate [BEMS 31/2, 31/4 — Cambridge University Library].

30 RAM, sub-committee on endowment and development, 13 April 1901; RAM, 15 April 1901.

III

TRAINING COLLEGE, 1901–1914

When the Duke of York (the future King George V) opened the York Wing of the Albert Memorial in 1899, the city took the opportunity to rename both the institution and the college. The college had laboured under the cumbersome title of Exeter Technical and University Extension College and was popularly referred to as the Technical School. For a few months in 1899 its official title was the Albert Memorial College. In 1900 it became the Royal Albert Memorial College, was often thereafter referred to as the Royal Albert Memorial University College, and became known to the general public as University College, Exeter. These were not the only changes in nomenclature. The Royal Albert Memorial had so sonorous a name that government by committee seemed inadequate. The Museum and Technical Education committee therefore became the Governors of the Royal Albert Memorial. The sub-committees were reorganised at the same time. Technical education was added to the responsibilities of the College Committee. There were also committees for Finance, the Museum and the Library. As time passed, College Committee created sub-committees of its own—for finance, the manual school, the hostel. All reported to College Committee, whose minutes were in turn received by the Governors who in theory had the power to reverse the decisions of College Committee. But as Clayden explained in 1908:

> As a matter of practice the report of the College committee is rarely questioned . . . .. All routine matters such as curriculum, arrangement of lectures, examinations, admission of students, discipline etc. are decided by myself in consultation with the four professors and the Mistress of Education, who form an Educational Council.[1]

On major matters of policy involving new expenditure, college autonomy broke down. Exeter City Council held the purse strings and the College and the Governors of the Royal Albert Memorial had to persuade the city before they could embark on costly new undertakings, such as the training of teachers.

For most of the nineteenth century the work of teacher-training was in the hands of the churches. Their training colleges supplied many teachers but even in 1900 little more than a quarter of the country's elementary school teachers had had a college training. Others had passed the certificate examinations by dint of evening study while teaching in the day. Many had been pupil teachers who stayed in the profession as uncertificated teachers.[2] Universities and university colleges began to offer teacher-training towards the end of the nineteenth century, and by 1900 sixteen universities and colleges had training departments,* with 1150 students in training, more than a quarter of the total at that date. For the most part, secondary or grammar school teachers were expected to teach by the light of nature. Cambridge (but not Oxford) offered to train secondary school teachers in 1879, and was followed in 1883 by London and in 1894 by Manchester. Women were humble enough to take advantage of these courses but few of the men who intended to make a career as secondary school teachers troubled to acquire a postgraduate certificate of education.[3]

Universities and colleges had been quick to take up teacher-training not only because it was useful work but because government made valuable grants both to the institution and to the students. Unlike the Church training colleges, which were wholly residential, the training departments attached to universities and university colleges were day training colleges. The Board of Education made a grant of £20 on account of each certificated teacher who had passed through a day training college and had completed eighteen months' satisfactory service. Maintenance grants were paid at the rate of £20 p.a. to women and £25 to men; a grant of £13 towards fees was also paid.[4] Colleges received additional grants on a per capita basis for teaching art, mathematics and science subjects. Each day student following the two-year certificate course could be worth as much as £25 a year to a training department.

In July 1901 Principal Clayden formally applied to the Board of

---

*'Training department' was the usual term until the second world war; it then gave way to 'department of education'. The students were known as 'students in training'. The term 'training college' gave way to 'college of education' in the 1960s.

Education to open a day training college. The application was granted, itself a tacit admission by the Board that the Royal Albert Memorial College was 'of university rank'. The Board attached various conditions to the establishment of a day training college: in the first year only women were to be admitted, to the number of 25; a proper 'practising school' would be needed where the students could undergo what was then called 'school practice'; and the Board insisted that the staff should be strengthened by the appointment of persons of high university training, one of whom was to be a woman graduate as lecturer in education.[5] Even before the College had received a penny of the Board's money it was able to make these new appointments. The city council agreed to vote the college the full proceeds of a penny rate under the Technical Instruction Act 1889 and there was also the prospect of more whisky money. Armed with these extra supplies, the college appointed three heads of department. W. H. Lewis the senior science master of Exeter School became head of chemistry and biology, but retained his post at Exeter School. H. F. Lunn was appointed 'Mathematical Master', and W. J. Harte who had been a colleague of Clayden's at Bath College became tutor in history and literature. Miss L. M. Epps was appointed 'Mistress of Method', that is lecturer in education.[6]

Thus strengthened, the college opened its training department in September 1901 with 25 women students. Forty were admitted in 1902 and in 1903 the Board of Education gave its blessing to the admission of 20 men as well. Thus by 1904 the college had 120 students in training $(2 \times 40 + 2 \times 20)$. Numbers were raised to 132 in 1907 and remained at this level for several years until in 1911 a further increase to 150 students took place, after the opening of the new building in Gandy Street.[7] The admission of men did not make the training department fully co-educational. The teaching practice of the women students was arranged and supervised by the mistress of method and other women members of staff. The admission of men necessitated the appointment of a master of method, A. W. Parry, formerly on the staff of Saint Luke's College. In 1904 when the college created its first chairs he became professor of education, taking his place beside Lewis, Harte and Lunn. By then Lewis had become a full-time member of staff, and it was settled policy to create only full-time posts, given the large number of day students in the college.[8] Naturally the teaching practice of the men fell to Parry and other male members of staff. Segregation of the sexes did not end there. One anxious parent received assurances to the following effect:

We have not found any practical inconvenience arising by the joint instruction of men and women; careful rules are made which are loyally obeyed. Our number of students is so large that it is necessary in any case to divide each year into sets and the men naturally fall into a distinct set for most subjects.[9]

Before the establishment of the training department the college was a merely local institution for local students. Those who came from outside the city boundaries lived in adjacent parts of the county and went home at the end of the day's (or evening's) work. The students in training came from further afield. When the department opened there was a chronic shortage of places for pupil-teachers who wished to complete their training and acquire a certificate; in 1900 less than half the qualified teachers could find a place in a training college or department.[10] From the start therefore Exeter enjoyed a healthy demand for the available places. It could not advertise for students until it had received the Board's formal consent to the opening of a day training college, not given until July 1901. The college had little more than two months in which to recruit its first intake of students and arrange for their accommodation. Despite the short notice there were more than enough applicants, not all of them from Exeter, or even from south-west England. Ten out of the first 25 women admitted came from Wales and in the first twelve years nearly 30 per cent of the students in training were Welsh.*[11] Concern for the welfare of these students led the college to lay down a policy for lodgings. At a time when most training colleges were residential and imposed severe restrictions on the use of leisure time— Sheffield kept its students in after tea—there was nothing unusual in Exeter's regulations, though they seem harsh by the laxer standards of the 1980s. One advantage of being a local authority institution was that the college could call upon the sanitary inspector to view lodgings before they were licensed for students. The college very properly insisted that landladies should provide a warm, well-lit room for evening study. It also required landladies to record in a diary the time at which students returned to their lodgings if they came in after 9 p.m.; if a student came in after 11 p.m. her landlady was to report her to the college next day. No student was to go out after 10 p.m. without college approval. Men students in training, first admitted in 1903, were subject to the same rules.[12]

*There was still a large contingent of Welsh students in the college in the 1950s but the connection has weakened since then.

From the outset Exeter wished to provide hostel accommodation, at least for women students in training whose homes lay outside Exeter. The Church of England already had a hostel, Sandford Hall, which the college licensed for Anglican women. In the absence of grants from the Board of Education, Exeter could not afford to provide a non-denominational hostel of its own and it was left to the friends of the college to act on its behalf. In 1902 Miss Montgomery formed a syndicate to buy 'The Vineyard'* in Castle Street, a pleasant Georgian house with a fine garden overlooked by the ruins of Rougemont Castle. Its large bedrooms became dormitories which were divided into cubicles by serge curtains. The students had the use of a common room and a study but the furnishings were austere and if the memory of an old student is to be trusted there was not one comfortable chair in the building. For the first two terms, until a regular appointment could be made, Miss Montgomery left her own home in Baring Crescent and acted as warden of College Hostel. The hostel accommodated 30 students and was therefore too small to house all the women students in training. To make good the deficiency the syndicate bought Bradninch House in Bradninch Place, Gandy Street, as an annexe for a further 20 students. When Bradninch House was demolished, together with other Queen Anne houses to make room for the new college buildings in Gandy Street, modern wings were added to College Hostel, providing single study-bedrooms and raising to 78 the number of students who could be accommodated. The college, however, was reluctant to admit more than 70 students and usually a somewhat lower number was in residence. The rules were strict. The hostel doors closed at 7 p.m. and special permission was needed if a student wished to stay out until 9 p.m. There were religious exercises daily; in the morning the reading of a psalm and three collects, prayers and grace; in the evening hymns and three collects, prayers and grace. Students apparently accepted this régime uncomplainingly; the only overt protest was a mild banter directed at the curfew by writers in the *Students' Magazine.*[13]

In 1906 the city council bought out the non-profit-making syndicate and placed the hostel under college control. In order to qualify for a building grant from the Board of Education the college had to guarantee that all hostel places went to students in training and from 1908 until a second hostel was opened after the war there were no hostel places for private students taking courses at the college. This was the

*Now known as Bradninch House.

price that had to be paid for help with the funds for the hostel extension.[14]

The training department developed naturally enough in a college that already had a flourishing pupil-teacher centre, and for some years large numbers of pupil-teachers continued to offer themselves for training, about a quarter of them from the county, the others from the city. Necessary as the pupil teachers might have been when the school population was growing fast before and after the Education Act of 1870, there were strong objections to their employment in the twentieth century. How could the Board of Education raise the quality of teaching in elementary schools if a quarter of the teachers were themselves half-trained, partly-educated apprentices? The ratepayers had the benefit of cheap labour in the schools, but established teachers and their trade unions disliked the pupil-teacher system for that very reason. With the growth of the secondary school population the need for pupil teachers was diminishing, for the secondary school could provide full-time education up to the age of eighteen whereas the pupil-teacher had only part-time education, during his or her years of pupilage. The scheme of training offered in Exeter, for example, was a two-year course leading to the King's Scholarship, which was the entrance examination to a training college. In the first year the pupil-teacher attended for instruction for the whole of Tuesday and Thursday each week and on Saturday morning. In the second year he attended four days a week and again on Saturday morning. The arrangement was not calculated to promote examination success. The King's Scholarship examination took place in the Lent Term of the second year, by which time the pupil-teacher had by no means finished his course of study. In 1907 therefore the system was changed so that the course was completed before the examination took place, and the last term was spent in the classroom, teaching others. By then the number coming forward to enrol as pupil teachers was falling fast and in 1909 the Exeter centre closed.[13] In an institution that had ambitions to be taken for a university college the pupil-teacher centre was somewhat embarrassing. It plainly taught at the secondary level and its closure was part of the long slow process by which the college divested itself of all but the higher branches of education.

That process had a long way to go in 1909. The college still bore the marks of its origin in the schools of art and science. The School of Art was by that time somewhat out of the mainstream of development except that it offered classes in art to the students in training. The School of

Science on its more practical side had developed into a small technical college, or manual school as it was then called. Until 1902 it had fewer than 30 pupils and was singularly ill-equipped. A class of 20 had to share one foot-lathe, for example. The influential local industrialist H. A. Willey had long taken an interest in the work of the school of science. He sent representatives to the United States, Germany, France, Australia, and Hungary to study manual schools there, and in 1900 submitted a report to the city council. His proposals alarmed Principal Clayden:

> The scheme for manual schools drags along. I hope I have turned it aside for a time at least but I am by no means sure . . . . The scheme would be excellent if it did not propose to use our rooms and our staff and part of our income. Curiously enough I cannot get Miss Montgomery to see that the appending of a boys' school to our work would effectually bar any expansion of the adult work, and would quite alter the Collegiate character of the place. Even if the boys occupied our class rooms in the mornings only it would effectively kill all idea of a University College . . . . Altogether therefore I feel anything but certain as to the future either for myself or for the work to which I have given the best years of my life. But . . . there has been a crisis of some sort almost every year I have been here and we have emerged safely from them all so far.[16]

The college emerged safely yet again. In 1902 with equipment provided by Willey the manual school moved to separate premises in Longbrook Street, Exeter. The number of day students increased, without, however, coming close to the numbers in the academic departments of the college. The new premises quickly became inadequate and by 1905 HMI were condemning the overcrowded conditions in which the school was conducted. Students, who had to have reached Standard VII before admission, studied for from one to three years. Despite poor facilities the school did good work and launched many young men into skilled employment in electrical and mechanical engineering, and as draftsmen and patternmakers. A few proceeded on Willey scholarships to university courses at Nottingham University College, or Manchester Technical College. Others left Exeter to find work with C. A. Parsons or Hawthorn Leslie in Newcastle, with Richardsons at Hartlepool, in Manchester, Calcutta, or Winnipeg. Like the pupil-teacher centre the manual school was, as Clayden saw, out of place in an aspiring university college, with its students admitted at the age of fourteen and taking practical rather than academic courses. But it remained a part of the college until 1918 when it became the responsibility of the city's education committee.[17] On the theoretical side the work of the science school continued, with evening classes that ranged from mathematics and physics to hygiene and telephony. Some of these courses reached a high standard but many were in the tradition of the science school as it had been in the 1880s.[18]

The college was in fact hard pressed to show that it did much work either by day or in evening classes that could rank as of university quality. It had indeed to assert that courses for the London matriculation or the London intermediate examination counted as university teaching.* For the number of students reading for degrees was small. It was in 1901, the same year in which the training department opened, that the college began to offer courses for the external degrees of the University of London. The first graduate was Janet Algar, an Exeter girl who took a general degree in science in 1904. The Governors of the Royal Albert Memorial marked the occasion by awarding her a special book prize of two guineas. By 1914, 44 students of the college had graduated, mostly with general degrees, and 1914 was the first year in which the number of graduates reached double figures.[19] One advantage of establishing a training department was that it might generate a supply of degree students. In 1891 the education department issued regulations which provided for a third year at training college in order that selected students might take a degree. Few Exeter students attempted this task before the First World War. For a pupil-teacher entering the training department the burden of work would have been severe. In his first year he would take the London Intermediate (five subjects for external students in arts, only four subjects in science). In his second year the Board of Education's certificate examinations in academic subjects and educational theory had to be tackled. Both first- and second-year study would be interrupted by several weeks of teaching practice. The third year was free from such distractions and could be devoted to preparing for the London external degree! In 1911 the Board of Education recognised that it was asking rather too much, and allowed students in training to take a four-year course consisting of three years of study for a degree followed by a fourth year of professional training. Unluckily for Exeter this more spacious scheme applied only in universities, not in university colleges.

On average only four students graduated in each of the years from

---

*The matriculation examination of London University was roughly equivalent to five good passes in ordinary level GCE; the intermediate, equivalent to five advanced level passes, was often taken in the first year of a three-year degree. The Higher School Certificate Examination was introduced in 1920, but many schools continued to prepare candidates for the London intermediate instead. In 1950 school certificate and higher school certificate examinations were replaced by ordinary and advanced level GCE.

1904 to 1914. The university department of the college would have been painfully small if these had been its only students. An unknown but probably not small number of students took the degree examinations but failed to satisfy the examiners. Larger numbers of 'university' students were preparing for matriculation and the intermediate—again not always with happy results:

Candidates for Matriculation and Intermediate

	Matriculation		Intermediate	
	Pass	Fail	Pass	Fail
Jan 1909	8	14	—	—
June 1909	16	18	8	4
Jan 1910	11	14	—	—
June 1910	—	—	7	18

These are the only statistics of this kind that are extant for the years up to 1914. There is no reason to suppose that they are unrepresentative. Nationally, failure rates were high among external candidates for London intermediate, averaging 50 per cent in arts and 90 per cent in science in the years 1908–10.[20] In any case it was the training of non-graduate elementary school teachers, not university work, that remained the principal business of the college until after the first world war. In 1912, for example, day students were distributed among the departments as follows:

University department	74
Training department	153
School of Art	50
Engineering and manual training	31
	308

In addition over 400 students were attending evening classes.[21]

There were 19 members of staff to teach some 230 students in the training and university departments. A modern university would regard a staff:student ratio of 1:12 as decidedly adverse. In a small college such a ratio posed several problems. Where 19 members of staff professed between them a dozen subjects teachers had to be generalists. Only physics, mathematics, education and English had the luxury of more than one member of staff. Frank Fletcher of classics and J. L. Sager of biology helped to supervise teaching practice as well as teach their speciality.* W. J. Harte doubled as historian and economist. In his earlier days in the college his duties had been even more varied. As Professor of History and Literature he undertook to teach Greek and Latin to intermediate standard, English history from Julius Caesar to George III with special courses on the reign of Edward III and the Civil War. He also took English grammar, précis writing and composition for London matriculation, and for the students in training he expounded *Hamlet* and *The Merchant of Venice* and Sir Walter Scott's *Old Mortality*. In 1906 when he was no longer needed for Greek and Latin he offered a course in ancient history instead. H. F. Lunn, principal lecturer and from 1904 professor of mathematics, was teaching mathematics in 1902 from matriculation to degree level; he also taught general elementary physics and helped Clayden with physiography and geology.[22] Such versatility was admirable, but more admirable in a grammar school than a university college.

Specialist teaching requires specialist books, and in this respect the college was fortunate in sharing premises with Exeter's public library. Although the Albert Memorial had hardly any money for the purchase of books the library had grown to a considerable size by the end of the nineteenth century, thanks to generous benefactors. Public demand for works of fiction was met for many years from the books of the Public Select Library, which were given to the city in 1871. At various dates valuable collections of works of reference—the Kent Kingdon bequest and the Fisher Library were the richest—came to the library by bequest or gift. By 1900 the lending library had 6000 books and unusually for a municipal library the reference section had many more—some 14,000. It was the reference library that mattered to the college. Students outnumbered all other readers there, but in a collection acquired by gift rather than purchase they found that some subjects were better served than others. Art books and historical works were well represented; the natural sciences apart from biology had not been so lucky. In 1904 therefore the college resolved to purchase some books of its own and the

*Frank Fletcher (1867–1956) devilled for Jowett, the Master of Balliol, from the age of 11. He was a classical exhibitioner at Balliol and won the Gaisford Prize for Greek verse in 1888. He was Jowett's secretary from 1889–93. He taught in elementary schools from 1895 to 1901 and was then a lecturer in education in various university colleges, and a sub-editor of the *Victorian County History* until 1909. In 1909 he was appointed lecturer in classics in Exeter and in 1928 was elected to the chair. He retired in 1933. J. L. Sager, a Cambridge biologist, had taken a post-graduate certificate in education. In their very different ways both might be regarded as fitted to lend a hand in the work of the training department. For Jowett's secretaries, see G. Faber, *Jowett* (1957).

present university library traces its origin to that decision. The first book grant was £50. Books from the city library were also set aside to form the nucleus of a college library. Students could borrow these books; other readers could refer to them. The college did not have its own librarian or even at that date contribute to the costs of library administration. The city librarian H. Tapley-Soper became college librarian as well, and retained both posts until 1933, when the college first appointed a librarian of its own.[23]

In 1904 the city council commissioned a report from Michael Sadler* on secondary and higher education in Exeter. He had kind things to say of the college:

> The remarkable development of the Royal Albert Memorial College shows that its work has met a real need . . . . It has filled a gap of somewhat irregular outline in the educational provision of the City . . . . [West of Bristol and Southampton] there is no other city which is so clearly marked out as a suitable seat for an academic institution.[24]

Sadler's words have been taken to mean that he plainly foresaw a bright future for 'the educational metropolis of the West',[25] but a more cautious interpretation is possible. He accepted that Exeter would be the natural site for a university college if one were ever established west of Bristol, but he by no means implied that such a development was certain to take place.

The advisory committee on (Treasury) grants to university colleges took an equally cautious view. In 1902 when degree work had only just begun it found that the college fell 'far short of the required standard in purely university work'. On the occasion of its visit in 1905 it toyed with the idea of a special grant from time to time to encourage institutions like the college to reach the required standards. Those standards the committee fixed at £1500 in fees from university work and £4000 in local income. On both counts Exeter fell woefully short of compliance. In 1907 the advisory committee made a careful survey of Exeter's standards in teaching and equipment and appeared to be reasonably satisfied. But the numbers pursuing post-matriculation work were small, and the college had not stirred the generosity of local benefactors. In common with Birkbeck College and the East London College [Queen Mary College], Exeter once more failed to get a grant. In 1909 the advisory

---

*Michael Sadler (1861-1943) was at the time professor of education at Manchester. He later became Vice-Chancellor of the University of Leeds and Master of University College, Oxford.

committee set more stringent criteria: satisfactory instruction in modern languages, classics, mathematics, the natural sciences, history and philosophy; a reasonable number of students; adequate buildings and equipment; and an income large enough not only for efficiency but also for superannuation. If Exeter could not meet the standards set in 1905 it is not surprising that the higher physical and financial standards of 1909 also defeated it.[26]

How could the college acquire the coveted status? One faint possibility was a link with Bristol, which became an independent university in 1908. Principal Clayden hoped to temper the connection with the University of London through participating in the privileges of the new university.[27] It is not clear what measures he had in mind and Bristol showed no interest in fostering a potential rival in its hinterland. If short cuts were ruled out, there was nothing for it but the slow process of growth through numbers, finance and quality of work done.

Financially it had been made plain that the Treasury helped those colleges that helped themselves. If a college could attract private benefactions or secure generous aid from local authorities it stood a much better chance of a Treasury grant. Exeter City Council was the only local authority that showed much enthusiasm for Exeter's infant college. It levied a penny rate for the library, which can be regarded in part as a subvention to the college. The penny rate levied in 1901 for technical instruction went entirely to the college, but by no means all of it for university work. The proceeds amounted to £900 in 1901 and for several years after, despite the continued growth of Exeter's rateable value. In 1908 an adjustment raised the sum to £1,150, the full value of a penny rate at that time.* Devon's contribution to college finances was much smaller and consisted of the payment of fees for Devon students who attended the college. Until Devon was ready to levy a penny rate for the use of the college, there could be little hope that local income would reach £4,000 p.a., the standard set by the Treasury. The principal paymaster was not the local authority at all but the Board of Education, which in 1913–14 contributed about half of the college's income in the form of grants for tuition and residence and fees paid for students in training.[28]

From the earliest days of the schools of art and science private benefactors had given money to help the work. Their subscriptions were

---

*The city council also passed over £1300 of whisky money, but this could hardly be regarded as local income.

treated as income and it was not until the end of the century that a permanent endowment was contemplated. No practical steps were taken to attract endowments, however, until 1911. The ambitious appeal then launched aimed at raising £30,000 in five years. Nearly £4,000 was promised in the first three weeks but by the outbreak of the First World War only £6,000 had been collected, most of it in large sums of £50 to £500. James G. Owen, later Sir James Owen, proprietor of the *Express and Echo*, headed the appeal committee. In a circular letter of a kind that became familiar in the inter-war years he put the case for generosity to the College:

We have provided Elementary Schools and Secondary Schools. We dare not stop there. We must complete the ladder by offering every facility for education of University standard. This we are doing under great disadvantages in Devonshire at the University College, Exeter, and we appeal to you with the utmost confidence to associate yourself with us in advancing the efficiency and scope of the Institution by providing it with a substantial permanent endowment.[29]

Lack of endowments did not stop the College from acquiring additional buildings. The York wing of the Museum, opened in 1899, was full two years later and in 1902 the first tentative plans were drawn up for a new building on adjoining land in Gandy Street and Bradninch Place. By 1904 all the houses in Bradninch Place and two properties in Gandy Street had been acquired. As part of the new building would serve the day training college, the Board of Education was prepared to make a capital grant. Building began in July 1909 and by Easter 1911 was complete. Gothic went out of fashion with the new century and Gandy Street as it has always been known was a red-brick building in the Georgian style. It had more than 20,000 square feet of floor space, over 40 rooms including a raked lecture theatre holding 60, some large lecture rooms, a purpose-built botanical laboratory, academic and administrative offices and common-rooms for staff and students. It did not entirely represent a net gain of accommodation since the old properties on the site had been used for teaching, as student common-rooms, and as an annexe to the hostel. Nevertheless, Gandy Street was an imposing and important addition to the capital assets of the College, the only building it could call its own, and the centre of college life for nearly half a century. The site was a restricted one of about an acre. There were hopes that the unbuilt land to the north could become the site of a great hall, but nothing more dignified than army huts has ever been erected there. With the acquisiton of the Streatham Estate in 1922 it was no longer necessary to think in terms of a cramped city-centre site and Gandy Street, no longer new, seemed much less desirable to those who had not known the makeshift arrangements that had preceded it.

The College did not sever its connections with the Museum when the Gandy Street building opened. It continued to need accommodation there and did not finally withdraw until the Faculty of Arts moved into Queen's Building on the Streatham Estate in 1958. Shortly afterwards in 1959 the old School of Art, by then a College of Art, also left the Museum for spacious new quarters off Topsham Road, thus ending a 90-year old connection between the Albert Memorial and technical and higher education in Exeter.[30]

It was not only in building that the College strove to show itself worthy of university status. Academic self-government has always been regarded as a necessary feature of a university. The college committee that reported to the Governors of the Royal Albert Memorial hardly ranked as an academic body. It is true that the Principal consulted the professors before attending college committee but that was an informal arrangement. The committee itself consisted of laymen and if any correspondence with a university body can be found at all it is with Council rather than Senate. In 1909 the college established a Board of Studies to report to college committee on academic matters. The Board consisted of the Principal, the four professors, the Registrar and the Mistress of Method. The other members of staff clearly saw this as oligarchy rather than self-government and in 1911 the Board of Studies was enlarged. Teaching was reorganised on a departmental basis* and the lecturers in charge of departments became members of the board. There was still no elective element in college government, but nearly half the academic staff now came within the pale of the constitution. Among those who thus gained a voice were J. W. Schopp the German-born lecturer in modern languages, and A. E. Morgan lecturer in English[31]†

Admissions policy is another matter where high standards are expected

*There were to be nine departments—biology, chemistry, classics, education, English, history, mathematics, modern languages, and physics.

†J. W. Schopp, a forthright scholar, was appointed in 1902 and became professor of modern languages in 1926; he retired in 1935. A. E. Morgan was appointed to a lectureship in English in 1910 and became professor in 1919; he moved to Sheffield in 1924, was Principal of University College, Hull 1926–35, Principal and Vice-Chancellor of McGill 1935–37. A civil servant during the Second World War he rose to be Assistant Secretary in the Ministry of Labour and National Service. He was Educational Controller for the British Council 1945–50. In 1954 at the age of 68 he began a third career as warden of Toynbee Hall, retiring in 1963. He died in 1972.

of university institutions. The College preferred to accept for teacher-training only those students who had passed London matriculation, or who could give 'satisfactory evidence of being likely to profit by a university course'. It was not always easy to adhere to this high-sounding principle. One difficulty was that students in training had often taken the Board's examination for the King's Scholarship; many had not attended a secondary school and it was only secondary schools that had the London matriculation or an equivalent qualification in view. A further difficulty was that the Royal Albert Memorial College was a local authority institution partly financed out of the rates. From the outset the college was expected to give preference to local students. In 1902 for instance all Exeter students who passed the King's Scholarship examination in the second division were guaranteed a place 'unless other sufficient reasons are brought before the committee'. Such a provision might well conflict with the ambition to admit students capable of profiting from a university course. The City Council particularly resented the presence of Devon students in the college, paying no higher fees than those chargeable to the sons and daughters of Exeter rate-payers. Devon, it was felt, was getting its teachers trained on the cheap at the expense of the City. The County Council appears to have felt no qualms of conscience on this score although about a quarter of the students in the College came from Devon. In the training department half the students came from beyond Devon — from Cornwall, Dorset and Somerset, and from South Wales. The City Council made no attempt to touch the conscience or the pocket of those more distant authorities. Devon in their view was the principal offender since its students attended all departments of the College; only the training department attracted students from further afield.[32]

The ideal university student combines high spirits with high thinking. The surviving evidence suggests that the typical Exeter student in the years before the First World War satisfied the first half of this formula more fully than the second, by establishing a tradition of good fellowship that while not excluding scholarship kept it firmly in its place. The College acquired its first playing fields in 1903 when it took over Exeter Cricket Club's lease of Gras Lawn in Barrack Road. In 1912 the College bought the land outright. The substantial contingent of Welshmen made the college a force to be reckoned with on the rugby field. In the three seasons 1911–14 the College scored victory after victory over the redoubtable old enemy, Saint Luke's College. When Saint Luke's won

10–5 in February 1914 it was their first victory in three years at a time when the sides met twice a season. In 1911–12 Exeter had in their XV Willie Davies*, a Welsh international three-quarter from Aberavon, but as Saint Luke's suffered some heavier defeats when he was no longer playing in the XV it is clear that the college was enjoying an unusual spell of sporting brilliance.

The origins of that expensive branch of student activity, the Athletic Union, go back to 1906 when the college first levied a subscription of ten shillings (50p) for sporting purposes.[33] Apart from sport, a popular student diversion was 'the social', an early-evening entertainment that was a mixture of dancing, songs and refreshments. For men only there was 'the smoker', a dinner party at which the more clubbable members of staff were welcome. In the small college of those days the staff took a prominent part in many student activities. They edited the *Students' Magazine* first published in 1898. They took part in debates: Miss Epps, mistress of method, proposed a tax on bachelors; J. W. Schopp championed tobacco. Politically the students steered a somewhat erratic middle-of-the-road course, if voting at debates is any guide. A motion that conscription was essential for the safety of the Empire was heavily defeated; on the other hand, there were narrow majorities in favour of capital punishment and against rate aid to voluntary hospitals.

In some respects the College was conducted more like a school than a university. As in schools (and training colleges at that time), men and women prefects were appointed and not only among the students in training, but in the university department as well. Half-term was observed: it ran from midday Saturday to Monday evening; the students petitioned for a longer holiday beginning after lectures on Friday and lasting until Tuesday evening. Only the first part of their request was granted. The men students in training practised initiation ceremonies on innocent freshmen or juniors, who were subjected to a mock medical examination and a comic general knowledge paper. Remarkably this boyish tradition survived the interruption of the First World War when the stream of men students in training almost dried up.[34]

Sporting, dramatic† and literary societies, field clubs and religious associations flourished before the formation of a students union in Exeter. By 1895 the university extension students had formed a Guild

---

*Davies also headed the batting and bowling averages in the 1912 season. His bowling analysis read: 105.4 overs, 20 maidens, 222 runs, 41 wickets.
†The dramatic society produced its first play in 1910, *The Importance of being Earnest*.

which put on a performance of *A Midsummer Night's Dream*. In 1900 the union or students' club, as it was indifferently called, was allowed to use some college rooms in Bradninch Place for refreshments and accommodation between lectures. Expenses exceeded revenue and after a few years no more is heard of a students' club.[35] In 1909 a more serious and successful attempt was made. Albert Howe, College wag and first 'mayor of the Borough of Bradninch', proposed the establishment of a Student Representative Council. The constitution, after amendment by the Board of Studies, provided for a council of eighteen, four representing the university department and fourteen the training department; ten of the fourteen students in training and two of the four university students were to be women. The Board of Studies suggested this concession to the suffragist movement as being an accurate reflection of relative numbers in the college. Council held its first meeting on 30 May 1910 with Principal Clayden, honorary president, in the chair. By November 1910 the student chairman was presiding over meetings.[36]

Various student societies — dramatic, literary, choral, and debating — affiliated to the union, together with the committee that ran the *Students' Magazine*. The union subscription was set at four shillings (20p). This was too small a sum to permit subvention of sporting activities. Instead the SRC undertook to administer a Central Sports Fund largely provided out of the pockets of members of staff and other voluntary contributors. Perhaps this fund rather than the College levy of ten shillings per head, first raised in 1906, marks the true origin of the modern Athletic Union.[37]

Intellectually undistinguished though the atmosphere may have been, it apparently pleased the students. A flourishing Old Students' Association quickly established itself with branches in several cities in Southern and Midland England and in South Wales. A high proportion of the members were inevitably teachers in elementary schools. Though they looked back affectionately on their two, or sometimes three, years in college they were in no position to make timely and handsome benefactions to their alma mater. As Europe plunged into war the Royal Albert Memorial College remained an unendowed institution little known outside Devon. The Board of Education, in allowing it to establish a training department, had virtually admitted that it detected in it the seeds of a university. In 1912 the college received an invitation to the Congress of Universities of the British Empire to be held in London in July of that year.[38] But the recognition that really mattered — that of the advisory committee on grants to universities and colleges — seemed well beyond immediate attainment. It needed the extraordinary hopes that modern war generates to bring recognition within the bounds of probability.

Notes

1 Letterbook 3, Clayden to J. N. Keynes, 31 March 1908 [University of Exeter archives].
2 H. C. Dent, *The Training of Teachers in England and Wales 1800-1975* (Hodder and Stoughton 1977), pp.12-14, 56.
3 Ibid., pp.33, 37.
4 Board of Education, *Code* 1903 (BPP 1903 LI); Advisory Committee on Grants to University Colleges (BPP 1907 LXIV), p.559.
5 RAM, College committee, 26 July 1901.
6 Ibid. n.d. but May to July 1901, 2 and 27 July, 6 August 1901.
7 Ibid., 7 July and 2 December 1902, 9 February 1903, 8 July 1907; letterbook, 1910-12, A. K. Woodbridge to Bishop of St. Germans, Truro, 7 March, and to H. Lloyd Parry, 11 April 1911.
8 RAM, College committee, 23 March 1903, 22 February 1904.
9 Letterbook, 1908, A. K. Woodbridge to E. Hackforth, 22 April 1908.
10 Dent, *Training of Teachers*, p.49.
11 Letterbook, 1913, A. K. Woodbridge to Miss J. D. Montgomery, 8 April 1913.
12 Dent, p.84; RAM 27 July 1901; *Students' Magazine*, October 1901 [Cambridge University archives, BEMS 31/10 — Cambridge University Library].
13 Memories of Miss Amy Shorto, Warden of College Hostel 1903-10, written in 1941; memories of Miss Blanche Moore, an early student in College Hostel and for 50 years a staunch supporter of the Old Students' Association and the College Club; *Students' Magazine*, November 1908, March 1914.
14 RAM, College committee, 6 April 1908.
15 Dent, pp.54-6; RAM, College committee, 6 June 1904, 8 July 1907; letterbook 1908-09, A. K. Woodbridge to J. Morgan, 9 March 1909.
16 Clayden to R. D. Roberts, Secretary to the Cambridge Local Lectures Syndicate [Cambridge University Archives, BEMS 31/5 — Cambridge University Library].
17 RAM, Sub-Committee on a day manual school, 1 and 15 December 1900, 19 January 1901; College committee, 3 December 1901, 15 September and 2 December 1902, 8 June 1905; manual school sub-committee, 4 July 1907; RAM, 3 June 1918.
18 Letterbook 1910-12, A. K. Woodbridge to J. W. Dodgson, Reading University College, 9 November 1910; *Calendar* 1910-1911.
19 RAM, 12 December 1904; *Calendar* 1920-21, University of Exeter, *Exeter University Register 1893-1962* (1970).
20 Exeter examination results are noted in a book recording attendance at committees, 1906-12 [box 3, University of Exeter archives]; *Daily Telegraph*, 29 February 1912.
21 Letterbook 1912, A. K. Woodbridge to the editor, *The Schoolmaster's Yearbook*, 26 July 1912.
22 *Calendar*, 1902-03, 1905-06, 1912-13.
23 AM, Finance Committee, 3 May and 3 August 1871; *Annual Report*, 1872, 1898; RAM, Library committee, 3 February 1902, 2 February and 30 November 1903, 4 January, 2 and 16 May 1904.

24 M. E. Sadler, *Report on Secondary and higher education in Exeter*, (City of Exeter, Education committee, 1905), pp.34, 61, 63.

25 Newton, *Victorian Exeter*, p.xvi; L. J. Lloyd, 'The University of Exeter: A Retrospect' in F. Barlow, ed., *Exeter and its Region* (Exeter, 1969) p.316.

26 Advisory committee on grants to university colleges, *Reports*, BPP 1902 LXXX, p.140; 1905 LX p.331; LXIV, pp.562, 689–92; 1909 LXIX, p.8; 1910 LXXII, p.325, 335–6.

27 *Express and Echo*, Exeter, 1 October 1909.

28 RAM, College committee, 1 June 1908; finance committee, 16 July 1908; 'Statement regarding the use made of the University College by Students residing in the county of Devon' (1908) [box 3, University archives]; letterbook, A. K. Woodbridge to S. Snodgrass, City Education Department, 15 June 1914; PPA, Statement of income 1913–14.

29 AM, Museum and technical education committee, 10 October 1898; RAM, sub-committee on endowment and development, 13 April 1901; *Western Daily Mercury*, 21 October 1911; letterbooks, A. K. Woodbridge to H. Epps, 15 February 1912, to Clayden, 2 January 1912; J. G. Owen to Sir Harry Veitch, 21 May 1913.

30 RAM, 15 April 1901, and 6 July 1904; Endowment Committee, 14 April 1902; letterbook, 1908–09, Clayden to R. Hawtrey [Secretary to the advisory committee on grants to universities and colleges] 1 July 1909.

31 Letterbooks, 1909, A. K. Woodbridge to H. F. Lunn, 19 January 1909; 1910–12, Woodbridge to H. Lloyd Parry [town clerk and secretary of college committee], 17 January 1911, and to J. W. Schopp, 29 March 1911.

32 RAM, College Committee, 29 August 1901, 27 March 1902, 5 March 1906; RAM, 11 December 1905; 'Statement regarding the use made of the University College by Students residing in the County of Devon' 1908 [University of Exeter Archives, box 3].

33 RAM, College Committee 22 June 1903 and 5 February 1906; RAM, 12 September 1903 and 5 February 1912; *Students' Magazine*, March, June and December 1912, March 1914.

34 *Students' Magazine*, 1906–14 passim; *The Ram*, Spring 1921. *The Ram* was the *Students' Magazine* under a new name and format; Students' Representative Council [hereafter SRC], 3 November 1910 and 22 February 1911 [University of Exeter archives].

35 AM, Museum and Technical Education Committee, 1 July 1895, 11 May 1896; RAM 9 July 1900; *Annual Report*, 1900; *Students' Magazine*, 1900–02, passim.

36 *Students' Magazine*, March and November 1910; SRC, 3 December 1909, 18 February, 26 and 30 May, 25 October, 3 November 1910.

37 SRC, 6 December 1910, 17 November 1911.

38 RAM, 20 May 1912.

IV

THE FIRST WORLD WAR
AND THE UNIVERSITY MOVEMENT

The college could not avoid the impact of war. Men students almost disappeared from the training and university departments but women took their place and numbers were not much reduced. Members of staff also went off to the war, and sixteen former students and two members of staff were killed. Not all those who went away saw much active service. Professor Lunn was a second-lieutenant in an anti-aircraft detachment near London—in Clayden's opinion, a good teacher wasted. Captain A. E. Morgan of the Royal Field Artillery was stationed at Topsham and an indulgent C.O. allowed him to live at home and to undertake propaganda work for the cause of university education in the South West. When A. K. Woodbridge, the Registrar, was called up, the College lost its administrative staff at a stroke. Woodbridge had been appointed Registrar and Secretary in 1904. He assumed the administrative duties previously performed by John Trott, Registrar and Lecturer in Physics, and by Miss Lake, who had served as secretary and accountant since 1901 for £80 a year. Clayden himself had undertaken a good deal of routine correspondence, for example with the Board of Education, because there was nobody else to do the work. The appointment of a full-time registrar relieved Clayden of this burden, but the administrative machine remained a rudimentary one. The typewriter acquired in 1904 was apparently for the use of the Registrar himself; secretarial assistance—and then for administrators only—was beyond the means of the college until the 1920s. The gap left by the call-up of the Registrar was filled by Clayden and H. Lloyd Parry, the town clerk, who between them undertook admissions, correspondence, and the accounts, beside their normal duties. The war required not only the men but the property of the College. Part of the main building in Gandy Street housed the staff of the local recruiting drive—without causing intolerable inconvenience. More seriously, College Hostel became a military hospital in 1915. The students moved to Hartwell House, a property in Pennsylvania leased by the college as a replacement. In the fullness of time the College bought the freehold, and Hartwell House later became Hope Hall.[1]

With the end of the war men flocked back to college. The training of men teachers had been virtually suspended for four years and emergency measures were needed to make good the deficiency. Men who had spent a year in training before military service were allowed to take their certificate after a further term's work. And for students in training and university students alike there were ex-servicemen's grants generous enough to attract larger numbers to universities than ever before. In the academic year 1920–21 there were 48,000 university students in the country, an increase of 70 per cent on 1910–11. Exeter shared in this post-war expansion. In October 1919 the College registered nearly 400 day students, a total that included 110 students in the School of Art. In 1920, the most crowded year, there were over 350 students excluding the School of Art, but including the new Department of Pharmacy.* The remaining open space behind the Museum and to the side of the main building in Gandy Street became a jumble of army huts, now silent and forlorn, but for nearly forty years a serviceable if unlovely annexe to the main buildings of the college and university.[2]

Numbers did not bring prosperity. The cost of living doubled during the war and went on rising fast until the middle of 1920 when the boom collapsed and prices began to tumble. College income increased little. It stood at over £13,000 in 1913–14, and had risen to less than £18,000 in 1919–20 when a deficit of some £5,000 threatened. Had academic salaries increased in step with the cost of living the deficit would have been much larger. Principal Clayden's salary rose by £100 between 1914 and 1920, an increase of 16½ per cent. On average the salaries of staff already appointed before 1914 increased by 57 per cent. Heads of department were by 1920 receiving less than the poorer-paid headmasters; and if the junior members of staff had been schoolmasters with an allowance for special responsibility they would have been earning more under the Burnham scale of 1920 than they received as college lecturers. The burden of sustaining the College seemed to be beyond the powers or at

*The manual or technical school was detached from the College in 1918.

least the will of the City Council. Devon, with 113 students in the College, contributed £275 to its income, Exeter, with 69 students, over £4,200.* The city let it be known that closure of the College was not out of the question. Devon had no training college of its own and would probably have had to establish one at considerable expense if Exeter's disappeared. It is probable that the rumours of closure were simply part of a diplomatic offensive designed to force Devon into joint support of the college. If that was the intention it succeeded. The county promised a grant at the annual rate of £4,000 a year, beginning in December 1919 with a grant of one-third of that amount for the remaining months of the financial year 1919–20. In return it was agreed to vest the management of the college in a committee composed equally of representatives of the City and County Councils. At length Devon had been brought to join with Exeter on equal terms in shaping the destiny of the College.[3]

Devon took the decision to become jointly responsible for the College, not out of fear alone, but also in hope. The hope was that a demonstration of local support would persuade the government to raise the College to the rank of a university. It may seem strange that high ambition should flourish during and immediately after a destructive war, but it is undeniable that the waste of lives and money produced feelings of optimism rather than despair. One manifestation of the national desire for 'reconstruction' was the movement to found a university in South-West England. Principal Clayden sketched a plan of campaign when he delivered his presidential address to the Devonshire Association in 1915. Pre-war aspirations to university status had centred round the Royal Albert Memorial College alone, but had been disappointed because the College plainly lacked the necessary resources. By 1915 interest had broadened to encompass other institutions of higher education in the South West. As Clayden saw it, the cathedral city of Exeter was the fitting home for academic work in arts and pure science; Plymouth with its naval and maritime traditions could develop its technical schools and the marine-biology station; and Camborne, centre of Cornish mining, already had a school of mines that could play its part in a federal university. In addition the South West had three training colleges — for women at Truro, for men at Saint Luke's, and the day training college attached to the Royal Albert Memorial. Finally at Seale Hayne near Newton Abbot there was a newly-founded agricultural college. To Clayden it seemed obvious that these institutions offered the chance to

*Much of this was whisky money, of course.

create a multi-faculty university strongly supported by the local community. The federal university of Wales provided a model on which a university for South-West England could pattern itself.[4]

Clayden left to younger men the hard work of converting his idea into a reality. The first step was formally taken in May 1917 with the establishment of a Committee for the Furtherance of University Education in the South West. The most active members of the committee were the secretary, Professor W. H. Lewis, and the publicity secretary, Captain A. E. Morgan, of the Department of English. W. P. Hiern, FRS, a distinguished botanist who lived in Barnstaple, was joint secretary with Lewis, adding lustre rather than executive power to the movement. Chairmanship of the committee fell to Sir Henry Lopes, Chairman of Devon County Council, 1917–1938. It was a happy choice. Sir Henry, a Devon landowner and soldier, had served as Conservative MP for Grantham from 1892–1900. When in 1910 he tried to return to national politics the electors of Torquay, in unusually radical mood, preferred a Liberal. For the rest of his life Sir Henry devoted himself to local causes, chief of which was Devon County Council; second only to that was his concern for the college at Exeter. As a natural leader of Devon society he gave weight and influence to any committee that he headed. But from the start he was no figure-head. His recruitment was one of the outstanding successes of the furtherance committee. Another important figure whose sympathies and interest were early enlisted was W. L. Munday (later Sir William Munday), a Plymouth solicitor and city councillor. The committee, and especially Lewis and Morgan, set to work to arouse opinion in favour of the proposed university. They spoke at meetings all over Devon and Cornwall and sought interviews with men of power or influence. Thomas Hardy, visited by Morgan, predictably suggested that the new university should be entitled the University of Wessex. 1918 was the tercentenary of the death of Sir Walter Raleigh, and for a time there was a real possibility that the Raleigh University would commemorate the buccaneering poet-historian. Sir William M'Cormick, chairman of the advisory committee on grants to universities, could not be neglected. He took the view that Bristol could give adequate academic service to Devon and Cornwall; he was not moved when Morgan produced a map and drew a circle centred on Bristol and embracing not only the South West but Oxford, Cambridge and London as well.

The immediate object of the committee was to secure local support for an approach to the Board of Education. Eventually in November

1918* a delegation proceeded to London for a conference with the Minister, H. A. L. Fisher. It represented many interests and most shades of opinion in the South West: the major local authorities — Devon, Cornwall and Dorset, Plymouth, and Exeter; men of letters and scientists — Quiller-Couch, W. D. Whetham [Sir William Dampier], W. P. Hiern; chambers of commerce, trades councils and trade unions, the Workers' Educational Association, schools, literary and scientific societies. The Minister saw littler merit in the deputation's case: federal universities had had an unhappy history; the University of Wales was a new experiment, but the earlier federation of Manchester, Leeds and Liverpool had broken up in 1903. Where, he asked, were the students, the staff and the money to come from? 'The frostiness of his attitude created a very vexed mood among those present.' [Morgan]. In an explanatory letter to Earl Fortescue a few days later Fisher did little to soothe ruffled feathers: he had meant to imply not that there could never be a university in the South West, but that it would take a long time.[5]

The leaders of the movement refused to be discouraged by this setback. For a time they hoped to overcome their financial difficulties by persuading the people of Devon and Cornwall to commemorate their war dead by establishing a university in South-West England.[6] Almost every parish in the peninsula has its grim witness in stone to the rejection of this idea. Nevertheless, in the face of steady pressure the Board of Education agreed to inspect the work of university standard. Why did the Board make this conciliatory gesture? At the time of the deputation in November 1918 the official attitude, reflected in Fisher's speech, was extremely hostile to the campaign for a university in the South West:

> To propose at this time of day to form a university out of a second-rate College at Exeter, mainly filled with Training College Students, a newly founded Agricultural College at Newton Abbot, a School of Mines at Camborne and a Technical School at Plymouth is a very tall order.

The officials advising the minister thought so poorly of the claim for a university that they had not even been very willing to see the deputation at all. They and the minister were somewhat surprised at the anger which was aroused by the rejection of the case put forward. An HMI stationed at Plymouth warned the minister that the Liberals might lose seats to

*Here and at a few other points, there are minor corrections, mostly of dates, to the story as told by Sir Hector Hetherington in *The University College at Exeter 1920-25*. Important sources, notably the Principal's papers, have come to light since he wrote. But his work remains invaluable as a first-hand and delightful account by the most important actor in the play.

Labour in Plymouth constituencies as a result of his attitude. If that argument sounds a little strained, there can be no doubt that the Department was impressed by the County Council's decision to grant £4,000 a year to the College in Exeter. Rate support for the College was now higher than that for Hartley College, Southampton, which was on the list of grant-aided university colleges. The Department was also puzzled and irritated by the whole question of university colleges. Exeter was not the only aspirant to university status: Stoke, Hull, Norwich and Leicester were all thinking along similar lines. In a memorandum dated 25 November 1919 the department showed impatience to settle the matter:

> It is most desirable that an announcement should be made as soon as possible which will make it clear that the list of university colleges will be closed either at once, or after Exeter has been admitted.[7]

It was in these circumstances that Sir Alfred Dale, a former Vice-Chancellor of Liverpool University, and a team of HMI came to Exeter in March 1920 to inspect the college and confer with local authorities about its future. Their report was thorough and friendly. They noted that in science, teaching was for the pass degree only 'but within its limits the instruction is thorough and efficient'. In history and modern languages 'the results, as tested by the Honours Examination of the University of London, are encouraging and both these Honours Schools show promise of growth'. As on previous inspections it was the poverty of the College that attracted adverse comment: teachers were too few and therefore had to cover too much ground; salaries were low and superannuation had still not been instituted; apparatus, books and periodicals were all deficient. Even with Devon's new contribution of £4,000 p.a. a deficit of more than £3,000 was expected in the year 1920–21. Politely they described the site of the College as restricted—a few years later Principal Murray used the franker expression 'absurd'. Nevertheless the report concluded favourably:

> It seems desirable to retain the College as a centre of higher education in the district that it serves . . . . Even as it now is, [it] supplies a foundation on which it is possible to build. It is doing good work already: it is capable of doing more work and better work. Poverty is the main if not the only obstacle . . . . Timely help may not only enable it to discharge more effectively its existing functions, but may also develop it into a centre of higher studies that should ultimately serve the South-West of England as a University institution.[8]

The signatories did not specify what form the timely help should take, but the case of the University of Wales gave grounds for optimism. In 1918 the government had promised to match £ for £ the income raised locally for the support of the Welsh colleges in federation. Devon and Exeter were already making substantial contributions and it remained to persuade Plymouth, Cornwall and perhaps Dorset to follow their lead. This important task fell to the new Principal, H. J. W. Hetherington. Clayden retired (a year early) at the end of June 1920 after 27 years in the service of the college. He had taken little part in the work of the Furtherance Committee, and the constitutional changes that followed the County Council's grant to the college made a convenient point for him to withdraw from the hurly-burly:

> Recent events have opened up a new era in the history of the College. Hitherto it has grown little by little, each new development meaning some small adjustment to the whole until the University Extension Centre and the School of Science and Art with which we started have become the premier educational centre of these South-Western Countries.[9]

Hector Hetherington, a Scots philosopher from Glasgow, was appointed Principal at the early age of 31. He had previously served as professor of philosophy in Cardiff, so that he came to Exeter with some knowledge of the politics of federal universities. A fluent and persuasive speaker, an efficient administrator and a man of force and charm, he was destined to spend almost the whole of his working life at the head of a college or a university. When he left Exeter in December 1924 it was to spend two and a half years in the chair of moral philosophy in Glasgow before becoming Vice-Chancellor, first of Liverpool, and then from 1936 to 1961 of his old university, Glasgow. Exeter was fortunate to have the services of a man of his ability. They were not cheap: he received a salary nearly twice as large as Clayden's—but as it turned out, it proved a wise investment of college funds.

Hetherington soon had a chance to demonstrate his powers of persuasion and leadership. On the evening of Armistice Day 1920 a group of students who had served in the war invited the Principal to dinner at Deller's Café. The party broke up in good order at a respectable hour and Hetherington retired to bed. The students did not. They armed themselves with brushes and red paint and spent the small hours daubing Saint Luke's College and the statues of Richard Hooker and of the local hero General Redvers Buller VC. They posted scouts to give warning of approaching policemen and completed their prank unmolested and without detection. When the damage became visible on the morning of November 12 the city and the town council seethed with indignation. Hetherington persuaded the culprits to own up to him, fined them, and told the police that he knew but would not disclose the names of the offenders.* After a few days and some private words between Hetherington and the Chief Constable, four of the students voluntarily surrendered to the police, appeared before the magistrates and were bound over to be of good behaviour. Their war record had been good, there was no political significance in the colour of the paint they had used, and the statues had suffered no permanent damage. All was forgiven and an affair that had threatened to diminish local support for the college ended with smiles all round. The students were well pleased with the sympathetic handling of the culprits; the city was not in the end sorry that the spirited exploits of a few ex-servicemen were being reported as far away as South Africa; and all who had the welfare of the College at heart must have been well satisfied with the Principal's deft manoeuvres.[10]

All his skill would be needed in the weightier negotiations that lay ahead. The constitution under which Devon and Exeter assumed joint responsibility for the affairs of the College was intended to be a temporary arrangement until the College could secure incorporation. Sir Alfred Dale's report had been encouraging and work was proceeding on a draft charter. Nobody in Exeter was versed in the mysteries of applying for a charter and advice was sought from the three university colleges already on the Treasury list† — Reading, Nottingham, and Southampton.[11] Quite by chance Hetherington came to learn that the chairman of the UGC strongly disliked the whole idea of a university college: if a college was doing a considerable quantity of university work it should enjoy the freedom to devise its own courses and to award its own degrees. If the UGC kept to this view, which its predecessor had expressed with some vigour as long ago as 1912, Exeter would have to jump straight from its lowly status as a training college with a small university department to full independence as an incorporated university. Whether it had the academic or the financial resources to take such a step unaided was more

*Six members of the Students Representative Council resigned on 16 November, presumably because they were among the band of painters.
†In 1919 the advisory committee on grants to universities and colleges became the University Grants Committee, Sir William M'Cormick continuing as Chairman. At the same time responsibility for universities passed back to the Treasury from the Board of Education. In 1964 responsibility for universities reverted to the Department of Education and Science [DES] as it was now called, and the UGC became a part of the DES administrative machine.

than doubtful. Hetherington therefore devised a tentative scheme under which a senior university would establish a Board of Visitors. The Board would take fledgling Exeter under its wing, approve the content of courses, oversee appointments of professors and head of departments, appoint external examiners and be represented on the governing body. Except that there was to be only one university to monitor Exeter's progress, the scheme closely resembled that devised after the Second World War for the University of Keele; but there is no evidence that Lord Lindsay of Birker was aware of Hetherington's earlier proposal.

On 3 December 1920 a deputation from Exeter attended a conference in London with the Board of Education and the UGC for further discussions on the future of the college. Sir William M'Cormick liked the idea of a Board of Visitors. Doubts about the supply of students were laid to rest by representatives of the local authorities, who pointed out the recent expansion of secondary education in the South West and added that proportionately more children attended secondary schools there than in the country at large (10 per 1,000 of population in the South West; 8.4 per 1,000 nationally). It was on the question of finance that Exeter's case came to grief. The UGC estimated that an annual income of between £40,000 and £50,000 was necessary to sustain an independent university. Hetherington's pre-conference calculations had assumed that £30,000 would be enough. Though taken aback, he rapidly worked out that a penny rate from Devon, Cornwall, Plymouth and Exeter would raise £20,000 and that on a pound-for-pound basis (as with the University of Wales) the UGC might provide the rest. M'Cormick did not have to reply to this somewhat impudent piece of arithmetic because Hetherington's allies promptly let him down: Exeter was already contributing the equivalent of a 4d rate but representatives of the other authorities could not commit themselves even to a penny rate, and the Plymouth delegate added that Plymouth would rather spend money on engineering courses in Plymouth. If the UGC had wished to avoid the recognition of Exeter as a university college, these damaging disclosures would have provided an admirable pretext, but M'Cormick assured the delegation that he would approach the Treasury without prejudice. He advised against proceeding for the present with a petition to the Privy Council about the charter, but left a clear impression of wanting to be helpful. In its annual report published two months later in February 1921 the UGC touched approvingly on the 'patron' idea and set the minimum income of an independent university at £45,000.

Two tasks therefore confronted Hetherington: to acquire a patron for Exeter, and to extract promises of substantial financial help from the local authorities of South-West England. For a patron he turned to the University of Oxford where he had friends, rather than to Cambridge, whose extension lecturers had inspired the original scheme for university work in Exeter. By April the ground had been well prepared and formal application was made to the Hebdomadal Council. By November, the Council and Convocation had sanctioned the appointment of a Board of Visitors. The other task involved money and was rather more difficult. Devon with Sir Henry Lopes as Chairman of the County Council and with no rival institution of its own to cherish made relatively little resistance. It was willing to vote the proceeds of a penny rate if and when the College secured its charter as an independent university. Plymouth had its technical schools and was ambitious to develop engineering; Cornwall sent as many students to the College as the city of Exeter, but looked more fondly on the Camborne School of Mines. Hetherington's powers of persuasion nevertheless carried the day. By the end of the year Plymouth had promised the penny rate and Cornwall £1,000*.[12]

With a patron and money found or promised, the College could look forward with some confidence to the visitation of the UGC in February 1922. Even before then prospects were brightened further by the likelihood of acquiring a splendid site for the projected university. This was the Streatham Estate, which occupied rising ground about a mile north of the city centre. Streatham Hall, an Italianate mansion, had been built in 1867 for Richard Thornton West, nephew of a London merchant and speculator, Richard Thornton, who died in 1865 leaving him about a million pounds. Some 11 acres of the estate were laid out as terraced ornamental gardens by Robert Veitch of the celebrated family of nurserymen. Many rare and valuable trees were planted to form an arboretum that is widely admired to this day. Thornton West died in 1878 and the property passed to his son Richard Bowerman West. On his death in 1900 it was put up for sale and outlying parts of the estate were built over (West Avenue and Thornton Hill). In 1906 the Hall and some of the land were offered to the City, but although the use of the hall as a hostel for students was considered no action was taken†. During the war

---

*In appendix II of *The University College at Exeter*, Sir Hector Hetherington postdated the conversion of Cornwall to October 1922. It was in fact a year earlier that R. G. Rows, already a supporter of the College, proposed and carried the grant of £1,000 a year conditional upon a university charter. (PPA, file 2).

†Probaby because the City had just bought The Vineyard in Castle Street and saw no need of a second hostel so far from the college.

Streatham Hall became a military hospital and in 1919 was again on the market, at £8,000. Sir James Owen, the proprietor of the *Express and Echo* and chairman of the college appeal, secured promises of £6,000 towards its purchase. This included £1,000 from Sir Henry Lopes who described the estate as 'the only available site for a future university'. The syndicate failed to secure the property. Sir E. Chaning Wills of Torquay next prepared to buy it for the college at £7,000 but died before he could persuade the vendor to accept so low a price for a mansion and 11 acres. After these disappointments came triumphant success. On Christmas Day 1921 Sir James Owen told Hetherington that Alderman W. H. Reed, a former mayor of Exeter, was willing to buy Streatham Hall for the college if and when its new status as a university was assured.

> Personally [wrote Hetherington to Owen] I think the place is very cheap at £8,000. It is an ideal site for a College — perhaps the very best in the whole South West.

It would be necessary (he added) to buy the 19 acres that stood between the Hall and the main entrance in Cowley Bridge Road, and he was confident that he could find a donor who would buy that parcel of land for the college. In addition, Streatham Farm was needed for playing fields and in the long run for an agricultural college. The farm occupied about 80 acres and had recently failed to reach the reserve price of £5,500 at auction. The total cost of acquiring the whole estate would amount to about £15,000 or £16,000.

> But [continued Hetherington] it will be well worth it to the College. We must not make the mistake that nearly all the new Universities have made by giving themselves too little room for expansion. In thirty years time the College will want every yard of that ground and unless we buy it now we shall have to buy it later at much higher figures. I have no sort of doubt that if Mr Reed is willing to become, in a sense, the founder of all this great development we shall have comparatively little difficulty in finding the necessary money to add this additional land. It's the first step that counts. One handsome and dignified benefaction is worth far more to the College than just the material aid that it brings. We must be in a position to say to the Grants Committee in February 'This is our site if you see fit to sanction the foundation of the new College'.[13]

During a fine spell of weather in mid-February 1922 the UGC came, saw and were conquered by Hetherington and the Streatham estate. When the committee returned to London on the evening of 17 February, their secretary sent Hetherington a telegram from Waterloo Station: the college would be placed on the grants list from 1 August 1922. A letter of confirmation followed in a few days:

[The UGC] believe that the existing College forms the nucleus out of which an adequate University College could develop, and they realise that any further postponement of a decision on the issue would result in a grave setback to the whole movement. At the same time they are not satisfied that the moment has come when the College can be advised to apply for the grant of a Charter [under a patron university]. Apart from questions affecting the numbers of the staff and students and the output of academic work of a definitely University standard, it is certain that the financial resources of the College fall very considerably short of the minimum provisions indicated as necessary in the Committee's Report . . . . The Committee fully recognises the disadvantages attaching to University Colleges constituted as they are at present and they do not suggest that advancement to this category of Institutions will remedy the existing educational disabilities of the Exeter College. Only the urgency of the special circumstances compels them to propose this exceptional and temporary solution of the difficulty.[14]

Although the UGC had given Exeter less than it asked for, Alderman Reed stood by his offer. It proved more difficult than expected to find donors to buy the rest of the estate outright, and the College borrowed on mortgage to complete the purchase. By May Day 1922[15] the newest university college had acquired an estate of more than a hundred acres that would have been the pride of any university lucky enough to own it. Beautiful by nature and by art it was set amid fields and farmland and enjoyed a wide prospect over the valley of the Exe to the west and south. Some thirty acres—the steep-sided Hoopern Valley—formed a barrier than had stopped the advance of housing northward from Exeter. That part of the estate it was impossible to build on. Much of the rest was not easy to develop—level ground is scarce on the northern outskirts of the city. But the difficulties of topography were as nothing to the difficulties of money—as the events of the next thirty years would make plain.

Historians are reluctant to attach too much importance to any one moment in the life of a man or an institution. The UGC visitation in 1922 and the consequent grant of university-college status were in a sense only the last moves in a game of academic chess that had begun in 1893. A beautiful estate and a persuasive principal simply clinched a case that had been growing more powerful for thirty years. Nevertheless, 1922 was a decisive year. Just as a chess-player with a won game may remain anxious until his opponent has actually resigned, so Exeter could not be sure that the undeniable advances made under Clayden and Hetherington would prove sufficient until the UGC gave them its stamp of approval. That the approval was forthcoming is remarkable enough, for Exeter was by far the smallest town in England with a university college, and remained so for more than 40 years. Everybody recognised that the position achieved in 1922 was not the final goal, but a halfway mark on the road to full university status. Few if any had an inkling that it would take so long to complete the journey.

Notes

1 *Students' Magazine*, June 1918; letterbook, 1917–18, Clayden to Ministry of Munitions, 17 December 1917; in 1971 when he was 85, A. E. Morgan recorded his memories of the war years in Exeter for the University archives — [hereafter Morgan MS]; RAM, special committee on college accounts, 28 and 31 October 1901; RAM, 6 January 1902; college committee, 4 and 11 January 1904; letterbooks, Clayden to Board of Education, 13 August 1917 and 3 February 1919; Hartwell House and College Hostel ledgers.

2 *UGC, Report 1929/30 to 1934/35* (HMSO 1936, repr. 1946), pp.52–3; *Express and Echo*, Exeter, 16 October 1919; PPA, file 14.

3 PPA, box file on finance; *Devon and Exeter Gazette*, 2 December 1919; RAM, 20 December 1919.

4 A. W. Clayden, 'The future of higher education in Devon' (*Transactions of the Devonshire Association*, v.47, pp.62–8).

5 Morgan MS; W. H. Lewis papers [University of Exeter archives]; Cambridge University Archives, BEMS 31/6; *Western Morning News*, 3 February 1919; *Western Times*, 1 November 1918.

6 Furtherance committee, 20 March 1918, 20 January 1919 [W. H. Lewis papers].

7 Board of Education, private papers, [Public Record Office (PRO) ED 24/1946]

8 PPA, endowment box file.

9 RAM, 5 January and 10 June 1920.

10 Hetherington, pp.28–9; *Western Times*, 13 November 1920; *The Ram*, Spring 1921; Student Representative Council, 16 November 1920.

11 Letterbook, Woodbridge to Registrar, Nottingham UC, 27 February 1919.

12 PPA, file 1 contains a long memorandum written by Hetherington for the conference of 3 December 1920 and notes on the proceedings of the conference; *Report of the UGC 1921*, Cmd 1163, pp.15–16; PPA, file 2; UGC agenda and papers [PRO, UGC 2/3].

13 W. G. Hoskins, 'Richard Thornton 1776–1865: a Victorian millionaire' (*History Today*, 1962, pp.574–79); John Caldwell and M. C. F. Proctor, *The grounds and gardens of the University of Exeter* (University of Exeter, 1969) pp.5–32; RAM College committee, 3 December 1906; *Express and Echo*, 22 Februray 1973; Owen to W. H. Lewis, 3 July, Lopes to Lewis, 5 July 1919 [W. H. Lewis papers]; PPA file 2, Hetherington to Owen, 27 December 1921.

14 PPA, file 2 — UGC to Hetherington, 3 March 1922, and Hetherington to Lloyd Parry 24 February 1922; unluckily, the agenda and papers of the UGC have no copy of the report that was prepared after the UGC visitation on 16 and 17 February 1922 [PRO, UGC 2/4].

15 *Express and Echo*, 6 May 1922.

Appendix to Chapter IV

Hetherington and the Charter in 1922

Before Hetherington received a formal letter from the UGC offering Exeter the status of a university college on the Treasury list, he had been sent a draft for comment. In a letter to Lloyd Parry dated 24 February 1922 he confessed that the offer

> is more than I hoped for when the Grants Committee came down. It brings two enormous advantages: (1) it gives us unequivocal status as a University Institution, and (2) it pledges the UGC to give us degree-granting powers whenever Parliament raises its grant to the old level of £1,500,000. It settles the principle that there shall be a university in Exeter.
>
> I am communicating this to you because, I think, that Mr Reed should be informed as soon as possible. His promise to give Streatham Hall to the College was, I understand, conditional upon our getting the Charter. But I think that though we shan't get the Charter itself for a year or two we shall have got all that the Charter stood for . . . . I hope that Mr Reed will be disposed to take the view that this new aspect of things substantially satisfies the condition that he very wisely imposed.

The question arises: Did Hetherington unintentionally mislead Lloyd Parry and Reed? The formal letter from the UGC refers to university-college status as unsatisfactory and temporary, but does not indicate how long such a status might last. As every academic knows, temporary buildings can last for forty years; why should a temporary status last any shorter time?

A few years later when he was back in Glasgow Hetherington had occasion to revert to the subject of the UGC's undertaking. In a letter to Lopes dated 18 May 1925 he praised the UGC for a piece of 'rare administrative courage for which Exeter can never be too grateful. We saved what mattered most to us. We were put on the list and for my part I was glad that we didn't have to move further than we were really ready to go'. That is, by 1925 Hetherington saw that Exeter was not ready for a charter, and appears to be saying that he had also seen it in 1922. This was probably wisdom after the event. In February 1922 he had been Principal for only 20 months and was 33 years old. He might well have taken more sanguine views then than at the ripe old age of 36! Whether Mr Reed would have given Streatham Hall to the College if he had expected a long delay before the Charter was granted must remain an unanswered question.*

*PPA, files 2 and 17; UGC minutes, 22 February 1922 [PRO, UGC 1/1].

PART II

THE UNIVERSITY COLLEGE
1922–1955

V

HETHERINGTON AND MOBERLY

Since the College was not immediately to become an independent university, it did not need to trouble the Privy Council for a charter. A more prosaic application to the registrar of companies was all that was necessary and on 26 July 1922 the college filed its memorandum and articles of association. The University College of the South West of England as it was henceforth called now had a constitution that closely followed the traditional model for provincial English universities. Its purposes were defined as to take over the work and assets of the Royal Albert Memorial College and its teacher-training department and to provide instruction in all branches of a liberal education and such scientific, technical and other instruction of a University standard as might be of service in professional and commercial life. Titular supremacy in the constitution was reserved for the Court, a large body of some 250 members widely representative of the society of South-West England. President of Court and of the College was the Duke of Cornwall, who was also the Prince of Wales, the future Edward VIII.*

Sir Henry Lopes became Deputy President and served until elected President in 1936 when the Prince of Wales succeeded to the throne. The lay body that in practice governed the college on its non-academic side was Council. A much smaller body than Court it was to meet monthly during term. Among the duties of Council were the appointments of staff and the establishment of a superannuation scheme. (The lack of such a scheme had long troubled the advisory committee and the UGC; for both of those bodies showed much concern to improve the status, salaries and conditions of service of university teachers). The idea of a

*The Prince had taken an interest in the work of the Furtherance Committee at the end of the war and it was his secretary Sir Walter Peacock who had suggested in 1918 that Raleigh might be a suitable title for the university.

patron university lingered on in one of the duties laid upon Council. Two of its members were nominated by the University of Oxford, and it was provided that Council should refer to a committee that included its two Oxford members the decision as to the status (professorial or otherwise) of the heads of department in the College. Council in effect replaced College Committee but with the difference that the membership of Council included three members of Senate. Senate itself was the old Board of Studies enlarged by the inclusion of two members of the assistant teaching staff and the tutor to women students. But unlike the Board of Studies, Senate was not a conventional but a written part of the constitution. Its powers were considerably smaller than the powers of a Senate in a full university. It could not devise or approve degree syllabuses; nor did it have any control over matriculation requirements. All such matters were in the hands of the University of London for whose degrees the University College offered tuition. Among other duties Senate reported on the qualifications of candidates for chairs and for the headship of departments; it made recommendations on the appointment of lecturers and a librarian; and it appointed assistant lecturers and demonstrators.[1] The influence of Senate was greater than its powers. Its members spent their working life in the college and knew its problems and needs more thoroughly than the lay members of Council. The views of Senate would therefore carry weight with Council even though as a matter of law Council was the more powerful body.

Recognition as a university college brought benefits in status but not in cash. The College remained as poor as ever, since the grant from the UGC simply replaced grants formerly received from the Board of Education. Indeed the College came out of the transaction rather worse off if anything, for one of the conditions attached to its new status was that it should join the superannuation scheme for universities (FSSU) at a cost of some £1,500 a year. Central government and the local authorities of the South West each provided well over a third of the income. The balance came mostly from fees, with small contributions from endowments and from the Law Society. The income of 1924–25 may be taken as fair example of college finances in the 1920s.

These figures look absurdly small in the light of modern prices and wages. But even in relation to the prices of the 1920s the income of the college was tiny, smaller than that of Southampton and much smaller than the income of Nottingham and Reading, both well-endowed by private benefactors. Indeed, Reading was soon to receive its charter of

Income in 1924-25[2]

	£	£
Endowments, unappropriated		674
Local authority grants		
Cornwall	500	
Devon	5000	
Exeter	3500	
Plymouth	1383	10383
Parliamentary grants		
UGC	6000	
Board of Education	6317	12317
Fees		4580
Law Society		600
Total		28554

incorporation as a full university (1926), thanks largely to its relatively strong financial position.

Exeter by contrast had to live within straitened means. While there was still some hope of full university status and the large income—both from the local authorities and the UGC—that would follow, Principal Hetherington had sketched out plans for strengthening departments by additional appointments. The number of chairs would have risen from three to ten and the number of non-professorial heads of department would have declined correspondingly; the only new departments immediately envisaged would have been music and geography*. In the longer run Hetherington looked forward to the separation of economics from history, of botany from zoology, and of German from French. The number of academic staff would have risen from 23 to 37, mostly by new appointments at the assistant lecturer grade.[3]† The creation of new chairs was not intended as a device for promoting incumbent heads of department, but as a means to increase Exeter's prestige by appointing men of distinction. There was enough money, in the event, for carrying out most of Hetherington's scheme. Six chairs were created and where the incumbent was judged worthy he was appointed. In this way F. H. Newman became Professor of Physics in 1923, J. W. Schopp of Modern Languages in 1926, W. S. Lewis of Geography in 1927, and Frank Fletcher of Classics in 1928. When the chairs of education and of mathematics were re-established in 1923 new men were appointed from outside—S. H. Watkins and T. A. Brown, both destined to give many

---

*Geography was already being taught by W. S. Lewis with help from Clayden, who was styled visiting Director.

†After the Second World War until its recent disappearance the assistant lecturer grade was temporary and probationary. Before the war assistant lecturers often enjoyed tenure.

years of service to the college. A. E. Morgan resigned the chair of English in 1924 and was succeeded by a young Cambridge scholar, Lewis Horrox. Thus in the course of the 1920s Hetherington's proposal to increase the number of chairs from three to ten was almost achieved. There matters rested; Exeter created no more chairs until after the Second World War; indeed when Frank Fletcher retired in 1933 the Chair of Classics lapsed until 1948.

Hetherington's other proposal also came to fruition. By 1928 the number of assistant staff had risen to 36, only one short of the number he had suggested as appropriate if degree-giving powers had been granted. Economics separated from history in 1926, and botany and zoology became separate departments in 1928. A department of music also came into precarious existence. Before taking any decisive step Hetherington sought advice from other university colleges. He intended to appointment Dr Ernest Bullock, the cathedral organist, as director:

> He is I believe a quite distinguished man . . . . He is also young and energetic and seems to have more commonsense than is usual with distinguished musicians.

Having received an encouraging reply from W. M. Childs, the Principal and future Vice-Chancellor of Reading, Hetherington went ahead. As in the old school of art the teachers in the school of music were to be paid out of the fees received. Students were admitted at the age of 16 and took courses in theory as well as instrumental or vocal training. Bullock recruited a large staff of hopeful teachers out of an even larger number of applicants, and Sir Walford Davies gave a lecture to inaugurate the school in October 1924. Pupils did not come forward in the expected numbers, however; in 1929 none of the five remaining part-time teachers had more than three pupils, and the school was not strong enough at any time before the Second World War to take its place as 'part of the cultural effort of the college'.[4]

Financially more profitable was the school of law established in 1923. The Law Society, anxious to improve the legal education of solicitors, was giving grants to law schools up and down the country. In return for a grant of £600 Exeter agreed to establish a Department of Law. A Board of Legal Studies was appointed widely representative of the legal profession in the South West and chaired by Sir Henry Duke, later Lord Merrivale, a Lord Justice of Appeal, and formerly member of parliament for Exeter. The Board appointed J. Griffith Morgan as lecturer and head of department.* He led a busy life lecturing to law students, mostly articled clerks, in Plymouth as well as in Exeter. Numbers were small at first but by 1926 there were nearly 40 students, ten of whom were reading for the LLB. The school had been safely founded, and ranked among the larger and more successful of its kind in the country.[5]

It is somewhat surprising that the College could make a considerable number of new appointments in view of the shortage of money. In part it was because college income grew. The 'parliamentary grant' allocated by the UGC rose substantially—to £10,500 p.a.—for the quinquennium 1925-30. Plymouth and Cornwall, though released from their promises by the failure to secure a charter, nevertheless agreed to make useful contributions to college income. In large part however, expansion was made possible only by paying low salaries. The standard professorial salary in Exeter (£800 a year) stood well below the salary that a professor could command in a full university. Lecturers and non-professorial heads received much lower salaries, without provision for automatic increments. Only the assistant lecturers, permanent and probationary, enjoyed the privilege of an incremental scale—within the range £250 to £350 a year. Secondary school teachers (male) were as well paid as Exeter's assistant lecturers and lecturers, though their conditions of work were no doubt less agreeable.

Men and women with the requisite combination of ability, energy and ambition, would not stay in Exeter on those terms. The first four heads of the Education Department—Parry, Forster, Dean and Wortley—all left after a comparatively short stay to become either at once or in due course principals of training colleges or of university colleges. Among assistant staff several notable men and women passed through the college in the 1920s. Dr Enid Starkie, the French scholar; Samuel Glasstone, an able inorganic chemist, a highly successful teacher and later the author of much-read text books; Geoffrey Lapage, a parasitologist bubbling over with projects and enthusiasm; R. E. Dickinson, a noted geographer; Bertie Wilkinson, the medieval historian. Two principals of the college —Hetherington and W. H. Moberly—left in quick succession for higher things—Moberly to be Vice-Chancellor of Manchester University 1926-34, and Chairman of the UGC 1934-49. Their successor John Murray was nearly tempted away after three years as Principal to become

*In 1927 Griffith Morgan became Director of Legal Studies and in 1948 first holder of the Bracton chair of law. He retired in 1957.

Vice-Chancellor of the University of Sheffield, but at considerable expense Exeter retained his services.[6] A small and struggling institution could rarely afford to match the salaries offered elsewhere and it was fortunate for Exeter that the supply of candidates for academic posts appeared to be fully equal to the demand in the inter-war years.* Most of the staff of the college were graduates of Oxford, Cambridge, or London. The earliest graduate appointments made in 1893 were almost exclusively of Oxford and Cambridge men and women. By the First World War there was also a substantial contingent with London degrees (perhaps acquired at a provincial university college) and the pattern then established held good until recent times. In the inter-war years at least two-thirds of the staff had first degrees from Oxford, Cambridge or London and the proportion was often higher—more than four-fifths in 1938–39, for example. These universities were the largest as well as the most highly esteemed, but between them they had only half the students in the country: their graduates therefore took a disproportionate share of the posts that fell vacant in Exeter, junior as well as senior.[7]

Students continued to be attracted mostly from the South West. The College had put its case for a charter in regional terms: it seems to have occurred to nobody that Exeter could supply anything beyond a regional need and students took the College at its own valuation. In 1928, for example, 84 per cent of the students lived in one or other of the four South-Western counties and no fewer than 16 per cent of the students lived in Exeter itself. South Wales with five per cent of the students supplied Exeter as generously as the Midlands and South-East England together. Only three per cent of the students came from overseas. But if Exeter continued to be a local college it was rapidly shedding its training-college coat. The 1922–23 session was the last in which the two-year certificate students outnumbered degree students. From 1923 onwards degree students accounted for more than half and by 1927–28 for two-thirds of the students. The College still took some pains to conceal how few of these students had got beyond the level of the London intermediate, but it is not too difficult to penetrate the statistical fog. In 1923–24 for example 39 students passed the whole and a further 18 most

*When W. J. Harte retired from the Chair of History in 1931 he was succeeded by Norman Sykes, later Dixie Professor of Ecclesiastical History in the University of Cambridge and Dean of Winchester. Candidates short-listed when Norman Sykes was appointed included four other men who later became distinguished professors elsewhere. In 1936 when W. F. Jackson Knight was appointed Assistant Lecturer in Classics, the field for a lectureship in classics at Birmingham included six men with firsts (Grant Robertson to Murray, 27 January 1936—PPC, 20).

of the intermediate examination. At that time the regulations required passes in four subjects: the 57 more or less successful students would therefore have taken a maximum of 228 papers between them, which leaves 109 papers unaccounted for. It follows that more than 80 students were reading for the London intermediate in the year in question out of a total of 187 'degree' students. Similar calculations are not possible for later years when less information was published but the number of students passing intermediate is known. It averaged 40 in the years 1922–30 when the average number taking a first degree was 42. Students were expected to spend one year on the intermediate and a further two years on their degree course. Roughly speaking, then, one-third of the degree students were preparing for the London intermediate, an examination that could equally well have been taken at a secondary school.*

The fall in the number of two-year certificate students was sharp, from 161 in 1922–23 to only 69 in 1927–28. An increasing number of students in training had the qualifications to read for a degree and the growth in the number of degree students in the 1920s reflected this fact. In every year from 1922–23 onwards over half the students doing degree work were grant-aided by the Board of Education and had pledged themselves to teach when they had completed their three-year course. In 1926 the Board at last allowed university college to accept students in training for a four-year course—three years of uninterrupted degree work followed by a year's professional training. Exeter accepted about 50 students every year. Had none of them fallen by the wayside some 200 students (over half the number in college) would have come from this source alone. The supply of 'private' degree students, that is of student privately financed or relying on scholarships, remained small, averaging less than 40 a year. Exeter had obtained the status of a university college, but it was still a training department at heart.[8]

Before the First World War the college had only one hostel, Bradninch Hostel in Castle Street, accommodating about 60 women students. After the war hostel accommodation greatly increased, not in response to pressure of numbers, but because the college like many similar bodies saw virtue in the hostel system. The UGC in 1921 commended the

---

*These calculations ignore examination failures. On the available evidence failure rates were high, averaging a little less than 30 per cent in degree examinations in 1927–32 (PPF, file 5). The results are likely to have been worse in intermediate—less than half the candidates passed in 1923–24. Candidates in intermediate who passed in three out of their four papers could redeem themselves by resitting the failed paper in November. This resource was not open to degree candidates.

building of hostels, and student opinion also favoured the practice. Exeter recovered College Hostel from the military in 1919 and retained the possession of Hartwell House, leased during the war when College Hostel was requisitioned. It was therefore possible to insist that all women students whose homes lay outside Exeter should live in a hostel. No fees were payable by students in training but the private students paid £1.15.0d. [£1.75] for single rooms in Hartwell House (there were very few), and £1.10.0d. per week for shared rooms. Since digs could be had in Exeter for £1.5.0d. and upwards, life in a hostel called for some financial sacrifice, as it has always done. At the same time the college brought two large private houses in Grendon Road near Livery Dole as a hostel for men students in training. Grendon and Frostleigh opened in October 1920 and served until the purpose-built Mardon Hall was ready in 1933. Streatham Hall, renamed Reed Hall to commemorate the notable benefactor, opened as a second hall of residence for men in 1925. Like the other halls* it had few single study-bedrooms, but a considerable number of large rooms with high ceilings shared by several students. Everyone recognised that converted private houses were a poor substitute for specially designed halls of residence, but without money what else could be done? In 1926 the UGC made a rare capital grant of £5,000. This with money given by Miss C. M. de Reyes made it possible to extend Hartwell House at no cost to the college. The hostel was renamed Hope Hall in memory of Miss Helen Hope of Bath. It was her legacy to Miss de Reyes (some £4,000) that was generously given to the College for the extension of Hartwell House. In 1927 Lord Astor gave £10,000 for a hostel at Plymouth. It opened in 1929 to the accompaniment of a paradoxical speech by Bernard Shaw and in the presence of a somewhat unwilling warden, Joseph Sykes, head of the Department of Economics in the University College.[9]

Astor Hall symbolised the federal nature of the university movement in the south west. It was only with the support of all the major local authorities that university-college status had been achieved in 1922. That support was given, particularly by Cornwall and Plymouth, because they expected that they too would secure university institutions in due course. Indeed, on one interpretation, the College at Exeter was only the first and a rather small instalment of the future university whose centre would lie in Plymouth:

---

*Terminology in the 1920s was confused but 'hall' was tending to replace 'hostel' as the usual expression.

It is intended that Plymouth shall be the main centre of the work . . . . While Plymouth is doing spade work and laying sound foundations it would be glad to see Exeter grow.[10]

Principal Hetherington would not have subscribed to that view of the matter but he did sincerely promote the idea of a federal university. It led him into an odd entanglement with Plymouth Technical Schools. Plymouth City Council was anxious to set up a faculty of engineering, teaching for London external degrees, but the UGC in 1924 would not support expensive new ventures in technological education. As a second best and in order to strengthen its academic claims Plymouth therefore proposed to give Hetherington the oversight of post-matriculation work in its technical schools.* The Principal of the Schools, W. S. Templeton, naturally disliked the implied demotion, and with Hetherington's support he was allowed to keep his title. Hetherington was given the title of supervisor and for a few months travelled twice a week to Plymouth to carry out his awkward duties. Moberly, who succeeded Hetherington in January 1925, continued the arrangement, but it was not to the taste of the third principal, John Murray. In 1929 in some acrimony he resigned his supervisory role to Professor W. H. Lewis, the Deputy Principal. In the meantime Plymouth and Exeter had embarked on a similar joint venture in commerce and economics. It too ran into difficulties. The Board of Education needed reassurance that Plymouth retained ultimate control over commercial education in the city and it reminded the authority that the UGC was at best lukewarm about schemes of condominium. The staff of the university college liked the scheme no better since they had to teach in Plymouth as well as Exeter. The head of the Department of Economics was justifiably angered at his unhappy lot:

I have suffered exportation to Plymouth and there compressed my space requirements to two rooms an alley and a corridor. Next year (1930–31) the absence of Mr Baster will impose extra exertion . . . . It hardly seems commensurate with the dignity and responsibility of my task as head of two Departments and as Dean to be remunerated at a scale £250 below the professorial scale.

The weakness of Plymouth's claim to be a centre of university teaching was that few students in the city's technical and commercial schools were doing work of degree standard. For example, much of the teaching of Sykes and Baster in economics was to young bankers seeking

---

*At the same time the school of pharmacy was transferred from Exeter to Plymouth as part of the scheme to develop applied science there.

qualifications from the Institute of Bankers rather than an academic grounding in the niceties of theoretical economics. In Murray's sceptical hands the Plymouth connection withered away. By 1934 the office of supervisor had fallen into disuse, and four years later the sharing of staff and all pretence of formal co-operation came to an end. Astor Hall became a children's home administered by Plymouth City Council; it was finally sold in 1954. [11]

Hetherington returned to Glasgow as Professor of Moral Philosophy in January 1925. His successor Moberly gave up the Chair of Philosophy in Birmingham to begin his long career in academic administration. When he too left Exeter in October 1926 to be succeeded by John Murray, the University College of the South West of England still showed strong traces of its humble origins. It was still a local college serving local men and women. By no means all of its teaching was of degree standard and its staff had less time for calm reflection than would now be considered desirable for university teachers. Postgraduate students were few, and were mostly to be found in the two lively science departments, chemistry and physics. More than half the students lived in halls of residence — a remarkable change in a few years. But the number of students in the College remained disappointingly static (318 in 1922–23 and 326 in 1926–27). Worst of all, the poverty of the College made the development of the Streatham Estate a remote and unlikely prospect. In 1922 Hetherington rashly suggested that for £20,000 the College could adapt and extend Streatham Hall for the teaching purposes of the whole College. The Town Clerk and the city architect doubted the feasibility of the proposal: 'I think it would be well if [we] discussed the matter before we met any further Committees.'[12] The mansion became a hall of residence instead, and it was left to John Murray to make a start on the move to Streatham.

Notes

1 PPA, file 23.
2 PPB, file 5.
3 PPA, file 1.
4 PPA, file 25; PPF, file 29; memorandum by (Sir) Thomas Armstrong, director of music 1929–33 (PPC, file 10).
5 PPA, file 21.
6 PPF, file 29; *Annual Reports*; Murray to Sir W. B. Riddell, chairman of the UGC, 17 December 1931 (PPB; file 21).

7 *Calendar* 1893-94, 1920-21, 1926-27, 1938-39.
8 *College List*, 1928; *Annual Reports*; PPC, file 14.
9 UGC, *Report* 1921 (BPP XI), pp.374-75; *Calendar*, 1920-21; *Annual Reports*, 1925, 1927, 1928; Hetherington, *The University College* p.21.
10 A Dufton [HMI, Plymouth] to H. A. L. Fisher, 3 and 8 December 1918 [PRO, ED24/1946].
11 Hetherington, *The University College*, pp.19-20; PPA files 6, 17; PPB, file 9; J, Sykes to Murray, 10 June 1930—PPC, file 13; PRO, ED 119/18; PPB, file 20; *Annual Report* 1931, and 1954.
12 Lloyd Parry to Hetherington, 29 June 1922 [PPA].

VI

THE MURRAY YEARS
1926–1939

John Murray became Principal of the University College of the South West of England in October 1926 at the age of 47, and held the office for 25 years. Though he achieved nothing as dramatic as Hetherington's coup in securing recognition by the UGC, he presided over and inspired two important phases in the growth of the College towards full university status: a period of consolidation and strengthening in the years before the Second World War; and a period of rapid expansion after 1945. When he retired in 1951 the goal of incorporation as an independent university was in sight.

Murray was born in the fishing port of Fraserburgh, Aberdeenshire, in 1879, the eldest son of Francis Robert Murray, fishcurer. He was educated at Robert Gordon's College, Aberdeen, and in 1896 entered the University of Aberdeen. He took his degree with honours in Greek and Latin in 1900, and in the following year went up to Christ Church, Oxford, on a Fullerton Scholarship. First-class honours in classical moderations (1903) and in *literae humaniores* (1905) led to a prize fellowship of Merton. In 1908 he became Student and Tutor of his old college, Christ Church, and in 1910 Censor. In 1915 he left Oxford for the Ministry of Munitions where he rose to be an assistant commissioner in the Labour Adviser's Department. In the general election of 1918 he stood as a Coalition Liberal in Leeds West and was elected with a large majority. He retained his seat in 1922 but came bottom of the poll in 1923 when the Conservatives fielded a candidate for the first time since the war. He made two further attempts to re-enter Parliament—at Kirkcaldy in 1924, and at Ripon in 1925—but the times were not propitious for Liberals. During the Lloyd George coalition Murray held

74

minor offices in the Board of Education and as chairman of the Central Committee on Trusts. His few speeches in the House showed a certain unorthordox radicalism; he was for example an early and lifelong advocate of family allowances.* But he opposed plans for the nationalisation of coal and the land, and disliked 'promise politics' as he termed the expansive projects of his leader, Lloyd George. It was with some relief therefore that he came to Exeter and laid aside his political ambitions — as it turned out, for ever.[1]

Murray was a tall commanding figure with a beautiful speaking voice. Where his sympathies were enlisted he was generous of his time and money to help past or present students or members of the staff. As a Highland Scot he claimed graphological powers denied to ordinary mortals: he could divine character, appearance, or incidents in a man's past life from handwriting.† He was fond of children and enjoyed reading aloud to them and to women students. As he wrote to a stony-hearted local authority in mitigation of a student's examination failure:

> She has plenty of sense and capacity without being first-rate in study, and she is sure to make her way in the world and to be a credit to those who take a share in helping her on. If she had not grown up such a fine figure of a young woman she would have been a better examinee, I fancy.

Cornwall education committee was unmoved and the student did not get a grant to repeat the year of study. The softer side of Murray's nature revealed in this episode was not often shown to the world. A fearless pugnacity was usually in the ascendant — whether he was dealing with the Board of Education, the UGC, Saint Luke's College, Exeter City Library Committee, or militant students. Where the interests of the College required it, he curbed his natural inclination to fight, and instead exercised diplomatic skills of a high order. It was by these less warlike methods that he kept on good terms over many years with a preposterously difficult rich man and secured for the College the largest single bequest that it had received up to that time. The long correspondence with this benefactor shows Murray at his best — firm in the defence of friends and principle, but conciliatory, understanding and patient in a good cause.[2]

Aberdeen and Oxford shaped Murray's academic ideals. In Aberdeen

---

*The University Library's copy of Eleanor Rathbone's *The Disinherited Family* was presented by Murray.
†See *Shinid* (1938) a humorous fantasy that he printed for private circulation, and *The Contemporary Review*, September 1950, 'Handwriting and Character'. There is reliable independent testimony to his skill in judging character from handwriting.

he saw a University that helped poor boys and girls to learning. He himself had climbed the educational ladder and he looked on Exeter as a college that could do in South-West England what Aberdeen did for aspiring Scotsmen like himself. In Oxford he saw the model of a university which cultivated learning and gentlemanliness through residence and the tutorial system. From these two models Murray drew inspiration for the college that he sought to create in Exeter. Hetherington and Moberly too thought along these lines; it was in other directions that Murray showed his originality. He was not content that Exeter should remain a provincial institution serving only the South West: he hoped to attract poor boys and girls 'from the dingier parts of England'; and to promote international understanding by mixing European, American and middle-eastern students with the native English. His international outlook was widely shared in a country desperately anxious to avoid a Second World War, but not many vice-chancellors or principals tried as hard as Murray to give their institution a strongly international flavour.[3]

If Exeter was to provide an educational ladder for able boys and girls of modest means, a system of scholarships was required. The costs of university education on the residential system were high. In 1918 when there were no hostels for degree students (unless they were women students in training) the bare cost of three years in Exeter—lodgings, fees, small sums for books and stationery—amounted to £189 13s. 0d.. This figure excluded pocket money, the expenses of travel, laundry and clothes. For students in training taking a degree under the auspices of the Board of Education the bare expenses were only £85 for three years. In 1938 when the college was wholly residential except for students whose parents lived in Exeter, the cost of tuition and residence amounted to considerably more—from £90 to £105 a year. A carpenter earning £4 a week, or a schoolmaster on £400 a year could not hope to keep a promising child for three years at such a rate without the aid of scholarships. The Board of Education grants to students in training considerably reduced but by no means eliminated the burden on parental incomes. State scholarships were not tenable at university colleges until 1946, and the scholarships awarded by local education authorities often pre-supposed daily attendance at the local redbrick university while continuing to live cheaply at home. From its beginnings in 1893 the Technical and University Extension College had offered scholarships to students resident in Exeter whose parents' income did not exceed £400 a year. Major scholarships remitted the whole cost of fees, minor scholarships half fees. When teaching for degrees began, the Governors of the Royal Albert Memorial awarded four open scholarships to university students, two at £30, two at £20 a year. By the early 1920s the college had at its disposal about 20 scholarships ranging in value from £15 to £40. Three of these were open scholarships, the others more or less restricted, the total annual value amounting to only £536. In 1927–28 the college was able to award scholarships to the value of £932 and by 1929 the sum had doubled to £1841. Six open scholarships (two a year) of £80 were all that were available to attract students from 'the dingier parts' of England. Most of the scholarships were local, especially to Devon— one open to the children of Devon freemasons, another to children whose parents had served in the war; others were restricted to particular towns—Northam, Bideford, Plymouth—or in the case of the Ballard Scholarships preference was given to boys who had attended the Ballard Institute in Plymouth. In 1935 the college enlarged its open scholarships further by offering ten a year, at £80 or £100 each. These were valuable awards and candidates competed from places as distant as Lincoln and Suffolk; a list of open scholars holding awards in 1935 shows that four came from Devon, five from other parts of south-west England and eight from the home counties, the west midlands and the west of England. Murray's ambition to make Exeter a national institution was beginning to have some success.[4]

Scholarship holders were not the only students attracted from other parts of England. Students in training and privately financed students were also coming to Exeter from further afield. In 1937 a quarter of the students came from other parts of England or from Wales; the proportion native to the South West had fallen from five-sixths (84 per cent) in 1928 to only three-fifths (59 per cent). The remainder of the students in 1937 (17 per cent) came from abroad. The high proportion of foreign and Commonwealth* students resulted directly from Murray's initiative. The first foreign students came from Germany. A former Oxford pupil of Murray's ran a co-educational boarding school in Schloss Salem, a castle belonging to Prince Max of Baden. Some pupils from this school came to Exeter for a term or a year to study English language and literature. In 1929 Murray undertook a lecture tour in the

---

*A portmanteau term not then in use but conveniently brief, and including students who would have been described as from the Dominions, the colonies, the mandated territories, India, or simply the Empire.

United States, one of its objects being the recruitment of American students for one-year courses in Exeter. During the world economic depression the number of overseas students grew only slowly, but with the revival of economic activity in the years 1935–37 the internationalisation of the college proceeded apace. The largest contingents came from Egypt and the United States with smaller numbers from the countries of Europe. In 1935 Henry Littler was appointed as the first tutor to overseas students. The post was attached to the Department of English where the tutors to foreign students are to be found to this day. Murray had every reason to be satisfied with his international enterprise:

> When I joined the College the students came almost exclusively from Devon and Cornwall and made a very parochial un-university society. They were little better than a Training College . . . . The influx of strangers, who are now [1939] a sixth of the whole has brought fresh air and a remarkable stimulus and broadening into the College.[5]

Another successful enterprise with an international theme was the summer school for foreign students instituted in 1928. A tradition of organising a summer school for English teachers stretched back to the years before the First World War. The school for foreign students was on a larger scale and in a good year actually made a substantial profit for the college. The numbers attending fluctuated with the state of trade and international politics. At its most prosperous in 1929 and 1930 the school had over 200 students for the three-week course but such figures were not approached again until 1936. At the first school in 1928 Harley Granville Barker, the distinguished actor-manager and dramatist, gave the inaugural address—on Shakespeare's stagecraft. In subsequent years Murray himself opened the proceedings with eloquence and charm. The pre-war summer schools laid less emphasis on English language and literature than their modern counterparts and instead offered a broad introduction to England and the English. In 1937 for example six lectures were given on the English language and nine on English literature out of 50 lectures in all.* There were also (as today) classes in reading and conversation and two and a half days were devoted to 'long motor excursions'.[6]

It was as well for the College that the number of overseas students was growing, for there was little long-term growth of numbers elsewhere. The number of students reading for a degree (including intermediate) reached

---

*At the thirtieth summer school in 1964 over half the lectures were devoted to English language and literature.

a plateau of about 250 in 1928 and showed no sign of permanently rising above that level for the rest of the inter-war period. The number reached 278 in 1929 and 284 in 1935 but was down to 219 in 1932 and 231 in 1933. In the last year of peace the number of degree students stood at 256. By recent standards these might seem discouraging figures but other institutions had a similar experience — the university population of Great Britain stagnated at about 50,000 students throughout the period 1920–38. Briefly in 1929–32 total numbers in the college rose to nearly 500. This prosperity owed much to the Labour government's proposal to raise the school leaving age to fifteen.* The Board of Education cajoled training colleges and departments to admit large numbers of two-year students in the attempt to provide enough teachers. For Exeter an expansion of the training of certificate students was financially rewarding but academically retrograde. In 1928 the college had only 37 such students; there were 185 by 1930 and the number was still over 100 in 1933. Soon after their departure the influx of overseas students once more gave a buoyant appearance to the college, but its main business — teaching for a first degree — grew very little. 1938 — the best year in the thirties for the output of graduates (64) — fell a little short of 1929 when 67 students had taken a first degree.[7]

Postgraduate students accounted for a tiny fraction of student numbers. There were never more than 13 full-time postgraduate students in Exeter, and even that number was not reached until 1936. In 1922 there had been only three. Nevertheless this small number of research students included some who were of the highest quality. H. J. Walke, who graduated in physics in 1932 and later took his MSc and PhD in Exeter, was awarded a Commonwealth Fellowship to continue his work on radioactivity in Berkeley, California. He published a stream of papers and at the time of his early death in 1939 he was George Holt Senior Research Fellow in the University of Liverpool working under the Nobel Laureate (Sir) James Chadwick. Had he lived it is likely that he would have had a distinguished career.[8] W. G. Hoskins, FBA, the doyen of English local historians, graduated BSc (Econ) in 1929, and later took his master's degree and doctorate at the University College. Happily his life has been long and fruitful and his imaginative and pioneering work in topographical and social history has inspired many imitators.†

*The proposal fell victim to the economic crisis of 1931, and the school-leaving age was not raised to 15 until 1947.
†In 1974 the University of Exeter conferred the honorary degree of Doctor of Letters on Professor W. G. Hoskins.

Although the number of degree students did not grow after the later 'twenties the total number of students did, because of the influx first of two-year certificate students and then of foreigners. The number of staff rose correspondingly and the student:staff ratio if anything was slightly lowered from just over to just under seven to one. Murray had few opportunities before 1945 to appoint new heads of department or new professors except in the Department of History. When Harte retired in 1931 Norman Sykes was appointed. He had little faith in the future of the college and left after only two years. His successor D. C. Douglas, a distinguished medievalist, left for Bristol in 1939 and R. R. Darlington, another medievalist, left for Birkbeck in 1945.* In other departments changes were few. The Chair of Classics lapsed when Fletcher retired in 1933; H. T. S. Britton already on the staff succeeded W. H. Lewis in the Chair of Chemistry in 1935 and a young Oxford don N. J. Abercrombie, was chosen to succeed Schopp in the Chair of Modern Languages. Abercrombie became a civil servant during the war, stayed on as a permanent official after it and rose to be Secretary-General of the Arts Council. It is clear that the College chose if it could not always keep able men for the chairs that fell vacant, but the methods of appointment were haphazard by recent standards. Not until 1952 did the College call on external assessors to give expert advice. The articles of association provided that the college should consult the Oxford members of Council before appointing to chairs, and Murray followed this proceedure before promoting Fletcher to the Chair of Classics in 1928. There is no further evidence about Oxford consultations. Murray's opinions of candidates for a non-professorial post in physical education are extant and show something of the qualities he was looking for.

A Pleasant straight unassuming; lack of distinction, but a worker.
B Slow slightly sleepy manner; ranging mind and resourceful; not very expressive though the stuff is there. An athlete. A good laugh and smile.
C Nice domestic type; not expressive; practically no teaching as yet. Cross-country — tennis.
D Small. Careful mind, persistent, shy; a practical type rather than a speculator. Soccer, tennis, swims.
E The only tall man of the five, and better 'class'. Acquisitive and expository rather than original. Interviews well. Nervous type. Acts: squash and golf.

The selection committee was unanimous in offering this post to B.[9]

Cardinal Newman saw the purpose of universities as the production of

*Sykes, Douglas and Darlington were all elected FBA in due course.

gentlemen. Murray agreed, or at least saw gentlemanliness as one of the qualities to be developed by attendance at a university. It followed that university teachers should be gentlemen themselves and if a member of his staff did not display the elusive qualities required of a gentleman he was regarded as unfit for high office in a university—or in wartime in the civil service. As part of the preparations against the Second World War, the government sought the help of universities in compiling lists of potential civil servants. Murray made certain recommendations to Sir Horace Wilson, the Permanent Secretary to the Treasury, recommendations which throw light on his attitude to his staff—and also on his judgement. Of two gentlemen whom he ranked equal first among his staff as prospective civil servants one did indeed have a highly successful career in public affairs, both during and after the war, but the other did less well. Government proved less fastidious than Murray and at a time of national danger preferred energy to elegance in its temporary civil servants: two men whom Murray damned as not or not quite gentlemen nevertheless attained positions of high responsibility in the wartime civil service.[10].

The concern to appoint gentlemen to the staff did not begin with Murray. Principal Clayden had aired similar views when new appointments were being made in 1901. 'It is very important to get *gentlemen*.' But Murray, unlike his predecessors, was in the habit of making his postulates plain for all to see, and few of his assumptions remained unspoken or unrecorded. The hall of residence was already a prominent feature of the University College when Murray arrived in Exeter, but only he took pains to put its functions beyond all doubt. A letter to the Warden of Merton College, Oxford, puts the matter starkly:

> Am I right in suspecting that some Oxford institutions are not the colleges they were? The intake of some is mainly boys from secondary schools, who are just as raw, morally and socially, as the intake of the modern universities . . . . With raw young men from poor homes and day schools the Hall methods as practised here in Exeter is damnably appropriate. I don't like having more than 60 of them in a Hall. Above that number their social crudity is intractable: they are on top, not you.

The process of 'gentling the masses' that had begun in the elementary schools of Victorian Britain was to be continued, for the able few, in halls of residence. This view of the hall's function was widely shared and was reiterated, less bluntly, in a UGC report of 1957 (the Niblett report on halls of residence) in an approving reference to the civilising influence of thick-pile carpets.[11]

When Murray arrived in Exeter the University College had four halls of residence—Bradninch and Hope for women, Reed and Grendon for men. They offered accommodation to some 200 students, or more than half the students in the college. Two of the halls were unsatisfactory. Bradninch was in the city centre and had few single study-bedrooms. Grendon was overcrowded and unhealthy. In 1928 the city's sanitary inspector roundly condemned its kitchen-quarters and means of storing food. The college was happy to sell these properties—Bradninch Hall to the County Council—as soon as new halls could be provided elsewhere. In 1931 the college brought a further 22 acres of the original Streatham estate from St Wilfred's convent for £5,100. The land lay to the north and west of Reed Hall and there on a sloping site close to Reed Hall was built Mardon Hall. Designed in a 'country house' style it opened in 1933 and provided accommodation, mostly in spartan double rooms, for about 80 men. Public rooms were provided on a comparatively lavish scale—a large common room, library, music room, games room and for the warden a reception room in addition to his private flat. There was no money for a permanent dining hall—and there never has been; a large hut suited Murray's sense of Scotch economy very well. A new hall for women opened in 1930, in a large house (Highlands) standing in eight acres of grounds. Renamed Lopes Hall, it was enlarged to accommodate 70 students. With the extension completed in 1933, the College sold Bradninch Hall, and its residents moved from the city centre to the new hall in St German's Road close to the Streatham Estate. The college acquired two further halls at this time by the purchase of large private houses. Kilmorie and two other large terrace houses in Pennsylvania Road became Kilmorie Hall (renamed Exeter Hall in 1939) and accommodated 36 men. Great Duryard, an early-eighteenth-century mansion set in 14 acres of handsome grounds, was acquired in 1935 and renamed Thomas Hall after C. V. Thomas, a Cornish solicitor and businessman who was chairman of Cornwall education committee and a friend and benefactor of the College.

The provision of halls of residence more than kept pace with the growth of numbers, and by the later 'thirties Exeter with Reading had three-quarters of its students in residence, the highest proportion in redbrick universities, though the university colleges at Nottingham and Southampton did not lag far behind. Regulations varied from hall to hall in Exeter, but everywhere remained strict, if less so than before the war. In 1927 for example the popular and respected warden of Reed Hall

K. M. Constable forbade noise during the hours 9 am-1 pm, 2-5 pm, 7-9 pm and after 10 pm on week-days; Saturday was free of such restrictions, as was Sunday after 2 pm. The hall closed at 10 pm though exeats were allowed till 11.30 pm — freshmen being limited to one exeat a week. Hope Hall granted exeats more liberally — but only till 10.15 pm. Bradninch Hall imposed silence for two hours every evening in the two winter terms and from 8.30 pm to 9.45 pm in the summer. Lights went out at 10.15 pm in the winter, and at 10.30 pm in summer. The custom of prayers morning and evening was maintained.[12] When the alternative to halls was lodgings students appeared to prefer halls. The UGC thought so in the twenties and its sub-committee (the Niblett committee) received evidence to the same effect from the National Union of Students in 1957. 'Social crudity' did not stand in the way of docile submission to rules that students would now scorn to obey.

To strengthen the claims of the College for a charter it was not sufficient to offer scholarships, appoint new staff, and provide halls of residence; new academic buildings were also needed to relieve overcrowding in Gandy Street by development of the magnificent but empty Streatham estate. In 1922 the college had acquired by gift or purchase some 120 acres (Streatham Hall 11 acres, Streatham Hall Farm 107 acres). As opportunity offered the College bought more land that had once formed part of the Streatham estate of Richard Thornton West: 17 acres (Northpark)* in 1929; 21 acres (St Wilfrid's land)† in 1931. The only good road on the estate in 1922 was the carriage-way to Streatham Hall, the present Streatham Drive, and it would therefore be necessary to build, when building became possible, fairly close to this road. In 1923 the college appointed as consulting architects two local men, Sidney Greenslade of Exeter and E. Vincent Harris of Plymouth. Their first plan for the development of the estate envisaged building on the land south of Streatham (Reed) Hall. Some felling of trees in the arboretum would have been necessary in the long run. But in 1925 the city began to construct a new road across the estate as part of a scheme for the relief of the unemployed. The new road linked the Cowley Road with Pennsylvania Road and incidentally provided better communications between the College's Hope Hall and the Streatham Estate. The road, which was formally opened in June 1927 by the Prince of Wales and was

*The Mathematics-Geology, Engineering (formerly Applied Science) and Amory Buildings now occupy this site.
†Mardon Hall and the Estate Services Centre have been built on part of this land.

named after him, gave the College more freedom in its plans to develop the estate: it was no longer tied to the rather small area between Reed Hall and the Cowley Road; it could build at any point along or near the Prince of Wales Road as well. Murray was quick to notice the new possibilites and it was he rather than Vincent Harris who first suggested a change of plan. 'The proper view point', he argued, 'appears to be the path along the top of the other side of the Hoopern Valley'. The College buildings should be disposed like trees in a landscape, to be admired from a distance. Vincent Harris was happy to adapt his plans in conformity with this idea and in 1931 produced a design for the 'Move to Streatham'.

The principal axis of the design was a straight line beginning behind Reed Hall and travelling in a southerly direction down what is now the Memorial Avenue to the Prince of Wales Road. If extended this line would have passed through the north tower of Exeter Cathedral. A subsidiary axis bisected the principal axis; if extended it would have passed through the college building in Gandy Street. Vincent Harris proposed to drive a grand processional way up the principal axis from the Prince of Wales Road to a chapel which would close the vista at the higher (northern) end. At the point of interception by the subsisiary axis the road forked and assumed the shape of a circus. Subsidiary roads followed an elliptical path round the principal way, and buildings were disposed in rigid symmetry and in complete disregard of the lie of the land along the roads sketched out. Some of the sites chosen by Harris have been built on. The Roborough Library stands where Harris intended it to be, and the Hatherly Laboratories where in the 1931 plan the arts building was to have been placed. Harris's 1931 plan envisaged biology laboratories where the second library was built in 1966.

Vincent Harris did not have a completely free hand to draw up a plan for the estate, since the building of the Washington Singer Laboratories had begun before his plan was made. But he appears to have had no difficulty in accommodating his designs to include the partly finished building. Originally the College had intended to use the site of the laboratories for the faculty of arts and the administration. The designs —for a classical building set round a quadrangle—did not satisfy Murray, who persuaded Council and the architect that modern laboratories for physics and chemistry should have first claim on college resources. Harris responded with an imposing building in the Dutch Renaissance style. It allowed for a considerable growth in the size of the two departments and in the view of F. H. Newman, the professor of physics and first director of the laboratories, 'would meet all that might be expected for science teaching and research in the South West for a generation'. In addition, the new building provided a large multi-purpose hall—suitable for gymnastics, plays, concerts and the conduct of examinations. It was to serve in all these ways for more than 30 years.[13]

The College erected only one other academic building on the Streatham site before the outbreak of the Second World War dashed all hopes of an early move to the promised land. This was the Roborough Library begun in 1938 and completed in 1940. The need for a library became urgent after 1933 when the arrangement with the city library broke down. The city completed a new library in Castle Street in 1931 more than 20 years after the Carnegie Foundation had first offered a handsome contribution to the work. The new library cost much more to administer than the old one in the Museum, and the City Council looked for a larger contribution than the £429 that the college had been paying towards library expenses. Murray who had little sympathy with and less understanding of the librarian's craft argued vehemently that the College was paying too much, not too little, for services received:

> The City Librarian's clear and informative account of library procedures and tasks suggests convincingly that a girl clerk able to type and a messenger boy, supervised by a librarian more or less honorary, could do the work and both have some time to spare. The College had already the boy. There are savings to be made clearly, on the £429 basis by breaking with the City Library . . . .

The College therefore appointed its own acting librarian. Miss K. E. Perrin (Mrs Allison) was well qualified for the work but like many university librarians at the time was accorded a low status and an even lower salary. Murray was right in thinking that (in the short run) the Library could be run more cheaply in independence of the city. Most of the College books had already been withdrawn into departmental or seminar libraries staffed by the city but housed on college premises. These books together with the other volumes previously kept in the city library were now collected together in rooms on the second floor in Gandy Street. Pass and certificate students benefited by the change for they now had access to all the books whereas under the system of departmental libraries they had been denied the use of the more specialised works deposited in the departmental collections. The Library was still tiny, but was growing fast. There had been about 5,000 volumes in 1922; ten years later there were 25,000. The college subscribed to nearly 200 periodicals against only 37 in 1920.[14] Pressure of space would soon force the College to built its own library, costly in itself and expensive to staff and maintain. In the long run a separation from the city library was no doubt inevitable; the economies that immediately arose could not last, and were followed by a permanent rise in the cost of library services.

The need for a library on the Streatham estate was already strongly felt when the UGC made its quinquennial visitation in 1934. But another four years passed before building began. Sir Henry Lopes, President of the University College of the South West, was raised to the peerage as Lord Roborough shortly before his death in 1938, and the Roborough Library commemorated his long and valuable service to the College. The plan of the library was simple; a large high-ceilinged reading room for about 150 students with stacks below and a gallery and some small rooms above. The capacity of the library was about 130,000 volumes. The accommodation was generous for a college with only 500 students and 45,000 books; it allowed for expansion — but not on the scale that was to be experienced in the years after 1945.

Scholarships, chairs, halls of residence, academic buildings — how were they financed? Slowly college income rose, mostly thanks to increased grants from the UGC. Each quinquennial allocation was larger (by about four or five thousand pounds) than the last, so that from 1936 onwards the college had an annual grant of £19,000 compared to the £6000 allotted to it in 1922. Not even the economic crisis of 1931 led to a cut in the UGC allocations. The [May] committee on national expenditure had proposed a large cut of £250,000 (about 14 per cent) in the UGC vote, but a Cabinet committee had substituted a lesser cut and for one year only. In the end the UGC did even better. Sir Walter Riddell, the chairman, was on holiday when the axe was poised to fall. He received the following telegram from the Treasury:

> If we avoid cut in your annual grant could we seize most of your Deposit Account instead? It would help. Please wire.

Sir Walter was happy to telegraph his agreement — which his committee readily endorsed. For the rest of the quinquennium the UGC had no reserves out of which to make occasional capital grants; otherwise it emerged unscathed. In 1936 even the seized deposits were restored to it.

From 1936 the UGC's grant to Exeter for the first time amounted to more than a third of college income and, also for the first time, exceeded the grants received from the local authorities. Those grants increased substantially in 1930 mostly owing to larger contributions from Devon and Exeter. In the crisis of 1931 the College met trouble halfway and itself suggested a five per cent cut in the grants it received. Only Cornwall exacted a larger sacrifice. The loss of income was therefore small and was recouped by a cut (it ranged from two to four per cent) in the incomes of the salaried staff—a good bargain for them at a time of rapidly falling prices. (They were to fare much worse in real terms in the inflation of 1974–76). Recurrent expenditure, after allowing for a persistent deficit in the halls account, remained well below income throughout the period, and a part of the heavy capital costs of the building programme was regularly met out of the surplus.[15]

Traditionally, universities raised capital—whether for buildings, chairs, scholarships, or general endowment—by an appeal to the public. The UGC had little money to spare for capital projects—Exeter received some small grants for the purchase books, help with the extension of Hope Hall, and a contribution of £10,000 towards the cost of the Roborough Library. These useful sums of money were not to be despised, but it was well understood that academic advancement depended in large part on private generosity. The universities and university colleges of the country launched a concerted appeal for funds in 1925. Exeter hoped to raise £100,000, but Moberly seemed doubtful about asking for so much. Murray, used to the hard knocks of politics, was more brazen and looked on fund-raising as 'a perpetual by-election'. He soon decided that the college needed not one hundred but five hundred thousand pounds and by 1928 was asking for three-quarters of a million. The organisation behind the appeal was rudimentary. An imposing appeal committee was headed by the Dukes of Bedford and Somerset and the not inconsiderable number of earls and other great landowners who lived or had interests in South-West England. The detailed work of fund-raising rested in practice on the shoulders of the Principal and the appeal organiser and his small staff. L. du Garde Peach, the playwright and one-time lecturer in the Department of English, was the first organiser. He was succeeded in 1926 by a racy Irishman L. M. Grayburn, who had been a banker and the best amateur jockey in India. Grayburn served without pay for nine years and most of the credit for the large sums raised must go to him and Murray. The appeal committee employed a succession of young ladies as canvassers and propagandists for the cause. They submitted shrewd and amusing reports to Grayburn and Murray, but were unable to raise large sums. With such a slender organisation behind it, it is not surprising that the appeal was cheap to run: only five per cent of the funds raised were absorbed by working expenses.[16]

The lot of an appeal organiser in the 1920s was not a happy one. The largest incomes were heavily taxed and rich men were subject to appeals from many quarters. Local hospitals for example were often competing with the university college for a limited supply of charitable money, to the disadvantage of the latter. Health had a wider appeal than education and many who were happy to see the poor restored to health were doubtful about the wisdom of educating the children of the poor when servants were hard to find. An unexpected difficulty cropped up during an appeal week in Torquay in February 1928. The best hostesses, it was discovered, kept Lent strictly and would not offer their support or their drawing rooms to the appeal. On another occasion an Exeter doctor refused to subscribe on the grounds that the need for good housing came first; the canvasser found his argument hard to counter. 'I'm bound to say I rather agree with him, I've never seen such slums anywhere, even in London.' The social structure of Devon militated against spectacularly large benefactions. Most of the wealthy families were landed rather than commercial or industrial. The claims on their charity were many and varied, and it was unlikely that any one good cause would attract large benefactions from that quarter. In the sixteenth and seventeenth centuries the largest benefactions had been made by merchants, and the nineteenth-century founders of university colleges—John Owens, William Armstrong, Josiah Mason, the Palmers—were all merchants or industrialists. When Exeter appealed for funds the local landed families responded with substantial donations—£2,000, £1,000, £500—but Sir Henry Lopes was the only Devon landowner who made, over the years, a really large contribution to the coffers of the College. The other large gifts came from men and women whose families were or had fairly recently been engaged in business. Such families were comparatively rare in Devon. Lord Glanely and Sir William Reardon Smith—both large benefactors of the College—were Devon men who had made fortunes as Cardiff shipowners. Washington Singer was a descendant of the sewing-machine manufacturer. W. H. Reed and C. V. Thomas were wealthy businessmen whose firms operated in South-West England. A. C. Ballard and E. J. Mardon, two of the most generous benefactors of the college, were living in retirement in Devon after lives spent the one in business and the other in the Indian Civil Service. The age of corporate giving had not yet dawned: men and women not companies were the principal benefactors of the college.[17]

When Murray arrived in Exeter the appeal had already raised over £30,000. Four years later in 1930 the sum raised or promised had risen to £259,000 and the number of individual subscribers had multiplied fifteen-fold to nearly 7000. In these four years the economic climate had on the whole favoured giving. The Wall Street crash in October 1929, rising unemployment and in 1931 a financial crisis made further large-scale fund raising impossible. The appeal organiser's young ladies continued their house-to-house canvassing in Barnstaple, Bovey Tracey, Honiton, Exeter and elsewhere. They picked up sums ranging from sixpence to a few guineas and more than earned their keep, but for all practical purposes the ambitious appeal for three-quarters of a million pounds was dead. In 1937 Murray tried again: the UGC had promised its grant towards the library on condition that the balance of the money— some £20,000—was raised by an appeal. The results were disappointing, for less than £9,000 was given.

In 1927 Grayburn optimistically calculated that he could raise a quarter of a million pounds from the region. He allowed for a refusal from 10 per cent of the population and for 25 per cent who would be too poor to give anything. But he expected per capita contributions ranging from 6d to £10 from the other families: 25 per cent, he estimated, could afford to give sixpence or a shilling (2½p or 5p), one per cent could afford £5, and half a per cent could afford £10. The pattern of giving proved to be quite different. Ten rich men and women gave £175,000 and most of the rest came in substantial sums of £100 or more. Refusals were much commoner than Grayburn expected, but most of the population in the South West could not be reached for lack of money and staff.[18]

Most of the money raised was earmarked for scholarships (usually closed or restricted), or for other specified purposes. Lord Glanely generously endowed a chair of agriculture because Devon was a farming county. The college did not teach agriculture at the time, had no plans to do so except in co-operation with the agricultural college at Seale Hayne, and was somewhat embarrassed by this surprising windfall. The four new large buildings completed between 1931 and 1940—the Washington Singer Laboratories, Mardon and Lopes Halls, and the Roborough

Library—cost £210,000. The College had at its unfettered disposal little more than half this sum. Capital that could not be saved out of current income had to come from borrowing, and a college that had always been poor now plunged into heavy debt. Sir Ian Amory, the treasurer, negotiated loans from the bank, at favourable rates of interest, but even his business acumen could not persuade banks to advance money at less than five per cent*. Faced with heavy interest and redemption charges the College took the unusual step of borrowing some of the endowments appropriated to specific purposes, such as scholarships, readerships, and chairs. This step as Murray candidly admitted was not to the taste of financial purists, but was not taken lightly or in secret. The consent of donors and of the UGC was sought and received before investments were cashed and the proceeds used to reduce debts to the bank.† Current income had to supply the funds for scholarships and chairs that would otherwise have come from investments, so that the financial saving to the college was small unless, for example, scholarships would not be awarded for lack of a suitable candidate. The principal gain from the transaction was the important one of reassuring the bank that its advances to the college could be confined within reasonable bounds.[19]

At their height in the later thirties college debts amounted to eighteen months' income. The UGC was seriously alarmed. Exeter's debt was almost the largest of any university institution and by far the largest in relation to resources and size. The decision to build the Roborough Library before the money had been raised added still more debt. Since the UGC had stipulated that its own grant of £10,000 was conditional upon the rest of the money being raised by an appeal, it had a legitimate grievance when Murray embarked on the project without knowing where the other £20,000 was to come from. When war broke out the College could look back on an eventful thirteen years under Murray's leadership. It had become a largely residential, almost cosmopolitan institution; it had begun the process of transferring its academic centre from Gandy Street to the Streatham Estate; it had attracted generous benefactions.

These achievements were not without their drawbacks and the College did not lack its critics. The building of laboratories for chemistry and physics on the Streatham estate separated the largest science departments from the rest of the College for a generation. The building of the

---

*In 1935 the bank agreed to accept 4 per cent for as long as the bank rate remained at 2 per cent.
†The process of restoring endowments began in 1946 and was completed in 1953.

Roborough Library separated the principal users of the library—the Faculties of Arts and Economics—from their books. This separation was a tiresome inconvenience rather than a serious obstacle to study, but it did for example prevent students from spending the odd hour in the library when, say, one lecture ended at 11 and another was not due to begin until 12. The presence of foreign students displeased those who preferred the college to live up to its name as the University College of the South West of England rather than see good Devon money applied to 'a university of the middle east'. A more serious criticism came from an unexpected quarter. Murray took some pains to establish links with American universities in order to attract students to Exeter for their junior year, and to promote exchanges between American lecturers and their Exeter counterparts. In 1935–36, Dr H. W. Simon of Columbia University spent a year in the education department on one such exchange. His lively young wife accompanied him and when she got back home she recorded her impressions in a best-selling book, published under the *nom de plume* Margaret Halsey. *With Malice toward Some* sold 300,000 copies in the United States in four months. It was issued by the Book-of-the-Month Club to its subscribers and launched its authoress on a career as social critic. She has since written several other books, including *Color Blind: A White Woman looks at the Negro* (1946); *The Corrupted Giant* (1963)—a study of American society; and her autobiography *No Laughing Matter* (1977). *With Malice toward Some* despite its title was kindly as well as amusing; it poked gentle fun at English food, the shyness of English students and the emptiness and snobbery of genteel conversation in Exeter's halls of residence. It was not a profound or damning attack on the college; but the memory of it lingers on in Exeter, even though copies of the book are now scarce.[20] The episode embarrassed the College, without deterring it from the continued pursuit of gentlemanliness through the residential and tutorial system.

Notes

1 W. Johnston, *Roll of the Graduates of the University of Aberdeen 1860-1900* (Aberdeen 1906); Oxford University, *Calendar*, 1910; *Parliamentary Debates* 15 June 1921, vol.143, col.538; *The Times*, 31 October 1924, 1, 3 and 8 December 1925; PPE, file 7; Murray to Sir F. Leyland-Barratt, 25 March 1929 [PPE, file 15].

2 Murray to the Secretary for Education, Truro, 10 June 1937 [PPC file 21]; PPG, files 13–22; *The Times*, 30 December 1964 and 2 January 1965: *Western Morning News*, 3 February 1965; University of Exeter, *Gazette*, no.30, April 1965.

3 Murray to W. Young, 6 May 1930 [PPC, file 7]; *Parliamentary Debates*, 28 March 1922, vol.152, col.1208; Murray to Lord Astor, 19 February 1929, [PPB, file 9].

4 Lloyd Parry to Headmistress, Secondary School for Girls, Devonport, 28 May 1918 [letterbook]; *Prospectus*, 1938 [PPC, file 23]; Bruce Truscot [E. Allison Peers], *Red Brick University* (1943) pp.20–21, 38–41; *Calendar*, 1893–94; Woodbridge to J. M. McLeod, 19 June 1908 [letterbook 1908]; *Annual Report*, 1923–24, 1934–35; L. J. Lloyd papers [University of Exeter archives]; PPG, file 10.

5 *College List*, 1937; Murray to Sir William M'Cormick, 24 March 1928 [PPF, file 29]; PPG, file 3; PPC, files 22 and 23.

6 Based on souvenir programmes in Box 10 of the University's archives and in the University Library; *Annual Report* 1933 ff.

7 *Annual Report* 1930 ff; PPF, file 10.

8 There is an obituary of Walke in *Nature*, 27 January 1940.

9 PPC, file 18; PPD, files 5, and 8; PPC, file 23.

10 PPD, file 1.

11 Clayden to R. D. Roberts, 28 May 1901 [Cambridge University archives BEMS 31/5 — Cambridge University Library]; PPF, file 16; UGC [Niblett] *Report of the sub-committee on halls of residence* (1957), p.13.

12 PPG, file 4; *The Ram*, July 1933; PPB, file 6.

13 *Annual Reports*, 1923 and 1925; W. H. Lewis papers [University of Exeter archives]; PPB, file 5; copies of the 'Move to Streatham' are in *Prospectus* 1931–32 and among the papers of the university librarian.

14 RAM, 5 April 1909; PPB, file 26; College Library Committee, annual reports 1920–33 [DRO].

15 UGC, 22 October 1931, and 18 February 1936 [PRO, UGC1 and 2]; PPF, files 6, 9; *Annual Reports*.

16 PPA, file 17; Hetherington, *The University College at Exeter*, p.22; PPE, files 5 and 19.

17 PPE, files 8, 22; W. K. Jordan, *Philanthrophy in England 1480–1660* (1959) passim.

18 PPE, passim; *Annual Reports*, 1927–38.

19 PPB, files 13 and 14; PPF, files 5–10, 18, 31; *Annual Reports* 1931–37, 1947–53; PPE, file 27.

20 PRO, UGC 5/2; *The Times*, 2 January 1965; Margaret Halsey, *With Malice toward Some* (Hamish Hamilton, 1938); there is a review of *With Malice* in *Times Literary Supplement*, 19 November 1938; *Annual Report*, 1936.

VII

THE UNIVERSITY COLLEGE
IN WAR AND PEACE 1939–1955

The Second World War, unlike the First, did not take the college by surprise. Despite strenuous opposition from some students an OTC was established in 1936 under the command first of Jackson Knight and then of A. H. Shorter, later the Montefiore Reader in Geography. Over half of the male students who returned to college in the autumn of 1939 had volunteered for active service by June 1940. When war broke out some of the staff volunteered to fight; others entered the civil service as and when government required. But opinion was far from unanimous, especially among the students, that the war with Germany was either necessary or just. In April 1940 a research student in economics was prosecuted for passing naval secrets to the *Daily Worker* (now the *Morning Star*). Early in May Guild Council in a gesture of protest agains the war refused to support the national savings movement. Later in the month when the German panzer divisions were already pouring into Belgium and northern France it was only by a narrow majority that Guild passed a motion of support for the Churchill government. The Principal, a patriot first and a liberal second, was incensed by these events. The two 'most ill-affected' students were sent down and an assistant lecturer in classics dismissed. Censorship of the students' newspaper the *South Westerner* was instituted and when in 1941 the students asked for it to be lifted Murray bluntly refused. Nor did Murray have much sympathy with conscientious objectors. If they applied for vacant posts during or for some time after the war they stood little chance of appointment.* In all these matters Murray was able to plead either pressure of public opinion, especially the lay majority on the Council of the College, or the

*Hetherington had acted similarly when he was Principal.

requirements of the Defence of the Realm Act. But there is clear evidence that he personally favoured tough measures and overrode the objections of colleagues who were as patriotic as himself but more tolerant.[1]

For the first four years of the war the number of students in College kept up surprisingly well. But this was only because evacuees took the place of students called up for war service. Some 70 students from the Central School of Speech and Drama occupied Lopes Hall in 1939–40 and Reed Hall from 1940 to 1942. In 1940 London School of Medicine for Women—200 students and 25 staff—joined the College, which was more crowded than it had ever been in peacetime. The School took over Thomas Hall and moved into slightly less cramped quarters in 1942 when the School of Speech and Drama returned to London. The medical students stayed only one more year in Exeter and with their return to London numbers fell sharply to 350 in 1943, and over 60 of these were cadets from the Royal Corps of Signals undergoing training in the physics department.[2]

In early planning against the outbreak of war the government had indicated a wish to use the Washington Singer Laboratories and Mardon Hall as hospitals. Professor Newman circumvented this design so far as the laboratories were concerned by arranging to let about half of the available space there to the Royal Aircraft Establishment (RAE). The RAE later moved to the Roborough Library, of which it occupied about a half, until 1943. When the evacuees returned to the London area in time for the German rocket attacks, the college looked around for new tenants for buildings that would otherwise have stood empty. The American Red Cross therefore took over Mardon Hall as a rest centre for American troops.

It is understandable that schools and research establishments saw little reason to stay in Exeter until the end of the war, for the city was heavily attacked from the air in the so-called Baedeker raids. Much of the city centre was destroyed by incendiary bombs in April and early May 1942. College buildings were among those hit in the final raid on Sunday 3 May. The registry, which occupied an old property on the far side of the alley leading from Gandy Street to Rougemont Gardens, was burnt out with the loss of most of the College records, including the minutes of Council and Senate. The handicraft hut, used for teacher-training in peacetime and for training munitions workers in wartime, was also completely destroyed.* The main Gandy Street building also caught fire

*A new single-storey registry was built on the site after the war.

in two places. Professor Newman having first checked that the Washington Singer Laboratories were safe, hurried to Gandy Street where he found the main building already alight. Staff, students and other amateurs were doing their best to contain the blaze. Newman found some firemen fighting a losing battle nearby and persuaded them to turn their attention to the threatened College buildings. They soon brought the fire under control and saved the main building from serious damage. Other College property escaped more lightly. There was some damage to the roofs of the Roborough Library and the Washington Singer Laboratories, but that was all. The heaviest personal loss was suffered by R. R. Darlington, the Professor of History: all his books and papers were destroyed when his flat in Southernhay burnt out.[3]

The destruction of records made the orderly administration of college affairs more difficult than it already was. Shortly after the outbreak of war the college established an emergency committee which took over most of the functions of Council and Senate. Those bodies rarely met during the war, and few records of their deliberations have been preserved. Not until the 1947–48 session was the normal peacetime routine restored; only then did the college resume the practice of publishing an annual report; only from October 1947 is it possible to follow the proceedings of Senate and Council in carefully preserved volumes of their minutes.

Prices rose much less in the Second World War than in 1914–18. The official and not entirely satisfactory cost of living index rose by 50 per cent in the six years from 1939 to 1945. Even this modest rise posed problems for a College whose income from Treasury and local authority grants remained unchanged throughout the war while its income from fees declined with the fall in student numbers. Until 1943 substantial rents were paid by the Royal Aircraft Establishment and the London School of Medicine for Women, but the American occupation of Mardon Hall by no means off-set the loss of income when the evacuees returned to London. By 1942–43 the College was running a substantial deficit and had given up setting money aside to make good arrears of maintenance when the war ended. The UGC, which knew of Exeter's predicament, was not alarmed and felt that no action need be taken. Where an institution was in serious difficulties (Southampton for example) the committee was ready to offer help. In some respects the war reduced college expenditure: members of staff called up for war service did not need to be paid unless their new salary was lower than the one they had received from the college. In the early days of the war some supplementation of income was called for, but as former members of staff worked their way up the military or civil service hierarchy their pay soon came to exceed their peacetime earnings. Those who stayed in Exeter found that their incomes stood still while prices inexorably moved upwards. In 1944 the college finally agreed to institute salary scales for lecturers and professors but the concession was a small one and, in fact, cost very little. There was to be no effective relief for the hard-pressed staff until the Treasury grant was doubled at the end of the war.[4]

One painless economy open to the College was to grow more of its food. Before the war the College gardeners directed by John Caldwell, head of the Department of Botany, had shown themselves masters of their craft by taking many prizes at local and national flower shows. On the outbreak of war their talents were put to other uses. Ten acres of pasture near Mardon Hall were ploughed and put down to potatoes and green vegetables. By 1942 eight men and two girls were cultivating 21 acres with the aim of supplying the halls of residence throughout the year. In vacations surplus produce was sold on the open market. The chief crops were potatoes and brussels sprouts, but the estate also produced small quantities of all the vegetables commonly grown. In addition Caldwell bought some chickens, pigs and rabbits, and a few goats. The enterprise was profitable even though the produce was conservatively valued at grower's prices, i.e. at the prices a grower would have received from a wholesaler. Since most of the produce went direct to hall kitchens, which would otherwise have had to buy at retail prices, the gain to college finances was considerable. In the crop year 1941–42, for example, the estate produced food valued at £1900* while the total cost of college grounds was £1800; (in 1935 when maintenance of the grounds had cost £1000 food worth only £100 had been produced). After the war Professor Caldwell somewhat reluctantly abandoned oversight of the college market-garden. But the work went on and large supplies of food were still being grown in the early 1950s. By then some fields were becoming exhausted through over-cropping and had to be rested. A Ferguson tractor was bought in 1953—the first concession to mechanisation—and an extensive programme of liming and manuring was instituted. Eventually market gardening was given up and the land sown to grass.[5] The inflationary rise in food prices since 1970 has not persuaded the University to try its hand at market-gardening again.

*Grower's prices.

At the end of the Second World War students flocked to British universities in unprecedented numbers as they had in the years after 1918. At the peak of post-war overcrowding in 1949–50, there were 85,000 students in British universities, an increase of 70 per cent over 1939. Numbers fell back a little in the early 1950s, but the trough was a shallow one—81,000 in 1953–54—and by 1957–58 numbers were approaching 100,000. In common with other university colleges and the smaller provincial universities, Exeter took rather more than its fair share of these increasing numbers. Before the war Exeter had had about 450 full-time students; but already in 1945 this number was far exceeded with nearly 600 students in college. At its highest in 1949 there were close to one thousand students. Numbers briefly dropped below 900 in 1954, only to resume their upward path in the following year. In most of the post-war years the proportion of foreign and Commonwealth students stood at something above ten per cent, close to the national average and considerably below the pre-war proportion*. In the early post-war years the growth of numbers was the effect of an influx of ex-servicemen. The Ministry of Education's scheme for Further Education and Training (FETS) awards allowed many ex-servicemen whose studies had been interrupted to resume their courses, and it encouraged many more who would not otherwise have contemplated it to go to university. However, by the early 1950s the number of ex-servicemen in universities was beginning to decline. Their gradual disappearance did not lead to a substantial fall in numbers because other forces were working towards university expansion. The size of the university population had always depended on the size of the secondary-school and especially of the sixth-form population. After 1945 an increasing proportion of children was staying at school until the age of eighteen—in 1952 six and a half per cent, in 1957 nine per cent. Not all who left school at eighteen were qualified or wished to go to university, but for those who did a more ample provision of scholarships eased their path. The number of state scholarships (tenable at university colleges from 1946) rose to 800 in 1947–48 from the number fixed at 360 in 1936. Local authorities were also awarding major and minor scholarships much more freely, though it was not until 1962 that they were obliged to make awards to all those accepted for admission by a university.[6]

The post-war expansion had been foreseen. In May 1945 the UGC

*For the past twenty years overseas students have been less than ten per cent of the student population in Exeter.

asked the universities and university colleges by how much they could expand 'ignoring financial considerations' and in the long run. After due deliberation Murray replied that Exeter could double its pre-war size in four or five years (which it did) and could grow to three times its pre-war size (i.e. to 1200 students) in the longer term. He reminded the UGC that the college lacked adequate current income, endowments, and halls of residence. No great increase of income from fees or from local authority grants was to be expected, and growth would depend in effect on the size of UGC grants. The UGC, armed with much larger funds than ever before, responded by doubling Exeter's grant in 1945, doubling it again in 1947 and then planning for a somewhat slower growth to the end of the quinquennium in 1952. Whereas before the war the college had received a third of its income from the UGC it now received two-thirds to three-quarters (and has continued to do so ever since). Dependence on central government funds did not stop there. Apart from a few splendid benefactions, particularly for the foundation of new colleges at Oxford and Cambridge, private capital has not been given as freely since the war for university purposes. If a university has needed capital for land or buildings it has generally turned to the UGC, which somewhat to its surprise found itself making capital grants much more readily than in the 1930s. One immediate problem that faced all universities in 1945 was how to make good the arrears of maintenance that had accumulated since the early days of the war. Exeter's requests for assistance were not met in full, but enough money was made available for Murray to remark: 'We shall be in velvet'. Substantial grants were also made towards the purchase of some large houses that the College acquired at this time— Crossmead, Birks Grange, Thornlea, and Duryard. These properties were mostly required as halls of residence. With the exception of Thornlea they all stood in several acres of grounds, which the university has since put to good use as the site of new halls. At the end of the war owners were happy to rid themselves of the incumbrance of a large house and grounds and to live more modestly in small properties.* The College was thus able to buy cheaply properties that with the land attached have since proved extremely valuable. At the time these long-run advantages were not foreseen. The College was more concerned to gain possession of the new premises as quickly as possible. That was not always easy. The

*The College considered the purchase of other properties as well: the Imperial Hotel close to the Streatham estate; and Peamore House on the Exeter by-pass beyond Alphington. The latter would have made a splendid but absurdly distant hall of residence.

National Fire Service occupied Crossmead until the end of the war. Thornlea, needed for the department of education (as the training department was now known), stood under threat of requisition for housing. But by March 1946 the City Council had decided not to oppose the change of use to academic purposes. Birks Grange, acquired in 1946, remained requisitioned until 1948 when the College took possession and housed 20 students there. The College had also been quietly buying up properties in the Pennsylvania district of Exeter adjacent to Hope and Lopes Halls. By the end of the war few properties in the immediate vicinity of Hope and Lopes remained in private hands and the College had come close to having a continuous block of property running from Cowley Bridge Road to Pennsylvania Road. As houses were acquired, they became annexes to Hope or Lopes—Ibsley House (Montefiore); Homefield (Lazenby), Spreytonway, St Germans. The purchase of Lafrowda and its nine acres in 1965 almost completed the process; there is now only one private house left in the Hopes-Lopes area. The College would have liked to round off its estate by acquiring Higher Hoopern Farm, 35 acres of land in the upper Hoopern Valley north of the Hope-Lopes area. The property was on offer in 1946 for £19,000, but the district valuer thought the price much too high and it was not until 1964 that the University acquired the farm. Even if the College did not own the farm it wished to have its future development reserved for college purposes, since in the encouraging and expansive post-war atmosphere there were good prospects for long-term growth. Under the Town and Country Planning Act of 1947 the College therefore proposed that the idea of a 'university precinct' should be incorporated into Exeter's town plan:

> Those who are responsible for the development of the college have no choice but to take long views. The present target of college numbers is 1200 students. When that figure is attained it is questionable whether growth could or ought to be halted . . . . The growth is likely to be gradual but steady. Not all of these lands and houses [Higher Hoopern Farm, the area between Birks Grange and Duryard House, houses in St German's Road] are needed now. But all are part of the long view of college expansion.

Exeter City Council was not averse to this proposal and in due course a university sphere of influence was delineated on the town plan. At the same time Vincent Harris revised his own plans for the development of the estate. Though somewhat less formal than his pre-war design they still paid little regard to the lie of the land and took as their starting point the commanding view rather than the convenience of the user.[7]

Agreeable as it was to plan for a hopeful future, present discomforts could not be ignored. Money was freely available to universities (if not to their employees) in the post-war world, but what could it buy? Even the simplest needs were hard to satisfy. In a world of shortages strange things happened. The College needed floor coverings for the old houses that it had bought for use as halls of residence. Was a Board of Trade licence required for the purchase of linoleum? The UGC—more down-to-earth than in the past—assured Murray that licences were not needed. When informed that linoleum, licensed or unlicensed, was unobtainable they advised the purchase of felt base. In the end the College 'did itself rather rather well' by bidding for second-hand matting at a local auction sale. The UGC was the relevant Government department when the College applied for deferment for laboratory technicians threatened with military service. As the UGC put it with sly humour: 'The District Manpower Board will normally consult the University Grants Committee before rejecting the application.' The UGC also found itself allocating a quota of constructional steel to universities and colleges. Because of the shortages—of steel, cement, and labour—the one building that the College started in the early post-war period took four years to complete. Begun in 1948 the Hatherly Laboratories for botany and zoology were not ready for occupation until 1952. In their restrained Georgian style they present a handsome front to the passer-by and conform to Murray's guiding principle that college buildings should be designed for viewing from the far side of the Hoopern Valley. The long delay in completing the laboratories added considerably to the cost. During the war Mrs Heath had left the College a handsome bequest of £25,000 towards laboratories for the biological sciences, but death duties and the delays in building left the UGC finding most of the money in the end.*[8]

The post-war expansion of numbers was too sudden for comfort. The College had doubled in size within five years and there was every sign that the number of students would rise further. The numbers of teaching staff and of administrators kept pace with the growth in student numbers, but until the completion of the Hatherly laboratories no extra accommodation became available for lecture rooms, staff offices, or laboratories and workshops. Newly-appointed staff, especially if they

---

*With the growth of its budget the UGC has become a larger and more professional organisation. Until the appointment of Moberly in 1934 even the chairmanship had been a part-time job. The modern UGC is able to offer universities expert advice on subjects as varied as catering services and the design of libraries.

were of junior rank, found themselves occupying cubby holes and odd corners, or sharing a room with other members of staff—a tolerable arrangement only in the vacations when there were no students to see or teach. Exeter was not alone in its overcrowding. All over the country universities were bursting at the seams. What was unusual in Exeter's situation was that despite its recent growth and its potential for further growth it still kept its old status as a university college. Thirty years and more after admission to the Treasury list and with three times as many students it was still without its charter of incorporation as an independent university empowered to award its own degrees.

Notes

1 *The Times*, 20 April 1940; *Western Morning News*, 1 June 1940; Guild minutes 7, 20 and 24 May 1940; PPD, file 2; PPB, file 29; PPF, file 23; *Express and Echo*, 18 May 1940.

2 PPF, files 10 and 30; PPG, file 10; John Murray, *The War and the University College of the South West of England* (Exeter 1943).

3 Murray, *The War and the University College*; Murray to E. V. Harris, 7 and 13 May 1942; Murray, *The University College of the South West of England: the war and the peace* (Exeter 1949); for Newman's part in saving the main building, personal communication from Neville Portman, lecturer in physics; PPB, file 18.

4 PPF, file 13; PPB, file 18; UGC, 18 February 1942 [PRO, UGC 1/2]; PPF, files 15, 16 and 30.

5 John Caldwell, 'The Department of Botany: a retrospect' (University of Exeter, *Gazette*, January 1970); PPD, files 3 and 5; PPF, file 24; *Annual Reports*, 1947 ff.

6 UGC, *University development 1952-57*, p.15 (Cmnd 534, BPP 1957-8 XVIII); PPF, file 31; *Annual Reports*, 1947 ff; *University Awards: report of the working party*. (HMSO, 1948) pp.4-5; Education Act 1962; Statutory Instrument 1962/1689.

7 PPF, files 18, 19 and 30; *Annual Reports*, 1951 and 1964.

8 PPF, files 18, 30 and 31; *Annual Report*, 1952; UGC, 4 November 1948 [PRO, UGC 2/29].

VIII

THE STRUGGLE
FOR THE CHARTER

Ever since the earliest days of the Exeter Technical and University Extension College the College authorities had hoped that one day Exeter would join the lengthening list of full and independent British universities. The achievement of university college status in 1922 made ultimate success probable if not certain. In general terms it was clear what future measures were required before Exeter could achieve its ambitions: stronger finances, new and worthy buildings, a larger and better qualified body of students, a growing academic reputation based in part upon the examination successes and subsequent careers of the students but principally upon the contributions of the academic staff to the advancement of learning. There were no exact criteria laid down by which to test whether Exeter had made enough progress to merit promotion from the university college to the university league. The standards set by the advisory committee on Treasury grants and later by the UGC tended to become more rigorous with the passage of time where they could be laid down with precision—in the field of numbers and finance. After the incorporation of Reading University in 1926 no further universities were created in Britain until Nottingham received its charter in 1948. The best that Exeter could do was to improve itself as much as possible, put out periodic feelers about a charter, and hope.

Financially the college remained weak until after the Second World War. It was only then that the debts incurred on building account began to be reduced. Within ten years of the end of the war they had fallen to a sum trifling in relation to the much larger income that the college then enjoyed. An unfriendly critic might argue that the post-war prosperity was solely the result of the munificence of government acting through the

UGC; but since all universities were by then heavily dependent on the National Exchequer no adverse comparisons could be made. The local authorities continued to support the College, their grants increasing somewhat in money terms, but as a proportion of total income and in real terms representing a much smaller contribution than before the war. Receipts from fees remained substantial at nearly 16 per cent of income. Fees had been raised from time to time not with any view to charging the full cost of tuition but to keep them roughly comparable with those charged elsewhere.

It is difficult to estimate the intellectual quality of the student population. Judged by their qualifications on entrance there was some improvement, reflecting perhaps a fuller provision of secondary schools rather than higher innate abilities. Judged by their academic performance at college the students displayed a bewildering range of talents ranging from brilliant success to dismal failure. A modern university faced with more applicants than it can accept is prepared to admit that it has made a mistake and will require unsatisfactory students to withdraw. The pre-war college, short of applicants, could not afford harsh measures. Private students with sufficient means could take their time over passing examinations: one student, admittedly an exception, spent eight years on his intermediate course. By the later thirties it was unusual for the college to admit students who had not had a full secondary education including two years in the sixth form. In 1937, 54 students were admitted to the four-year course for students in training. 30 of these students had passed intermediate or the higher school certificate; another 21 had taken one or other of these examinations, had failed and had nevertheless been admitted. Only three had not proceeded beyond matriculation (five good passes* in the School Certificate examination, equivalent to ordinary level GCE). Unsatisfactory as the record of some of these students might seem to a modern admissions tutor, their educational qualifications were regarded with some satisfaction by the College as representing a considerable advance on former days. After the war, with applicants clamouring at the doors of universities, the College was more selective. In 1945 the Faculty of Arts admitted 118 students: 28 had completed the intermediate examinations, 66 had passed two or three of the four subjects required and only 24 (20 per cent) were without any part of the intermediate on entry. By 1947 the college was requiring a full pass in intermediate (or

*The five passes had to include English language, mathematics and Latin.

exemption from it*) from science students and arts students reading the more popular subjects — English, French, history and geography. Lower qualifications secured admission to the less crowded departments. At the same time the ready availibility of state and local authority scholarships and of grants to ex-servicemen led to a sharp reduction in the number of students in training. It was no longer necessary for students to bind themselves to teach; there were other ways to finance a university education. In 1946 less than a third of the students were pledged to teach. In 1948 the Ministry abolished the pledge and the student in training taking a four-year course gradually faded from the scene.[1]

In 1949 the UGC undertook a perfunctory and impressionistic survey of academic opinion about the relative abilities of past and present students. Universities did not report that more meant worse. It was felt that proportionately there were fewer outstanding students, but that on the whole there was little difference between the average student of 1938 and 1949. The particular comments submitted from Exeter conveyed mixed impressions; some departments thought highly of their recent students; others noted a decline in the proportion of outstandingly good — and of outstandingly weak — students. A review of degree results in Exeter appears to confirm the latter view.

Class of degree awarded: per cent

	1928–32	1948–51
I	11	6
II	44	61
IIIor Pass	46	33
N	257	711

The fall in the proportion of students awarded a first-class degree is statistically significant although the numbers are small. The rising proportion of students securing a second-class degree and the corresponding fall in thirds and passes is even more strongly significant in statistical terms, and may well reflect a genuine improvement in examination performance. But the improvement is not large enough to confirm the impression of a post-war golden age in the world of universities. The presence of a large body of ex-servicemen among the student population stirs happy memories among some who were then university teachers. They nostalgically recall the enthusiasm, energy and

*Until 1942 London University declined to recognise the Higher School Certificate of other examination boards as an equivalent to its own intermediate examination. Students who had taken and passed the 'wrong' examinations at school were obliged to take London intermediate in the November of their first year in the college.

maturity of the men and women who had returned to their studies after war service. In Exeter such students never accounted for more than a third of the student population, but they strongly impressed their teachers. The impersonal examiners for the London University external degrees do not appear to have been so readily appreciative. It is not hard to see why. A fighter pilot, a commando or a former WRNS officer will not be tongue-tied in the presence of his or her tutor like a boy or girl fresh from the grammar school. But poise, self-confidence and a knowledge of the world are of only limited help in the examination hall. Knowledge of affairs may be of some value to the historian, the student of literature, or the economist; but probably not to the mathematician, the physicist, or the linguist. The qualities that commended ex-servicemen to their teachers were personal rather than intellectual and gained them little credit under examination conditions. Information about examination failures is understandably scanty. The surviving evidence suggests a paradoxical state of affairs before the war. Between 1922 and 1928 the Department of Chemistry entered 24 candidates for degrees: fifteen were awarded firsts; seven seconds; two pass degrees. Yet for the College as a whole in the six years 1927–32 27 per cent of candidates failed their degree examinations. In 1948 (when the College could afford to be more selective) only six per cent failed. In 1956 and 1957, however, (the only other years for which statistics are available) the failure rate had almost returned to the pre-war level, with 23 per cent of candidates ploughed. At least some of the disappointed candidates re-sat their examinations in the following academic year, either in November or in June, but it is not known how many succeeded at the second attempt. Not much of this fragmentary information was published, and when it did appear in the annual reports of the College it was not presented in a readily comprehensible form. The high rate of failures could therefore have done little (if any) damage to the reputation of the College even if other colleges and universities had fared better. So far as the UGC could discover there was a considerable wastage rate among the students of many British universities; 13 per cent of the students admitted to the University of Liverpool in the years 1947–49 left without a degree, not all of them for reasons of academic failure; of students admitted to University College, London, in the years 1948–50, 18 per cent failed to take a degree; and a large-scale enquiry on the 1952 entry to British universities showed a wastage rate of 16 per cent, 11 per cent for academic and five per cent for other reasons. The wastage rate at Exeter was perhaps rather higher than the national average, but the College could put some of the blame for this state of affairs on the difficulties of teaching for the external degrees of the University of London.[2]

For what careers were Exeter students preparing themselves? In a report to the UGC in 1944 Murray made high claims: during his time in the College new outlets had been found—the church, the civil service, law, medicine, business. The students in training twenty years earlier had found posts in elementary schools: more recently in secondary schools, technical and training colleges and in universities. 'In short', he concluded 'the careers show the professional spread characteristic of a university'. This was painting too rosy a picture. It is true that a considerable number of students entered the legal and banking professions but they had already done so before enrolling as students. They came to the college part-time in order to pass the examinations of the Law Society or the Institute of Bankers. If they and the overseas students are excluded it appears that in the nineteen-thirties more than half of the students became teachers. In the early thirties, when the College was training a large number of two-year students, the proportion was considerably higher (over 70 per cent). As elsewhere the graduate teacher counted himself lucky to get a post in a secondary school. During the depression three-quarters of Exeter's graduate teachers went to teach in elementary schools and in 1937 when teaching posts were somewhat easier to find, rather more graduates went into elementary than into secondary schools. A period of unemployment after graduation was not uncommon in the teaching profession. In 1937 for example eight out of 54 students leaving the training department were still without posts at Christmas. But it was unusual for teachers to remain unemployed for longer than one or two terms. Graduates who did not intend to teach were rarely unemployed. Not all secured jobs commensurate with their qualifications but graduate unemployment was not a serious problem in Britain in the inter-war years by comparison with other European countries, or with the employment prospects of the less well-educated in Britain. Some employers—local authorities, banks and insurance companies prominent among them—rarely employed graduates except in technical posts. Industrial firms were beginning to offer general traineeships to graduates, but mostly took university men and women for research work or technical positions. The Department of Chemistry sent graduates to the laboratories of the government chemist, of ICI and of J. Lyons and Co. The tiny Department of Zoology, which until after the war had only a handful of honours students, supplied the British Museum with a deputy keeper and was the first department of the University College to have one of its former students appointed to a professorship.* Joseph Sykes, the head of the Department of Economics, believed that a degree in economics or commerce offered more varied job prospects than a degree in an arts subject. But his carefully compiled statistics belie his confidence. He had no difficulty in showing that two-thirds of his former students were working in business —banking, administration, accountancy or secretarial posts. But this was hardly surprising since many of them were part-time students seeking a professional qualification. The handful of students with a commerce degree (BCom) did work in business but not always in responsible posts. The students who had read for the BSc (Econ) on the other hand tended, like the arts men, to become teachers. The advantage was that rather more of them (two-thirds) taught in central or grammar schools or in technical colleges, and only one-third in elementary schools. Before the war it was unusual for Exeter students to work in the civil service. An economist, (Sir) Robert Taylor, became a distinguished member of the colonial service. There were few openings in social work or personnel management.[3]

After the war more varied job opportunities presented themselves to Exeter students. Relatively few were bonded to teach, even before 1948 when the pledge was abolished. Those who chose teaching as a career and had science degrees easily found posts; for the arts graduate competition was stronger but no teachers found the threat of unemployment as oppressive as it had been before the war. The College careers advisory service remained rudimentary; relatively few students in those halcyon days of full employment approached the service, and the careers of post-war graduates are therefore poorly recorded. It is clear however that industry and commerce were more willing than they had been before 1939 to employ graduates in non-specialist posts—men in sales or general management, women in personnel management or as secretaries. Exeter students rarely aspired to the highest branches of the civil service, contenting themselves with posts in the executive grade or in specialist work like tax offices. Journalism, social work, hospital administration were just a few of the many areas of employment opening up to the

*J. E. C. Raymont who graduated in 1936. In 1946 he was elected to the Chair of Zoology of University College, Southampton. The Royal Albert Memorial College also had its professor in G. R. Clemo, FRS, who held the Chair of Chemistry at Durham from 1925 to 1954.

graduate in the years after 1945. If Principal Murray had waited a few years before claiming that the careers of Exeter graduates showed the 'professional spread characteristic of a university' he would have been more accurate.

Exeter was unusual among university colleges, let alone universities, in the narrow range of subjects taught. If law and economics are classified as arts-based subjects (a view still held by the UGC) then Exeter was a two-faculty university college—arts and the natural sciences. Teaching of medicine had never been taken beyond the first MB, or of engineering beyond intermediate. The College had surrendered the manual school in 1918 and the art school in 1922 to the education committee of Exeter City Council and never showed much disposition to recover the lost ground. For many years Plymouth was the destined site for a faculty of engineering and the Camborne School of Mines for a faculty of mining technology. Seale-Hayne Agricultural College according to plans drawn up in the later 1920s would have provided a faculty of agriculture, with lecturers from Exeter offering a grounding in chemistry and biology; the connection with Seale-Hayne (never more than tenuous) lingered on into the 1950s and its Principal was for some years a member of Senate and titular professor of agriculture. In 1936 Murray assured the UGC that all propaganda for a federal university had stopped and that the federal idea was dead. Without federal connections Exeter seemed likely to remain a two-faculty college for a long time.

Of the faculties, arts with law and economics was the larger. Physics and chemistry were large vigorous and successful departments but they stood almost alone as standard-bearers for science. The honours school of mathematics was relatively small and even fewer students read for honours in botany or zoology. After Clayden's retirement in 1920 there was no full-time geologist on the staff until 1947. In 1931 after the Washington Singer Laboratories made it possible for chemistry and physics to take large numbers (if larger numbers offered) arts outnumbered science students in the proportions 4:3. In 1947, despite the post-war popularity of science, arts (with economics) outnumbered science by 2:1. The science students were admittedly better qualified: hardly any were reading for intermediate, and virtually all the postgraduate students in the college were to be found there, mostly in chemisty. But without the backing of applied sciences like medicine and engineering the scientific side of college work could hardly expect to equal the combined weight of arts and social studies.

In a college with 500 students and more than a dozen departments, even the larger departments had a small establishment. Physics, chemistry, mathematics, English, history and geography each had from three to five members of staff to cover the syllabuses for London degrees, for the London intermediate and for the two-year certificate course. Hours of teaching were inevitably long by more recent standards in provincial universities and it was only slowly that the College could approach to the tutorial ideal that was part of Murray's plan. In smaller departments like economics two men covered an enormous range of teaching: not only branches of economics that would today be allotted to specialist teachers, but also statistics and economy history came within their purview. In 1930, for example, Joseph Sykes was lecturing 23 hours a week: he was based in Plymouth but travelled to Exeter on three days of the week to teach there. The other economist Laurence Helsby* (later a distinguished civil servant and as Lord Helsby the Master of St Peter's Hall, Oxford) lectured for 15 hours a week and travelled to Plymouth on five days of the week. Despite the burden of teaching, several members of the College — Newman, Britton, Sykes, Caldwell, Douglas, Mallison, and Jackson Knight prominent among them — found time to pursue their researches and publish a substantial number of books and/or papers.

The post-war expansion doubled the number of students and of staff, and gave more time for reading, reflection and research. Economics grew with particular speed and the once hard-pressed Joseph Sykes shocked the Principal by reporting that he and his staff taught for no more than seven to nine hours each in a week. The economies of scale offered by expansion were not always as substantial as in the Department of Economics. Laboratory work in the sciences and language classes in French, German and classics tended to maintain the number of 'student-contact hours' for teachers in those subjects at a higher level. Nevertheless, the burden of teaching must have lightened considerably in the post-war years.

The more plentiful supplies of money allowed the College to expand its range of teaching within the limit of arts, natural sciences and social studies. A little German had been taught in the pre-war department of modern languages, though the main concern had always been French. In 1947, with the appointment of H. B. Garland, German became a separate department. In the same year with the appointment of A. Stuart the teaching of geology was put on a regular though at first far from

*HonLLD Exon 1963.

satisfactory footing. There was little space for the storage of specimens, for rock-cutting or photography, and a laboratory with 30 benches was a demand that could not be met for several years; it was not until 1950 that a second geologist was appointed.* The teaching of politics and public administration began in a small way before the war with the provision of a Diploma in Public Administration (DPA) for local government officers. After the war the staff (attached to economics) grew, and teaching began for a degree in government within the London scheme for the BSc(Econ). As with politics, the teaching of sociology began in response to demands for a vocational course. In 1947 the College received unsolicited applications for a course in social administration and not all the applicants could be persuaded that the DPA was really what they wanted. The College therefore appointed the rector of Watchet the Rev. J. V. Langmead Casserley, as its first (part-time) sociologist, and embarked on teaching for a diploma in social administration (DSA) parallel to the DPA. Within a few years the college was teaching for the sociology degree of the BSc (Econ).

Post-war prosperity also made possible the creation of new chairs. Within the space of two years in 1947 and 1948 the College almost doubled the number of professors by establishing new chairs in botany, zoology, economics, law and German, and by re-establishing the chairs of classics and philosophy. Except in classics the incumbent head of department was promoted to the chair, usually after long years of service. Levine, the new professor of philosophy, had joined the staff in 1921; Griffith Morgan (law) in 1923; Sykes (economics) in 1925; Harvey (zoology) in 1930; and Caldwell (botany) in 1936; only Garland had joined the College since the war. F. W. Clayton came from King's College, Cambridge to the Chair of Classics. The previous head of the Classics Department G. V. M. Heap moved to the new post of academic secretary; he resigned in 1950 to become an antiquarian book-seller.[4]

When Murray arrived in Exeter he formed an unfavourable view of the university college, as he recalled in 1946:

> The college was quite unfit, in my opinion to give degrees in 1922 and for years after. I took it on in 1926 and had a sharp disillusionment and all but threw it up . . . Hetherington's colleagues in 1922 may have shared his view [that the college was unequal by itself to carrying a University Charter]: any patronage that would have got them undeserved degree rights they would have jumped at. What they did not deserve then they do now (1946).

*D. L. Dineley, now Professor of Geology, Bristol.

It did not take Murray twenty years to change his mind. Already in 1934, after no more than eight years as Principal, he sounded out the UGC about the prospects for a charter. Though apparently sympathetic the UGC pointed to the lack of endowments and of a library. Within a few years the Roborough library had been built and after the war the more generous provision of government funds made the lack of endowments seem relatively unimportant. Since the elevation of Reading in 1926 no new universities had been created in Britain, and no university colleges were admitted to the Treasury list after Exeter in 1922 until Hull and Leicester secured that privilege in 1945. The lack of recent precedent made the business of applying for a charter more difficult. There was a firm resolve to approach the authorities as soon after the end of the war as possible, but some confusion as to who the authorities were and how to approach them. Reading appeared to have forgotten how twenty years before it had set about the business and neither Nottingham nor Southampton threw any light on the subject. Whether this was from ignorance or prudence is not clear; both had the same ambitions as Exeter, and both achieved university status before Exeter despite their professed innocence of the correct procedure. In the absence of enlightenment from without Murray fell back on his own political experience and organised a large and powerful deputation as if he were a member of Parliament asking the President of the Board of Trade for a certificate of industrial development for his constituency. In law the issue of a charter is a royal perogative exercised on the advice of the Lord President of the Council. The then Lord President Herbert Morrison was in no position to judge the merits of the case for himself and asked the UGC to received the deputation instead. Somewhat unwillingly Sir Walter Moberly agreed, on condition that the deputation was small enough to fit into the UGC's far from spacious offices. This did not augur well, and Murray's 'reconnaissance in force' had a frosty reception. Robert Cecil, Marquis of Salisbury, who had held the office of President of the College since 1945, introduced the deputation but Murray was naturally the principal speaker. Although more than ten years earlier he had pronounced the federal idea dead it had a prominent place in the scheme he laid before the UGC, if only because he was surrounded by representatives of Plymouth, Cornwall, Saint Luke's and Seale-Hayne. The UGC had never cared for a federal solution to Exeter's problems; the particular version of federalism proposed in 1947 had the added complication that it required the approval of the Ministry of

Education so far as Plymouth and Saint Luke's were concerned. But Exeter had taken no steps to sound out or alert the Ministry—and this was not the only point at which the college case had been inadequately prepared. The deputation came away empty-handed. In its report to the Lord President of the Council the UGC flatly rejected the federal scheme:

> The Committee do not consider that these plans are either desirable or possible even in a remote future.

The College should develop in arts and cognate subjects and in pure science. Yet as things stood in 1947 the UGC was not disposed to recommend a charter for the College even if it confined itself to arts and pure science. There were only a dozen research students in the college, and the committee was 'not satisfied the academic staff of the college are generally of the distinction and quality which is required in an institution of full university status'. Oddly enough a not wholly different academic staff was considered worthy of full university status only eight years later. Thirteen of the 18 professors in the college in 1955 already had chairs (or the headship of their department) in 1947, and nearly half of the non-professorial staff of 1955 were also in post eight years earlier. Unless the UGC had changed its standards the academic judgement it made in 1947 was contradicted by its judgement of 1955. It may be that even in a confidential report to the minister the UGC was unwilling to be entirely frank and that it advanced the lack of academic distinction as its prime reason for advising against a charter while concealing another reason that it held to be more weighty. Principal Murray—pugnacious, ageing, a daring financier and erratic schemer—has been widely regarded in Exeter as the real obstacle to early achievement of university status. If the UGC shared this view it took good care to conceal the fact, even from the Lord President of the Council. It had condoned Murray's financial expedients in his days of poverty in the 1930s; it had not protested much when he started to build the Roborough Library without raising his share of the capital in advance. When the UGC distrusted a domineering figure in the life of another institution—Nottingham University College—it was not afraid to say so. It therefore seems unlikely that it would have kept silence if it had regarded Murray as unfit in his old age to be the head of a full university. The true explanation is probably very simple: the university colleges of Nottingham, Southampton, and Hull were growing much faster than Exeter in the

Plate 7 *Laying the Foundation Stone of the Gandy Street Building, 1909*

Plate 8 *Gandy Street Building, the centre of college life from 1911 to 1958*

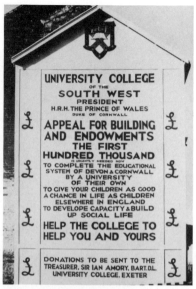

Plate 9   *College Hostel Cubicle
c 1913*

Plate 10   *University College
Appeal 1926*

Plate 11   *Gandy Street 'Cafe' between the Wars*

Plate 12 *The Prince of Wales and Principal Murray: Laying the Foundation Stone of the Washington Singer Laboratory, 1927*

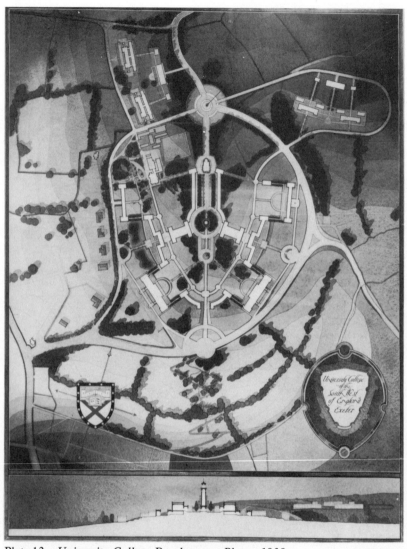

Plate 13 *University College Development Plan c 1930*

Plate 14   *Washington Singer Laboratories, opened 1931*

Plate 15   *Mardon Hall, opened 1933*

Plate 16   *Roborough Library, opened 1940*

Plate 17 *The Registry 1942*

Plate 18 *Laying the Foundation Stone of the Hatherly Laboratories, 1948*

Plate 19   *The Queen in the Roborough Library, 1956*

Photograph: *Express and Echo*

THE FIRST COUNCIL OF THE UNIVERSITY OF EXETER

BACK ROW.—PROFESSOR J. GRIFFITH MORGAN, PROFESSOR J. SYKES, A. G. BARTLETT, PROFESSOR A. T. PRICE, ALDERMAN H. J. PERRY.

MIDDLE ROW.—W. G. TAMLIN, PROFESSOR A. DAVIES, PROFESSOR J. CALDWELL, COLONEL ROLAND WARD, PROFESSOR J. LEVINE, Dr. H. H. MACEY, PROFESSOR E. BARLOW, PROFESSOR L. A. HARVEY.

FRONT ROW.—ALDERMAN H. G. MASON, Dr. L. K. ELMHIRST, Mrs. F. M. PUGH, PROFESSOR H. R. GARLAND (Deputy Vice-Chancellor), Dr. J. W. COOK (Vice-Chancellor), Mr. E. G. LAMPARD-VACHELL (Pro-Chancellor), R. ROSS, ALDERMAN W. T. SLADER, R. W. TURNER (Treasurer), Sir ARTHUR REED, PROFESSOR S. H. WATKINS.

ABSENT.—ALDERMAN VINCENT THOMPSON, Sir John DAW, J. A. DAY, Dr. H. J. HEWITT, PROFESSOR A. C. T. W. CURLE, W. J. F. CRUTTWELL.

EXETER

Plate 20   *The first Council of the University of Exeter, 1956*

Plate 21   *Three Vice-Chancellors (left to right): Dr F. J. Llewellyn 1966–72;*
Dr Harry Kay 1973–; Sir James Cook 1955–66

Plate 22   *Queen's Building – Faculty of Arts, 1958*

Plate 23   *Chemistry Laboratories (1965)*

Plate 24   *The Geology of Ireland*

Plate 25   *Cornwall House – The Lounge*

Plate 26   *Lafrowda Flats*

Plate 27   *Outdoor Swimming Pool*

Plate 28   *Exeter University XI – UAU Champions 1979–80*

Plate 29   School of Education (Saint Luke's) 1978

Plate 30   *Aerial View of the University Estate 1980*

Photograph: John Saunders

years after 1945, and were therefore stronger candidates for advancement to university status; the UGC or at least some of its members was disinclined to advise the creation of too many universities in a quinquennium; Nottingham received a charter in 1948, Southampton in 1952, Hull in 1954. In a country where change proceeded at a decent measured pace Exeter's turn would come. The UGC recognised this almost as soon as it had rejected the 1947 application. Papers prepared for a meeting of the Committee early in 1948 pointed out that Reading, Sheffield, and Bristol had all been considerably smaller than Exeter when they received charters. The UGC had not ruled out an eventual charter for Exeter — despite its unusually narrow base in arts and pure science.[5]

Principal Murray resigned in July 1951 at the age of 72 after twenty-five years' service to the college. With all his faults he had provided firm and inspiring leadership, raised large sums of money, and made a start on the transfer of the College to the Streatham Estate. His ideal of a fully residential college was close to achievement in 1939 and even in the rapid growth of numbers after 1945 more than 60 per cent of the students continued to live in halls of residence. He had done more than any other man to advance Exeter towards university status. After his retirement the college had several heads in quick succession. Professor F. H. Newman became acting principal until a successor could be appointed. Newman had been head of the Department of Physics since he came to Exeter in 1919. He was appointed the first professor of physics in 1923 and was director of the Washington Singer Laboratories from their opening in 1931. Despite poor health he published many research papers and with V. H. L. Searle a standard textbook *The General Properties of Matter*, as well as shouldering the heavy teaching duties of a busy department. He took up his post as acting principal in August 1951, but died in the following May. S. H. Watkins, who succeeded Newman as acting principal, had held the chair of education and psychology in the college since 1923. He served until the arrival of the new principal in the autumn of 1952. The new Principal, Sir Thomas W. J. Taylor, a bluff Oxford chemist, had been the first Vice-Chancellor of the new University of the West Indies from 1946 to 1952. Unhappily his relaxed and informal reign did not last long for he died on holiday in Italy in the long vacation of 1953. Professor H. B. Garland, Vice-Principal of the College, became acting Principal and served until J. W. Cook took up the post of Principal in September 1954. Professor Garland came to Exeter after war service in the Royal Artillery and in the military government of Germany from 1945 to 1947. His administrative experience was to serve him in good stead during his term of office as acting Principal. For it was during that period that the final preparations were being made before submission of the claim for a charter. When Exeter became a full university he served as Deputy Vice-Chancellor from 1955 to 1957. His work in the field of eighteenth-century German literature earned him high honours—the DLitt of the University of Cambridge and the Goethe Medal of the Goethe Institute. The abilities that make a good administrator and a distinguished scholar are best known to a small circle. As the university's first public orator Professor Garland's powers were plain for all to see. His graceful and polished eulogies of honorary graduands, spiced with wit and impeccably delivered, were models of their kind. In 1977 the university saluted his many services by conferring on him the honorary degree of Doctor of Letters.

When the new Principal arrived in the autumn of 1954 the college had had six heads in little more than three years. A period of stability at the top was due and duly came. James Wilfred Cook was born in 1900. Before he was twenty years old he had secured a first-class degree in chemistry and a lectureship at the Sir John Cass Technical Institute, London. From 1929 to 1939 he worked at the Royal Cancer Hospital with Sir Ernest Kennaway; he became Reader in Chemical Pathology in 1932 and was elected FRS in 1938. In 1939 he left London for the Regius Chair of Chemistry in the University of Glasgow. From 1950 to 1954 he served on the UGC, and in 1954 the Royal Society conferred on him the Davy Medal, the highest award it can give to an organic chemist. The new Principal apparently fitted the popular stereotype of a scientist: cold, just, precise. The reality was less simple: he had a sardonic sense of humour, he was a good judge of wine and cigars, and he had a considerable respect for the traditions that he met in Exeter.[6] His appointment heralded the grant of a charter.

The rebuff administered by the UGC in 1947 prompted the College to prepare its next submission more thoroughly. Instead of a political gesture —the deputation en masse—the College drew up a petition, a draft charter and draft statutes. This tedious but necessary work fell on the new academic secretary, A. G. Bartlett (who succeeded G. V. M. Heap in 1951) and on Professor H. B. Garland. Their proposals went first to Senate and then to the Charter Committee, a joint committee of Coucil and Senate. By the end of 1953 Senate had approved draft instruments, and little remained to be done by the time the new principal

E LIZABETH THE SECOND

by the Grace of God of the United Kingdom of Great Britain and Northern Ireland and of Our other Realms and Territories Queen, Head of the Commonwealth, Defender of the Faith.

TO ALL TO WHOM THESE PRESENTS SHALL COME, GREETING!

WHEREAS a Humble Petition has been presented to Us by the University College of the South West of England praying that We would be graciously pleased to constitute and found in Our City and County of the City of Exeter a University for the advancement of knowledge and the diffusion and extension of Arts, Sciences and Learning and to grant a Charter with such provisions therein in that behalf as shall seem to Us right and suitable:

AND WHEREAS We having taken the said Petition into Our Royal consideration are minded to accede thereto:

NOW, THEREFORE, KNOW YE that We by virtue of Our Royal Prerogative and of Our Special Grace, Certain Knowledge and Mere Motion have willed and ordained and by these Presents Do for Us, Our Heirs and Successors will and ordain as follows:

1. There shall be and there is hereby constituted and founded in Our City and County of the City of Exeter a University by the name and style of "The University of Exeter" by which name the Chancellor, the Pro-Chancellor, the Vice-Chancellor, the Deputy Vice-Chancellor, the Treasurer and all other persons who are for the time being members of the University of Exeter pursuant to this Our Charter and the Statutes of the University of Exeter shall be and are hereby constituted and incorporated into one Body Politic and Corporate with perpetual succession and a Common Seal with the power to assume Armorial Bearings which shall be duly enrolled in Our College of Arms and in that name to sue and be sued with power

(without any further licence in mortmain) to take, purchase, hold and also to grant, demise or otherwise dispose of real and personal property. Provided that the value of such real property excluding such lands tenements and hereditaments as may be for the time being occupied by or on behalf of the University of Exeter for the transaction of its business and the carrying out of its purposes shall not exceed in the whole in annual value £50,000, such annual value to be calculated and ascertained at the respective periods of taking or purchasing the same and which University shall have the constitution and powers and be subject to the regulations in this Our Charter prescribed or contained.

2. The University of Exeter hereby incorporated is hereinafter referred to as "the University."

3. The objects of the University are:

(a) To provide to the full extent which its resources from time to time permit for research and instruction in the humanities and sciences and other spheres of learning and knowledge of a standard and thoroughness required and expected of a University of the highest standing and to secure the advancement of knowledge the diffusion and extension of Arts, Sciences and Learning and the provision of a liberal and professional education.

(b) To provide and maintain halls of residence, colleges and other accommodation for students and other members of the University.

(c) To hold examinations.

The Charter

took up his appointment. The formal decision to petition the Privy Council for a charter was taken by the Court of the University College of the South West of England on 14 January 1955. The petition recited the early history of the movement for higher education in Exeter. It recalled that Alderman W. H. Reed

> presented part of the estate known as the Streatham Estate to the College with the result that together with its subsequent purchases the College now owns more than 200 acres of land on the northern fringe of the City of Exeter, a site of great beauty and ample convenience, upon which its later buildings have been erected. The site is capable of accommodating any further expansion which may be required.

The petition concluded with these words:

> Having regard to the matters hereinbefore stated this College with a history which extends over nearly a century, and established in a city whose cultural tradition extends unbroken over a period of a thousand years has now so far developed its work of University education and the dissemination of sound and humane learning as to justify the grant of free and independent status as a University, and the grant of a Charter would enable it to make its full contribution to the expansion of University education which it is one of our national aims to secure.

The College did not have to wait unduly long for a decision. On 28 October 1955 the Clerk to the Privy Council wrote a letter to the College's solicitor and parliamentary agent:

> I am directed by the Lord President of the Council to inform you that the Queen was pleased, at the Council held by Her Majesty today, to approve the grant of a Charter constituting and founding a University within the City and County of the City of Exeter under the style and title of 'The University of Exeter'.

The Charter passed the Great Seal on 21 December 1955 and on that day the University of Exeter formally came into existence.[7]

Notes

1 PPF, files 9, 17.
2 UGC agenda and papers for 27 October 1949 [PRO, UGC 2/30]; PPF, file 5; Standing Committee, 8 September 1948; *Annual Reports*; UGC *University development 1952-57* pp.20-1 (BPP 1957-58 XVIII).
3 PPF, file 30; *Annual Reports*, 1933-37; PPF, files 5, 9; *Graduate employment: a report of the 1937 Congress of the National Union of Students* (NUS, 1937) pp.16-19; PPD, file 12; PPC, file 18; Exeter University College Club, *Bulletin*, March 1936; PPC, file 11.
4 There is copious documentation of relations with Seale Hayne in PPB, files 21, 23 and

24; UGC interview with representatives of UCSW, 12 June 1936 [PRO, UGC 5/2]; PPC, file 18; publication are listed in the annual reports; PPF, file 2; PPD, files 10 and 11.

5 Murray to Lord Lindsay of Birker, 30 July 1946—PPF, file 30; *Annual Report*, 1934; PPB, files 11 and 12; UGC, 4 December 1947 [PRO, UGC 1/2 and 2/28 and 29]; Sir James Cook reported in the *South Westerner*, 14 October 1965.

6 *The Times*, 25 October 1975; University of Exeter, *Gazette*, February 1976 for an appreciation of Sir James Cook by a fellow chemist, Professor H. N. Rydon.

7 University of Exeter, *Gazette*, No.1, December 1955; the text of the charter and of other legal instruments (statutes, ordinances, regulations) are to be found in the *Calendar*.

PART III

THE UNIVERSITY OF EXETER:
THE FIRST TWENTY-FIVE YEARS

IX

THE TRANSITION
TO INDEPENDENCE

The constitution of the new university was not markedly different from that of the university college. Court, a large representative and unwieldy body, remained the nominally supreme organ; Council, consisting predominantly of laymen, held sway in all non-academic matters. Senate was the highest academic body: it now had a somewhat larger representation of assistant staff (at least six as against three in the Senate of the university college) but retained its character as a body composed largely of professors and heads of department. The new constitution made no concessions to federalism; the Faculty of Agriculture disappeared and with it the lingering connection with Seale-Hayne; and the Principal of Saint Luke's College ceased to be a supernumerary member of Senate. There were four faculties—arts (including education), science, social studies, and law. Some changes in terminology flowed from the creation of the university: President, Deputy President and Principal became Chancellor, Pro-Chancellor and Vice-Chancellor. The Marquess of Salisbury who had served for ten years as President did not wish to assume the dignity of Chancellor. His sister Mary, Dowager Duchess of Devonshire, became the first Chancellor of the University and gave the University gracious service for the first 16 years of its life, resigning in 1971. Lord Amory succeeded her as Chancellor in 1972. As Mr Derick Heathcoat Amory he had held the office of Treasurer of the University College from 1935 to 1943, the post filled with great acumen by his father, Sir Ian Amory, from 1926 until his death in 1931. After war service (he was severely wounded at Arnhem) he entered the House of Commons in 1945 and quickly made his mark. Made a junior minister when the Conservatives returned to power in 1951, he was Minister of Agriculture from 1954 to 1958 and Chancellor of the Exchequer from 1958 to 1960. In that year, to the public surprise, he voluntarily relinquished his high office and went to the House of Lords as Viscount Amory of Tiverton. From 1961 to 1963 he was British High Commissioner in Canada. He became joint Pro-Chancellor of the University of Exeter in 1965. From 1972 until his death in 1981 he presided with wit, good humour and distinction over the fortunes of the university, and endeared himself to many a degree congregation with his apt and amusing valedictory addresses.

The constitutional stucture altered little, but the powers of the new university greatly exceeded those of the old college. The power to grant degrees—the essential difference between the old regime and the new—brought many consequences in its train. Exeter no longer had to accept the fiat of the University of London about entrance qualifications, and could devise its own degrees and syllabuses, and conduct its own examinations. These changes greatly extended the work done by the department of the academic secretary (who had in 1954 been restyled the academic registrar). The growth of the college had already prompted the appointment of a larger administrative staff. When A. K. Woodbridge, registrar since 1904, retired in 1947 Principal Murray saluted him as the record Registrar.

> No other in Britain has held a University Registrarship for his long term of 43 years. It is not only a record time. He has suffered all the hardships, the deprivations, the squalid makeshifts and growing pains of a hungry and impecunious college. He has suffered from students, colleagues, committees and principal . . . . His equability has been a lesson for them all . . . . If ever a man has deserved to be called sweet-natured it is the Registrar, and sweetness without any loss of manly force or weight.

On Murray's reckoning he did the work of three men, and it was therefore in keeping with college traditions to appoint two men in his place—G. V. M. Heap as academic secretary and Sir Alexander Campbell as registrar. Sir Alexander, an experienced educational administrator, did much in his five years in Exeter to establish a tradition of careful finance just when for the first time money was relatively plentiful. Before the war parsimony in little things had been the price to be paid for daring plans of capital spending that were almost more than the college could afford. After the war the College and later the University lived within its means year after year. It got little thanks for its pains and less money until at length in 1979 the UGC acknowledged that Exeter was not only under financed, but likely to remain so for some time to come.

The transition to independence presented some awkward problems. Many members of the academic staff had had no experience of examining at degree level. Should students enrolled before independence continue with London degrees? What effect would independence have on the number of applications? All these difficulties or imagined difficulties were smoothly overcome. In 1955 in expectation of the early grant of a charter the University of London admitted Exeter into a 'special relationship' for examination purposes. Under this arrangement the rigours of the external degree were moderated: Exeter's teachers set and marked the final examination papers, subject to assessors appointed by London. It was a kind of tutelage that gave inexperienced members of staff of the new university a gentle introduction to the mysteries of examining. In 1956, 1957 and 1958 when there were still substantial numbers of students reading for London degrees matters reverted to their normal course, with London University resuming full responsibility for the examination process. Some departments hurried to escape from thraldom to the external degree system: students who had been admitted in October 1954 were in these departments allowed to opt for an Exeter degree, so that the university first awarded a few substantive degrees in 1957. In other departments students entering in 1955 had the choice of reading either for London or for Exeter degrees, and it was not until 1959 that virtually all graduands took Exeter degrees.

During the transition period Exeter was teaching for two sets of syllabuses—its own and London's. It would therefore have been difficult to make any sudden break with the past and in broad outline the content of Exeter's degree syllabuses for some years followed the London model. Where experiment was possible was in the timing of examinations. Except in law and social studies, London degrees were awarded on the results of one examination at the end of the third year. Exeter, strongly influenced by a powerful contingent of Cambridge men among the professoriate, opted instead for a final examination divided into two parts taken at the end of the second and third years. Eccentrically the Faculty of Social Studies examined its students at the end of the first year, called the examination part I, and disregarded the results in assessing the class of the degree. After some years a few departments, notably English and history, returned to the undivided final examination at the end of the third year. But to this day students in most departments are required to sit university examinations as part of their degree at the end of their second and third years.

Experiment was also possible in new combinations of subjects. In the main, Exeter accepted the departmental organisation of teaching and examining that characterised provincial universities; for each honours degree there was a corresponding department—English, mathematics, economics. The general degree—three subjects studied less intensively —was familiar from the London connection, and continued afer independence. The novelty, perhaps inspired by the example of Keele, was the introduction of joint or combined honours. Unlike at Keele, there was no foundation year, and combined honours, again unlike at Keele, were allowed only among subjects that were related, or were taught in the same faculty.* It was not possible for example to read for a combined honours degree in English and chemistry, but alluring combinations—English with French, Greek or philosophy; chemistry with botany, physics or geology—were available. The temptation to multiply the number of permitted combinations has proved almost irresistible. By 1978 the number had reached 78 and the preparation of a university timetable was proving too difficult a task even for a computer. Periodic pruning has not stunted the academic imagination, and fertile brains continue to hatch new schemes.[1]

Those who had believed that students came to Exeter for the sake of the London degree were happy to see their fears proved groundless. Exeter, like Nottingham, Southampton, Hull and Leicester, prospered as an independent university. Applications grew much faster than places, and the more difficult it became to secure admission to a university, the more universities candidates applied to with a further apparent increase of applications per place. In a good year in the 1930s, the University College could expect three or four candidates to apply for each place in the training department, where most degree students were to be found. In a less successful year there might be only two applicants for each place. Thus in 1931, 168 candidates applied for 50 places in the training department, half the candidates coming from South-West England; but in 1937 there were only 110 applicants for 54 places. By contrast in 1956– 57, the first full year after the grant of a charter, there were four applicants for each of the 500 available places; in the following year there were 3,250 applications for 500 places, and five years later there were

---

*This convention has broken down in recent years and the University now offers, for example, degrees in chemistry and law, and in chemistry and economics.

over 10,000 applications for 800 places. All universities were experiencing heavy demand but few enjoyed such an embarrassing press of applicants as Exeter. The establishment of the Universities' Central Council for Adminissions (UCCA) in 1962 did little to abate the flood, for until 1970 the scheme allowed candidates to apply to as many as six universities. The demand for places at Exeter continued to grow and by 1970 the University was handling 16,000 applications for 1,300 places.

Students chose to come to Exeter for a variety of reasons—they could be academic, personal, social or domestic. Small-group teaching and the residential system appealed to some, the scenery and soft airs of the South West to others, the knowledge that older friends were already up at the university to still others. The beauties of the University's own estate might have appealed to the scientists whose laboratories were situated there, but until 1958 students in arts and social studies had cramped quarters in the city centre—except for the library which being on the Streatham estate was at an inconvenient distance from the lecture rooms in Gandy Street. This separation of books from readers was not destined to last much longer. Before the charter was granted, the UGC had made funds available for a new teaching building on the Streatham estate, designed to house the Faculties of Arts and Social Studies, together with the Departments of Mathematics and Geology. Building operations began in 1956 and on 8 May Her Majesty the Queen and Prince Philip visited the site. Her Majesty presented the charter of incorporation to the Chancellor and unveiled the foundation stone of the new building. As far as is known, this is the only occasion on which the monarch has personally presented a charter of incorporation to an English university on its own estate. Two years later, Queen's Building, as it was named, was ready for occupation and the decisive step had been taken in the transfer of the University from Gandy Street to the Streatham estate. More buildings would be needed before the transfer was complete: the administration remained for the time being in Gandy Street and was joined by the Department of Law and the lecturer in psychology; the students had no adequate union building; and there was no worthy hall for ceremonies and examinations. In celebration of the charter, the University held a congregation for the installation of the Chancellor and for the conferment of honorary degrees. In the absence of a Great Hall, the University hired the Savoy cinema, now the ABC, for the ceremony. The honourary graduands fittingly included two former principals of the College, Sir Hector Hetherington and Dr John Murray.[2]

When this ceremony took place, Leicester, the last of the old University Colleges, was about to receive its charter and become, like Nottingham, Southampton, Hull and Exeter, a fully independent university. Only the University College of Keele remained under tutelage — of a much less irksome kind than that involved in teaching for the London external degree. This group of universities had about 7,000 students out of 70,000 attending English universities. The older provincial universities had four times as many, but even Manchester, the largest of them, had fewer than 5,000 students. London, Oxford and Cambridge had as many students as all the other English universities put together. Another 20,000 students attended Scottish and Welsh universities. Of the 24 universities on the Treasury list, Exeter ranked 21st, ahead of Leicester, Manchester College of Science and Technology (now UMIST) and Keele. Within a generation the British academic scene was to be transformed by unprecedented growth, a process in which Exeter was ready and willing to play its full part.

Notes

1 PPG, file 1; PPF, file 30; Senate, 1 November 1978.
2 University of Exeter, *The Charter Year 1955–1956; Annual Reports.*

X

THE STUDENTS

In 1955 the University of Exeter had almost a thousand students, not many more than in the crowded post-war years of the late forties. Admissions in 1955 were sharply higher than in the previous year and total numbers rose by more than 10 per cent, reversing the downward trend of the early fifties. In only one year (1972) since the charter was granted have numbers failed to rise. With hindsight it can be seen that the granting of the charter coincided with the beginning of a long period of continuous growth, but in 1955 nobody envisaged the scale of expansion that was to come. The UGC had once remarked that in British universities 'by a curious coincidence it seemed that the ideal number [of students] was always a little in excess of the existing number'. And Exeter was by no means immune from that engaging illusion. When numbers stood at 1,000, Vice-Chancellor Cook thought 1,500 or even 2,000 students might be a feasible aim; any further growth would destroy the 'intimate character' of the university. Within a few years, as numbers grew, the dangers seemed less forbidding. In 1959 the university agreed in response to UGC encouragement to plan for 3,000 students by 1970. After the publication of the report of the committee on higher education [the Robbins Report] in 1963, the University agreed to a quicker, advance—to 3,000 students by 1967. In 1967 a target of 5,000 students by 1980 was set, and in 1972 there seemed to be a real prospect of growth to 6,500 students in the middle eighties. Indeed Lord Holford assessed the ultimate capacity of the site as 11,000 students. The world economic depression that began in 1973 put a stop to these flights of fancy. More recent plans have drastically reduced the prospective size of the university. Even with the absorption of Saint Luke's College of Education in 1978, numbers are now unlikely much to exceed 5,000. 'The steady-state university' was briefly the fashionable phrase, as the headlong growth of the years 1955-75 came to an end.

How did the actual growth of numbers compare with the plans agreed between the University and the UGC? 1,000 students were registered for the first time in 1956, 2,000 in 1964 and 3,000 in 1968—only one year later than had been promised in 1963. It took seven years to add another 1,000 students and despite the addition of about 600 students from Saint Luke's College, numbers scarcely reached 5,000 in 1980*. Rates of growth were at their highest in the early 1960s and over the longer period 1955-1970 averaged 8½ per cent per annum. The rate of growth (including Saint Luke's) halved in the 1970s and for the years 1970-77, before the merger had taken place, the growth rate averaged only 3½ per cent per annum.

In admitting more and more students, Exeter was following national trends. In small part the growth of universities was a response to demographic pressure, the so-called 'bulge' in the birth rate. The number of births in the years 1946-48 exceeded those of 1936-38 by 35 per cent. Other things being equal, universities might therefore have expected to admit 35 per cent more students in 1964-66 than they had ten years before. They actually admitted nearly twice as many students because more children were staying on at school and acquiring the qualifications that would gain them entry to a university. There has been a nine-fold increase in the number of advanced-level candidates since 1950, and the proportion of school-leavers with two or more advanced-level subjects has steadily risen. It had already reached nine per cent of school leavers by 1963-64 and stood at nearly 14 per cent in 1976-77.[1] It is small wonder therefore that British universities have grown fast since the war.

Before 1939 the University College like most university institutions served as a regional university; it was well named the University College of the South West of England. In 1928, over four-fifths and in 1937 three-fifths of the students had their homes in Devon, Cornwall, Somerset and Dorset. The post-war expansion coincided with a change of student habits: more and more wished to attend a distant university. This new fashion was already evident in the crowded college of the late fifties: less than half the students came from the South West and nearly a third from London and South-East England. By the mid 1960s, the new pattern was well established. Less than a fifth of the students came from

*These figures refer to full time students taking courses of at least one year's duration. This is the UGC definition of a full-time student.

the South West, less than a tenth came from overseas, the rest from other parts of England and Wales, principally southern England. Exeter was becoming a southern university. Principal Murray had attracted some students from what he called the dingier parts of England. More recently, the university has attracted students from prosperous parts of the country and in particular from suburban London and its hinterland.

Students have been coming not only from more prosperous parts of the country but from the more prosperous homes — from Esher rather than the East End. Nationally, expansion of university education has done little to change the social composition of the student body. In British universities the proportion of students from working-class backgrounds held remarkably steady for many years at rather less than 30 per cent of the whole*. Exact figures are not available for Exeter until 1958, but it is clear that in the thirties most students came from relatively poor homes and had attended county secondary schools. Matters had not much changed by 1958 when more accurate information became available. In that year, 31 per cent of the students graduating appeared to be the children of working-class parents (social classes IIIb, IV and V in the Registrar General's classification). Half the students could be classified as falling into social class IIIa (skilled non-manual); rather less than 20 per cent fell into classes I and II (professional and managerial). Figures for graduands in 1968 and for admissions in 1975 (the graduands of 1978) show that Exeter has diverged sharply from the national pattern. In 1968 the parents of 42 per cent of Exeter graduands had professional or managerial jobs, and in 1975 the proportion had risen to 56 per cent. In the same years the proportion of students from working-class homes stood at only 11 per cent and 12 per cent respectively. By the mid 1970s, Exeter students came predominantly from prosperous and in some cases from wealthy homes.

This shift in the social origins of students is not the result of deliberate university policy; indeed some admissions tutors regret the low proportion of working-class students in the present-day university. Why then has Exeter become socially somewhat exclusive? Part of the reason lies in the peculiar social composition of southern England, the university's largest catchment area. Heavy industry in particular and all industrial employment is under-represented in southern England. The presence of the principal offices of central government in Westminster

---

*The proportion has been falling in the very recent past and only 23 per cent of university entrants in 1979 had working-class parents.

and of the commercial and financial services of 'the City' go far to explaining the high proportion of white-collar workers who live in the London area. However, the difference between London and the rest of the country is much less than the difference between Exeter and the average British university, and cannot explain much of the preponderance of students from professional and managerial families. The explanation lies rather in the similarities between Exeter and the ancient universities. Principal Murray deliberately modelled the University College on the Oxford pattern, emphasising residence and so far as practical, tutorial teaching. Tutorial teaching (one or two students) never became a typical feature of Exeter life, though teaching in small groups has flourished. Residence has remained characteristic. Moreover, the University has removed itself from its cramped quarters in the city centre to its beautiful and no longer empty Streatham Estate; it offers scenic attractions different from but not less gracious than those of Oxford and Cambridge. Many students (or their parents) appear to regard Exeter with Durham, Reading and a few others as acceptable substitutes for Oxford or Cambridge. Such students are likely to be the children of professional or otherwise prosperous parents: it is well known that relatively few candidates from comprehensive schools or sixth form colleges present themselves for admission to the ancient universities.[2]

Despite the rapid expansion after 1945, the University College held to the principle of residence. Having neither the money nor the materials for new halls of residence, it bought a few large old homes for conversion into halls or annexes to halls. These purchases went some way to house the larger numbers, and when the charter was granted, 60 per cent of the students still had places in hall. It remained a requirement of the College that students should spend at least part of their time in Exeter in a hall of residence. Those not resident in hall had to live in lodgings approved by the College. The supply of such lodgings in a small provincial city was limited and a policy of university expansion therefore required the provision of new halls of residence — but in ways strikingly different from the pre-war pattern.

Mardon Hall may be taken as the pre-war ideal since it was the only hall then entirely purpose-built. Financed by the College appeal it housed about eighty students, mostly in double rooms. There were communal washrooms, and a large wooden hut served as a dining room. These spartan features were offset by lavish provision elsewhere: a large reception room; a common room, library, and music room. Built in what

Murray termed a 'country-house style', Mardon Hall was intended to provide in its public rooms at least something of the atmosphere of a gentlemen's residence. In the planning of its post-war halls of residence, the University has been more circumscribed. The UGC has provided the funds and has laid down building norms with which the University architects have had to comply. In many ways the new halls are superior to the old: each student has a single room complete with wash-basin; and the dining rooms are as solidly built as any other part of the hall. For reasons of economy, however, the new halls have been built to a much larger scale: each has housed about 150 students and three or four halls have shared catering facilities. Each hall has a rather meagre common room; the television room and bar, like the dining room, are shared among the residents of the grouped halls. Partly because of shared dining facilities the formal dinner, an aspect of life to which much importance had attached in the smaller halls, gradually died out. The less gracious cafeteria service that took its place was not calculated to promote civility or high-toned conversation between the students and the warden. The change symbolised the retreat from the high conception of hall life that had ruled in pre-war days. The University continued to hope that halls of residence would act as centres of light and learning, as a civilising influence on the student body. But the new halls proved too large to develop the corporate sense so strongly felt in the old, and in the more impersonal atmosphere students were less willing to submit to restraints whether imposed by a student committee or (worse still) by the warden.

The University could not reasonably have been expected to foresee these difficulties when the design of the new halls was under consideration in the late 'fifties and early 'sixties. The first group of new halls was built in the grounds of Duryard House which with 13 acres had been bought in 1946. Ten years later the damp and crumbling Queen Anne mansion was closed and put up for auction. The property failed to reach the reserve price and was withdrawn. This was a lucky escape. The University was soon planning to house 300 students on the site and eventually built three halls there with accommodation for 450 students. Sir William Holford, the University's new architect, carefully restored the old house at considerable expense, and preserved as many of the fine trees in the park as was humanly possible. (Some students in Murray House may feel that he preserved too many since only distance can lend enchantment to the view of a Wellingtonia). Two large halls were built parallel to the Cowley Bridge Road, from which they were shielded by a bank of elms*. Each hall was five storeys high and constructed on the staircase plan. Named after principals of the University College, Hetherington and Murray Houses opened their doors to students in 1963. A companion hall for women students, Jessie Montgomery House, was set decently apart on the other side of the catering and common-room block that all three halls shared. Jessie Montgomery opened in 1964 and two years later a fourth hall (Moberly House) was completed nearby on the south side of Argyll Road.

The first three halls on the Duryard site formed part of the programme of expansion under which the University was expecting to admit 1,500 or 2,000 students. By 1959 when a total of 3,000 students was being envisaged, it became necessary to plan for many more places in hall. Birks Grange, a Victorian mansion that accommodated some 20 students, was set in extensive grounds that Holford had marked down for development as early as 1957. The original house was demolished and in its place rose three more halls—named after Devon hills. The Birks Halls—Brendon, Haldon and Raddon—opened in 1965–66. Like the Duryard Halls they shared catering and common-room facilities. Two more halls were built in the traditional style—an annexe to Crossmead Hall, and Ransom Pickard† House as an annexe to Lopes Hall.

By 1967 when the last of these halls was completed, the restraints of communal life, light though they were in the newer halls, were becoming irksome to most students. Life had always been more expensive in hall than in private lodgings. Before 1914 the College Hostel had charged £1 a week when good lodgings could be had in Exeter for 14 or 16 shillings (70 or 80p). In the late 1950s hall fees of £4 a week compared with lodgings at £3.10s or £3.12s.6d (£3.50 or £3.62½). Had students been looking for cheapness alone the landladies of Exeter would have had cause for rejoicing. However, it was cheapness with independence that they sought, and old-fashioned lodgings with a perhaps too motherly landlady were no more to their taste than the pastoral care of the warden. Flats and cottages (in town and country) became the favourite residences and by 1978 only 200 students (four per cent) were living in lodgings where meals were provided.³ The University responded to the changing taste of the time by building flats in the grounds of Lafrowda, a house in St Germans Road acquired in 1965. The flats, occupying high ground

*The trees have since died of Dutch elm disease and have been felled.
†Col. Ransom Pickard was a distinguished Exeter physician. He was a vice-president of the College from 1940 until his death in 1953 and a friend and generous benefactor of the College and the University.

overlooking the Hoopern Valley, were largely financed by mortgage from a building society—itself a novel proceeding—with a little more than a quarter of the capital provided by the UGC. The accommodation was arranged in groups of 12 study-bedrooms with cooking, cleaning and washing facilities. Common rooms were not provided and academic supervision was kept to a minimum with a solitary tutor providing an official presence and some pastoral care*. The adjacent Cornwall House, also newly built, provided the common-room facilities that were otherwise lacking. The first block of flats housing some 300 students opened in 1971. A further block completed in 1975 and 1976 brought the total number of places up to 720. The flats though spartan and noisy are popular. They are always fully occupied, partly because the rent (which includes the cost of heating, lighting and cooking) works out at less than half the hall fees. The tenants can eat well and still have money to spare by comparison with students in hall. Most places in the traditional halls of residence are nowadays occupied by first-year students. Hall life gives them an opportunity to make friends and get their bearings. They may not wish to spend three or even two years in hall, but they value the chance to spend a first year there. Broadly speaking since 1955 the University has provided additional places in halls and flats for 2,000 students and the proportion of students living in university accommodation remains roughly unchanged—about three-fifths. Few students live at home—less than 300 out of 5,000; the rest for the most part take private flats or cottages.

From time to time, hall fees have been a matter for dispute between students and the university authorities; without the conference trade they would have been higher and even more contentious. In the 1930s the summer school and a few other courses made a useful contribution to hall revenues. The summer school resumed in 1947 and by the following year was attracting almost as many students as in the pre-war years. The conference business grew more slowly. In the summer of 1954, for example, fewer than twenty, mostly short, courses were accommodated in halls of residence. Thereafter the trade more than kept pace with the growth of university accommodation. By 1970–71 it amounted to a fifth of hall revenue and the University found it worthwhile to employ staff whose full-time job was conference business. Lafrowda Flats stage I opened in 1971, allowing the University to go into the business of holiday letting. By 1978–79, conference fees and holiday

*There are now (1982) two tutors.

lettings amounted to more than half a million pounds, a quarter of halls and flats revenue. The season was a short one. Students went down at the end of June, and relatively little business was done after late August. The University preferred to attract conferences with at least an educational tinge. Thus in the summer of 1976 it ran its own summer school and provided facilities for a French teachers' course organised by the British Council, both of these courses long-standing commitments. Librarians held their annual conference in Exeter and the Geological Society organised a meeting of their engineering geology group. Of the six dozen groups that the University accommodated in the summer of 1976, two others may be mentioned to illustrate the variety of interests represented. In August a small party of cricketers from Brislington School spent three days in the Birks Halls. For a week in July, 150 karate enthusiasts assembled in Lafrowda for their summer course. At intervals each day they emerged into the open air, dressed in white robes and frightening the ornamental ducks with their battle cries; their summer course has now become a regular fixture. Exeter is better placed than many universities to attract the conference and holiday trade, but a benign climate and beautiful scenery will not answer correspondence or prepare room lists. The considerable success in attracting visitors owes much to the initiative and energy displayed by the University's conference office and domestic staff.

The reluctance of students to submit to the restraints of hall life was one example of a general shift in relations between the student body and the University. In the past youthful high spirits had taken the form either of boisterous behaviour (painting the Buller statue red, or tying a shirt to the top of North Hessary Tor television mast) or of devotion to a radical cause (the republican side in the Spanish civil war, or in more recent times the campaign for nuclear disarmament). To university authority, students had traditionally shown considerable deference. It is possible to trace the rise of 'the student estate' back to the 1880s when in Scottish universities student representative councils began to be constituted.[4] But it would be wrong to imagine a steady growth of student militancy from that day to this. The troubles that broke out in British universities in the mid 1960s blew up suddenly, took most people by surprise, and owe much to the circumstances of the time. In Exeter, student unrest before the mid-1960s was rare. When in 1921 the University College promulgated new details and highly restrictive regulations, the students tried hard within the conventions of the day to persuade Principal

Hetherington to relax the rules. Until then regulations for students had been simple, requiring little more than regular attendance, orderly behaviour and the wearing of gowns by matriculated students. The new regulations required students to be in their rooms by 10 pm and forbade them to enter hotels or public houses within the city, or to hold supper parties in hotels without the Principal's permission. Landladies were encouraged to report to the College students who were out late at night. The Students' Representative Council was much alarmed at the powers thus conferred on their landladies:

> With certain landladies, as soon as they realised the power in their hands, the students' lives would be extremely miserable.

Negotiations with Hetherington were unavailing and it was not until 1926 that the curfew was lifted from students in lodgings. The rule against entering public houses took various forms over the years. In 1937–38 it read simply: Students may not enter hotels or public houses; from 1939 the more ambiguous term 'must not frequent' (later "may not frequent") was employed. For ten years from 1926 to 1936 there were even regulations about the dress of women students. They were required to wear with their gowns 'costumes of plain colour and cut, or dresses of plain colour and cut which have long sleeves'. Sunday observance was strict: college grounds and tennis courts were closed on Sunday except that by 1939 tennis was permitted on Sunday afternoons. Sports grounds were not thrown open for Sunday play until 1970. But the other regulations were drastically amended in 1959. They then took the form proposed by the students in 1921:

> Students are expected to conform to a reasonable standard of behaviour and failure to do so will constitute a breach of University regulations.

In appearance this rule represented the position that held before 1921, but notions of reasonable behaviour have changed somewhat over the years, and Principal Clayden would be more than a little surprised if he could visit the modern University of Exeter and observe its manners and customs.[5]

Discontent with college regulations, first evident in 1921, broke out again in the years from 1936 to 1940. One bone of contention was hall rules, which in a largely residential college touched most students. The dispute centred on late-night passes, and the hour at which halls normally closed their doors. The College was somewhat more liberal than it had been before 1914 in that halls stayed open until about 10 pm (the rules varied a little from hall to hall) and late passes were available— more freely for men than women. Failure to secure concessions led students to make more radical demands—a staff-student committee, access to Senate minutes, even attendance at Senate in a non-voting capacity. Murray was not the man to countenance such changes and it did not occur to students that if peaceful persuasion failed they might take stronger measures. They therefore achieved nothing and many years passed before these matters again disturbed the peace of the University.[6]

Acquiescence in the existing balance of power between university and students persisted until the mid-1960s. In 1963 the student newspaper, *The South Westerner*, published an article about wastage—the discrepancy between the number admitted and the number graduating three years later. The article suggested that the rather puzzling statistics pointed to a failure rate of about 20 per cent. The Vice-Chancellor, Sir James Cook, who had no better figure to produce, regarded the article as untimely and irresponsible. Publication of *The South Westerner* was temporarily suspended. The students made no protest at this exercise of academic power. In the following year, after members of the rugby club had staged a near riot in the Ramshackle, the students' bar, the Vice-Chancellor again acted decisively by closing the bar until the Guild of Students enacted more satisfactory rules for disciplining disorderly students. On this occasion 300 students in general meeting formally deprecated the University's handling of the affair. The students also held a silent march of protest, at the end of which they handed in a petition, and promoted a boycott of the student refectory. These were mild reactions by the standards of the next few years. The deteriorating climate showed itself in 1966 when another ban on the appearance of *The South Westerner* was simply ignored—an act of defiance that would have been very surprising only a few years earlier. But these troubles were as nothing to those that confronted Dr F. J. Llewellyn (now Sir John Llewellyn), who succeeded Sir James Cook as Vice-Chancellor in October 1966. Sir James had the good fortune to retire before the storm broke.

The University's second Vice-Chancellor came to Exeter after a varied and unusual career in teaching, research and administration. He read chemistry at the University of Birmingham, graduating with first class honours in 1935 and taking his doctorate in 1938. He was appointed to a lectureship in Birkbeck College, London, but spent most of the war directing research into explosives for the Ministry of Supply. He returned briefly to English academic life at the end of the war and in 1947 was elected to the Chair of Chemistry in the University of Auckland, New Zealand. A crystallographer himself, he established a school of crystallography in Auckland during his eight years there. In 1956 he became a full-time administrator on appointment as Vice-Chancellor of the University of Canterbury, New Zealand. In 1961 poacher turned gamekeeper when Vice-Chancellor became chairman of the New Zealand UGC. From 1962 to 1965 Dr Llewellyn was also chairman of the New Zealand Broadcasting Corporation and it was during these years that a television services was introduced. Although never known to raise his voice above the quietest conversational tones, he had a powerful presence. He could be blunt, but he was also humorous, conciliatory and willing to delegate authority. Before taking up his new appointment in Exeter, he was asked by a student journalist how he saw relations between himself and the students. He replied: 'Well, I hope they'll be my friends. I certainly hope to meet them, talk to them and find out what they're thinking.'[7] Talking to students and about their demands was to take up more of his time than he could have foreseen.

Students sought redress for a number of grievances during these turbulent years. Among the earliest to be raised and settled were questions of discipline and regulations in hall. Then, with the growth of the student population and of the sums of money handled by the Guild of Students, the duties of the Guild officers became more onerous. A sabbatical year—first for the President, later for the Deputy President and Treasurer—was demanded and after some considerable delay conceded; sabbatical officers now number five. More contentious was the demand for student representation on committees of Council and Senate. Senate, and less certainly Council, were willing to allow students to serve on committees where their interests as consumers made it seem reasonable. Thus, students were admitted to Library Committee and to the Joint Committee on Catering and Residence. Student insistence that justices must be seen to be done led to their inclusion on *ad hoc* disciplinary committees. Most academic departments established staff/student committees which met from time to time to discuss matters of common interest. In negotiation with the university the student leaders knew that they had widespread support among their members. The quiescent mood under which general meetings of the Guild could transact no business for lack of a quorum had passed away, and by 1966 large attendances at general meetings became usual. At moments of high excitement, as many as half the students in the university would attend meetings at which they would roundly and almost unanimously condemn the procrastination of the authorities and threaten direct action unless their latest demands were promptly met. It was not long before the concessions already made came to seem unimportant; a genuine sharing of power, it was argued, required that students should be represented on the highest bodies in the University—Senate and Council. The first tentative mention of this possibility appeared in *The South Westerner* in 1964 but it was not then taken up.[8] In the early months of 1968, the demand was for nothing more than representation on committees; at the end of 1969, it was proposed to transfer some of the powers of Senate to a Student Affairs Council on which students should have 50 per cent representation. From this point it was but a short step to demanding 50 per cent of the seats on Senate. The Vice-Chancellor, Dr Llewellyn, though a formidable man, was ready to make some concessions. Where the students asked for half the seats, he offered them six* and refused to improve his offer. Constitutional difficulties would have delayed even this change if the students had insisted on direct representation on Senate. Instead a novel body, the Board of Senate, was proposed, consisting of the full Senate with the additional six students. Its powers were considerable, though personal matters, for example reports on students, were reserved for Senate proper. Even without recourse to the Privy Council for permission to amend the University's constitution the negotiations were protracted. The question of representation was raised in the autumn of 1970, conceded in principle in the following spring, and finally implemented when the Board of Senate held its first meeting on 7 February 1973. It had taken nearly two years to convince the students that six seats were all that they could have. The negotiations sorely strained their limited fund of patience, and called for all the powers of conciliation that the Vice-Chancellor and his right-hand man the late Professor G. K. T. Conn could muster. Since then the device of a Board of Senate, though cumbersome, has worked well. The decisions of the Board are by convention ratified without debate in the Senate that immediately follows. Students attend the Board and sometimes join in the debates on the academic government of the University but they suffer from two serious disadvantages: they are heavily outnumbered, and unlike most other members serve for only one or at most two years.

*Senate was more than 60 strong at the time.

Nobody could pretend that the balance of power in the University has been substantially altered by the changes that have been so ardently demanded and so slowly and reluctantly accepted.

The struggle over representation on Senate had been preceded by other struggles — representation on committees, access to personal files, visiting hours in the halls of residence, the hours of opening of the library, hall fees, the right to live in flats rather than hall or approved lodgings. On all these matters except access to personal files and the level of hall fees, the University gave way. Since the struggle over Senate representation, the battles have continued. Some hardy annuals — hall fees and the rent for university flats — can never have a final settlement in an inflationary age and are repeatedly matters for conflict. New grievances crop up — the provision of a day nursery for the children of students, the fees charged to overseas students, cuts in the government's educational budget. Some of these disputes ought to be for discussion between students and the government, but the hapless university has served as a useful proxy for a distant department of state. The Library and the administration building have been occupied — to the severe discomfort and embarrassment of those who work there — in demonstrations of anger against the Department of Education and Science. Laboratories, lecture rooms and the offices of academic members of staff have so far escaped this peculiar form of protest — other universities have not been so lucky. Although often threatened, 'direct action' was not taken by Exeter students in the exciting disputes that culminated in the grant of representation on Senate. It is only since then that there has been a little resort to physical force — rent strikes and the occupation of university buildings. But it is doubtful if these happenings reflect a further worsening of relations between the University and its students. The suspicion of authority and the strong sense of alienation that characterised the later sixties and early seventies seem to have passed. Youthful impatience, a touch of exhibitionism, a strong lead from the National Union of Students and a determination not to be outdone by the militants in other universities, go far to explain the rather minor breaches of the peace that have occurred in Exeter in the last few years.

To list student grievances does not account for the conflicts that have taken place. Similar grievances could have been found at any period in the history of the University and the University College, had the will to protest been there. A necessary condition for conflict was a shift in the student view of his relationship with the University. In the past the student had been content to accept that his role in the University was like that of an apprentice in a guild, occasionally boisterous but usually deferential. More recently the student has seen himself either as an oppressed subject seeking full rights of citizenship, or as a militant trade unionist confronting an unreasonable employer. On these views the boycott, the rent strike and the sit-in become legitimate forms of conflict. But, it may be asked, why did students lose faith in the old analogy of apprentice and guild? The underlying reasons must be sought outside Exeter. The period of highest tension coincided with the Vietnam War, which poisoned relations between the American government and many American students. While no direct link can be traced between a war in South-east Asia and a demand for student representation on the Senate of the University of Exeter, there is a probable indirect connection. The troubles in Berkeley, Paris, Berlin and the London School of Economics reached a climax in the late sixties and early seventies; they were clearly inspired by student protest against the Vietnam War and the social system that was held to have fathered it. Where others led, Exeter was willing to follow — at a respectful distance. The growing self-confidence of the student body was encouraged by the rapid growth of British universities. Governments evidently attached importance to higher education and students felt that they were a valuable, perhaps even an indispensable, part of the future labour force. In 1967 the Latey report recommended that the age of majority should be lowered to 18, well aware that there would be repercussions in universities and colleges:

> Much of our evidence suggests that the present state of the law leads to uncertainty and serious friction between students and college and university authorities . . . . By not being forced to act like parents we hope that colleges will all the more effectively act like colleges and that students will the more easily respect this situation and abide by its conditions.

Subsequent events have scarcely justified this hope. The report was accepted by the Government and most of its recommendations became law in 1969. Lowering the age of majority, itself in part a result of youthful discontent, encouraged that discontent by the contrast drawn between the status of students as students and their status as citizens. One President of Exeter's Guild of Students clearly had this contrast in mind when he observed:

> I've been here for four years; my professor has been here four months. Yet he has a seat on Senate and I haven't.[9]

In the circumstances it would have been surprising if Exeter had avoided the troubles of the period. That it escaped more lightly than many other British universities was partly owing to its social composition. As one student President wrote in a tone tinged with regret: 'Conditions at Exeter, far from industrial areas, with relatively affluent students, a beautiful campus and conservative traditions have not been conducive to extended radicalisation of the student body.' The University had a much smaller contingent of students in the apparently militant field of social studies than the University of Essex or the London School of Economics. The large Faculty of Arts implied an unusually high proportion of women students, who had traditionally proved disappointing material for militants, whether in student politics or trade unions. Some of the credit for Exeter's escape from the worst consequences of student militancy must go to the University authorities. They have refused to act the part of the bullying employer, preferring patient negotiation to a display of power, and expressing bewilderment rather than anger at the unreason of man. On many points at issue the students achieved everything that they wanted, but now that the tumult has died down it can be seen that the University stands unshaken and in essentials almost unchanged.

It was noticeable that the ardour of the students cooled each year as the season of examinations approached and attention was redirected to the 'proper' business of a university. Assessment by written 'unseen' examination did not escape criticism by students in their radical mood, but the criticisms were not pressed and other methods of classifying students—for example by continuous assessment—are still relatively unimportant. Just as there has been stability in the examination system so has there been only slow change in the class of degree awarded in Exeter:

First degrees awarded 1955-78 (percentages)

Class of Degree	1955	1959	1968	1978
I	5	4	6	5
IIi	15	27	26	33
IIii	26	42	45	51
II undivided	19	—	—	—
III or pass	35	27	22	12

In 1955 the degrees were still London degrees though examined by Exeter staff under the 'special relationship'. The table relates only to single or combined honours degrees; the general degree has over the years attracted a diminishing number of students and in 1978 less than three per cent of finalists took such a degree. It will be seen that the proportion of first-class degrees awarded has remained virtually unchanged. In some subjects it is notoriously difficult to achieve a first, and even upper-second-class honours are sparingly awarded. Law and economics, following national patterns, fall into this category. Other departments take a more favourable view of their students and (it is fair to say) an increasingly favourable view. The University of London awarded many third-class degrees. As the influence of London's example faded from memory, so too did the third, until in 1978 it accounted for only 12 per cent of the degrees awarded. Second-class degrees have always been typical, but the balance in favour of the lower-second-class degree is nowadays less marked. Perhaps because minimum standards for entry have risen, failures are now rare, whereas under the London external degree they were not uncommon. By national standards, Exeter is sparing of first, thirds and passes and seems a little generous with upper-second-class honours.[10]

Whether the improved results recorded since 1955 point to abler and more hard-working students, declining standards, better teaching methods or a fairer system of examination is a difficult and important question. Pessimists have long feared that 'more means worse'; that expansion of student numbers would let weaker candidates into universities and perhaps weaker dons into senior common rooms. These fears have not been confirmed by experience. The average student appears to be as capable and as conscientious as he or she was when the University of Exeter secured its charter. Expansion in the university sector has proceeded *pari passu* with expansion in the schools, where it is clear that much talent had lain hidden in the days when sixth-forms were small and sixth-form colleges non-existent. It could indeed be argued that many students, particularly in the natural sciences and in economics, come up to university better prepared than in the past. School syllabuses in mathematics, chemistry and physics are more ambitious, but not more daunting to the young, than they were a generation or two ago. Exeter has been lucky in that most departments have had a large number of applicants for each available place. Over the university as a whole, the ratio of applications to places reached a peak of 15:1 in 1965. It never fell below 10:1 even in the early seventies when the number of places available each year exceeded 1,500 and when the UCCA scheme had been amended to allow candidates a choice of only five universities. By the end of the seventies demand had surged again: in 1980 more than 22,000 candidates applied for a mere 1,600 places, a ratio of 13:1. The most popular departments—English, geography and law prominent among them—were embarrassed by the number of applicants. Some departments, on the other hand, experienced periods of relatively low demand. In the late sixties and early seventies, for example, Exeter like other universities found it difficult to fill its quota of places in major departments like physics and chemistry. But a recent shift of opinion among sixth-formers has restored the popularity of the sciences, natural and applied, and the University's physics, chemistry and applied science laboratories are now comfortably full of well-qualified students. A buoyant demand for places at Exeter allows admissions tutors to demand high marks at 'A' level. In the circumstances, it is not surprising that the proportion of graduates awarded upper-second-class honours is somewhat above the national average.

Teaching methods for the most part have continued in the time-honoured ways. Principal Murray hoped to make the tutorial a typical feature of Exeter teaching. In the old Oxford sense of a meeting between the tutor and one or two students, the tutorial is extravagant of manpower and has not become the usual method of instruction in Exeter. Teaching in small groups, however, flourishes under a variety of names (tutorial, essay class, seminar) and complements the more impersonal instruction afforded by lectures. Language departments and the sciences tend to provide a great deal of formal instruction; students of history, philosophy and the social sciences have more time for private study. These differences of approach arise in part from the nature of the subject and in part by tradition. Only in the past twenty years has educational technology had an impact on teaching methods, mostly in the language departments. The University's first language laboratory was installed in Hoopern House some distance from the Faculty of Arts in Queen's Building. In 1974, the University established a Language Centre in Queen's Building under the direction of Dr R. K. K. Hartmann. The centre is much more than a language laboratory: it is equipped with a variety of audio-visual aids and its staff offer instruction not only to students reading languages for a degree, but also to other members of the University who wish to improve their linguistic skills. Dutch, Arabic and Japanese are among the languages on offer. The teaching of linguistics is another and increasingly important function of the Language Centre. The language laboratory represents one way of improving teaching performance, made possible by advances in communications technology.

The University has also tried to improve the efficacy of the traditional teaching methods—the lecture and the seminar. In 1975 it established a teaching services centre under the energetic aegis of Dr Donald Bligh. He has sought, with the help of his technical staff, to teach the dons how to teach. Just as in the interwar years the grammar school master supposed that he could teach by the light of nature and was reluctant to admit that there was any art to be learned, so too in more recent times a university lecturer trained to teach would have been hard to find. The Teaching Services Centre exists to change this state of affairs. Judged by results, Exeter's traditional teaching methods were not inefficient, and they have certainly not changed enough since the charter was granted to explain the better academic showing of recent generations of students.

The academic attainment of students may be of absorbing interest to their tutors, but government, taxpayers and the world at large are more concerned with what students do for a living when their expensive education has come to an end. Reliable information about the employment of former students is hard to come by and what little is known comes from the University's appointments service. The University College and the University have long offered some vocational guidance to students, but for many years the service functioned unsystematically. Before the war there was an appointments committee, which published an annual booklet, *Vocational Guidance*, listing the jobs recently obtained by Exeter students and giving advice on prospects. In the 1950s the careers advisory service (if it may be so dignified) was one of the many responsibilities of the Secretary of the College and the University. One of the clerks in his department devoted part of his time to the work. But A. F. Nickels was no ordinary clerk; he wrote poetry and novels in his spare time and during his war service in the navy maintained a lively correspondence with Principal Murray, who encouraged his ventures into authorship*. He lived with his mongrel dog in a caravan on the outskirts of Exeter and cycled to work with the dog seated in a basket attached to the handlebars. Once at work, the dog hung quietly about the office until it was time to go home. Its master had no special expertise in the field of student appointments and in 1960 the service was put on a more organised basis when a Deputy Registrar, Mr D. W. J. Morrell, took charge, though this was by no means his only duty. It was not until 1964 that the University created a full-time post of Appointments Officer; in the following year it strengthened the

*Jonathan Cape published his novels—*They Wanted Wine* in 1952 and *Eventide* in 1954.

organisation by establishing an Appointments Board on which local employers as well as the University were represented. For some time A. J. Saunders, the first appointments officer, worked single-handed, interviewing and advising students, addressing meetings in and outside the University, arranging visits by prospective employers, soliciting the views of academic departments on the abilities of their students and reporting those views and his own to interested employers. As the number of third-year students grew and a tradition of registering with the Appointments Board was established, the burden of work necessitated further appointments. Today the appointments officer, Richard Langley, heads a small team that has the task of encouraging second-year students to think about their future and of advising finalists (and students who leave university prematurely) about career opportunities.

It is from the work of the Appointments Board and its predecessors that we can learn what happened next to most students after they had taken their degree. The information is incomplete* because there has always been a large group who have made no long-term plans or if they have, have not communicated them to the University: some of these students are unemployed, some temporarily employed in jobs of low status; some are doing Voluntary Service Overseas; about half have simply not replied to questionnaires. This 'miscellaneous' category of students amounted to about 15 per cent of the total in the early sixties, but has recently been larger—from 25 to 30 per cent. Setting these students aside, and considering only those for whom definite information is available, it becomes clear that the last twenty years have brought important changes in job opportunities for graduates. Traditionally Exeter students had been preparing themselves for careers as schoolteachers, and as late as 1959 and 1960, 37 per cent of Exeter graduates proceeded either to a teacher-training course or directly into employment as teachers or lecturers. Opportunities for direct employment of the untrained graduate teacher have worsened in recent years: private schools and the universities are among the last refuges of those who disdain to learn the art of teaching, and in the years 1976–78 only two per cent of Exeter's graduates went directly into teaching.† Numbers proceeding to teacher-training held up well and indeed grew until the

---

*Such statistics as there are refer only to first appointment or first course of postgraduate training. The subsequent careers of most students are unknown.

†In 1979 there was a sharp jump to 11 per cent. This is owing to the inclusion of BEd students from Saint Luke's College, professionally as well as academically qualified to teach.

recent national cut-back in the training of teachers, but the proportion of students taking such courses has fallen drastically: 30 per cent in 1959–60, 20 per cent in 1964–65, 11 per cent in 1977–78. The civil service and local government have been taking a slowly increasing proportion of Exeter graduates—less than five per cent in 1959–60, and in recent years seven or eight per cent. Nationally, the entry of young graduates into the civil service increased rapidly in the early 1970s largely because of recruitment to the executive grade, which had formerly been the preserve of non-graduates: in 1970 fewer than 600 graduates entered the grade; in 1975 over 1,800, in 1978 1,400. It is to this grade that most Exeter graduates look when they seek a career in the civil service. Smaller numbers enter specialist branches like the inspectorate of taxes or the scientific civil service. Only two or three a year enter the élite administrative grade but since the total entry to the grade fluctuates between 100 and 200 a year, Exeter is well represented by comparison with other provincial universities.* The relative success of Exeter in this field probably reflects the privileged educational and social background of recent Exeter students. Twenty years ago it was almost unknown for Exeter students to enter the administrative grade.

Teaching and the public service now provide jobs for only a minority of the graduates who proceed straight into employment. The great expansion of job opportunities for graduates since the war has been in the field of business: accountants, personnel officers, management trainees, research scientists in industry—these are the careers increasingly sought by graduates, from Exeter and elsewhere. Before the war, students of science often found industrial or commercial employment, but the arts graduate who looked beyond teaching or the public service for a career was rather unusual. Since 1945 prejudices have been breaking down: the arts student is less likely to spurn the chance of working in business; and firms no longer need convincing that arts graduates can be usefully employed. By the early 1960s from 14 to 17 per cent of students in arts, law and social studies were finding employment in business; the proportion had doubled by 1978. For recent years it is possible to distinguish between the arts graduate and the graduate in law or social studies. The arts graduate still seems somewhat reluctant to enter the world of business: in 1978 only 22 per cent of arts graduates,

---

*Oxford and Cambridge still supply over half of the entrants to the administrative grade of the civil service despite the best efforts of the Civil Service Commission to widen the basis of recruitment.

but 48 per cent of graduates in law or social studies took jobs in industry or commerce. Even the science student is now less likely to enter business than the lawyer or the economist, for in 1978 40 per cent of scientists found such employment. It is the rise of accountancy as an employer of graduates that has drawn so many students into the world of business. In 1965 only three students are recorded as having entered accountancy offices; in 1978, 98 (8.6 per cent of all Exeter graduates) did so, nearly a quarter of the graduates who found employment in the private sector. Most of these students had law or social studies degrees, but a few arts men and women and a considerable number of scientists (23) jumped on the accountancy bandwagon. Other professions seem likely to recruit many graduates in the future: solicitors have already begun to do so; building societies are now looking for graduate trainees, and the fire service is the latest employer to declare an interest in the graduate market.[11]

The generous salaries offered by many firms seem to be distracting students—in Exeter as elsewhere—from further courses of full-time training after graduation. Twenty years ago, half of Exeter's graduates undertook a teacher-training or secretarial course, or enrolled for a higher degree. By 1978 little more than a quarter of the graduates troubled to acquire further qualifications before seeking employment. But they have not rejected the path of further study. For solicitors, accountants and tax inspectors paid employment and the pursuit of professional qualifications go hand-in-hand. It may well be that those who enter paid employment immediately after graduation have chosen the harder road, in physical and mental, if not in financial terms.

Students through the ages have looked back on their university days as among the happiest of their lives. There is every reason to think that Exeter students share these feelings. Their job prospects on graduation are not to be despised. The system of small-group teaching that flourishes in Exeter has enabled them to get to know their teachers as familiar and friendly rather than distant and forbidding figures. Their three years will have been spent in a university that occupies a spacious, beautiful and well-kept estate. They will probably have lived for at least one year in a hall of residence set in the near idyllic surroundings provided by large grounds handsomely adorned with shrubs, trees and grass. It is a fair inference from Exeter's relative freedom from disorder in the late sixties and seventies that the University was making a comparatively favourable impression on its students, even in those difficult years. And the popularity of the reunions sponsored by Exeter University Club provides further evidence that many former students have happy memories of their university.

Employment of students after taking first degrees

	1959 and 1960		1964 and 1965		1977 and 1978	
	No	%	No	%	No	%
1 Employed in UK	146	25.7	327	37.2	901	43.3
Civil Service ⎱ Local government ⎰	26	4.6	70	8.0	173	8.3
Teaching	43	7.6	56	6.4	36	1.7
Industry, commerce	77	13.5	201	22.8	692	33.2
2 Further training	295	51.9	552	46.7	634	30.5
Teacher training	168	29.6	172	19.6	226	10.9
Research	68	12.0	144	16.4	204	9.8
Other training	59	10.4	94	10.7	204	9.8
3 Miscellaneous	127	22.3	142	16.2	545	26.2
TOTAL	568		1021		2080	

Notes

1 UGC, *Report 1929-30 to 1934-35*, p. 33 (HMSO, repr. 1946); University of Exeter, *Gazette*, December 1955, April 1956; DES, *Statistics of Education*.

2 PPC, file 11; PPF file 5; I am grateful to the Universities Central Council for Admissions (UCCA) and to Mr Peter Lee, Admissions Officer of the University of Exeter, for supplying data on the social origins of students in 1958, 1968 and 1975.

3 William Holford and Partners 'A report to the Works Committee on the building programme in the years 1960, 1961 and 1962' (1957); *Annual Reports*; Joint Committee on Catering and Residence, 29 November 1978.

4 E. Ashby and M. Anderson, *The Rise of the Student Estate* (Macmillan, 1970).

5 Changes in regulations can be traced in the *Prospectus* and the *Calendar*: Student representative council, 21 October and 21 November 1921.

6 *The Ram*, Spring 1937; Guild Council, 13 February and 13 May 1940.

7 *The South Westerner*, 17 October and 17 November 1963; Guild General Meeting, 1 December 1964; *The South Westerner*, 28 October 1965, 3 and 17 February 1966.

8 *The South Westerner*, 11 June and 26 November 1964.

9 [Latey] Report on the age of majority (BBP 1966-67 XXI Cmnd, 3342); *The South Westerner*, 6 June 1968 and 26 November 1970.

10 For degrees awarded in England, see DES, *Statistics of Education*, volume 6 (published annually).

11 Appointments Board, *Annual reports*, especially 1963-64 ff; Appointments Board, 4 May 1979 for civil service recruitment; Civil Service Commission, *Annual reports*, 1971-1978; exact comparision with other universities is not feasible because of the different 'mix' of subjects. Since 1962 the UGC has published an annual report on the first employment, or first destination, of graduates.

XI

THE DEPARTMENTS

When the University received its charter in 1955, it was as a university in the legal sense of that term — a guild or corporation of scholars. It was not a university in the popular sense of an institution that professed all or most branches of higher learning; it would not have counted as a university for the Manchester bus conductor who was in the habit of calling out: 'College of knowledge, all the faculties — we hope'. The scope of Exeter's teaching was rather narrow — on the arts side English, French, and German, Latin and Greek, philosophy and history; in social studies, economics, geography, law, politics, psychology and sociology; in the natural sciences, chemistry, physics, geology, mathematics, botany and zoology. There was no school of medicine, of engineering, of architecture, or of fine art. Not all the subjects taught had yet attained to the dignity of separate departments: psychology was the handmaiden of education: politics a sub-department of economics; sociology a sub-department of philosophy. The large and powerful departments were English and French, history and geography, mathematics and physics, and chemistry.

The subsequent growth of the University has been shaped by various forces. The UGC as spokesman for the government and the government's view of the national interest has sought to influence the direction of developments. The University itself, as a self-governing corporation of scholars, has had its own vision of the future, which it has endeavoured to promote within the guidelines laid down by the UGC. Both the UGC and the University represent a collective wisdom, long views, an attempt to plan ahead. The wishes of prospective students represent forces of a quite different order — personal, discrete, unpredictable. From the interplay of these differing conceptions — the plan and the market — has emerged the University as it stands today.

The UGC was seemingly well placed to impose its view of the future.

As principal paymaster it could refuse to finance developments that it thought unwise; it could suggest developments that it held to be desirable; and it could do all this in the confident belief that a poorly-endowed University would be happy to attract the funds of which the UGC was custodian. The committee had no power to direct universities; it needed none—the purse is mightier than the sword. The academic independence of universities was scrupulously preserved: no institution was obliged to accept funds for the expansion of (say) engineering, or social studies; but few senates were so high-minded as to refuse the offer of funds for expansion, even into areas that would not have been their own first choice.

The UGC plans for Exeter have wavered little from a persistent desire to expand the science-based departments more rapidly than the arts-based. (In UGC terminology, those who are not science-based are arts-based, and arts-based subjects therefore include geography, law and psychology as well as the disciplines commonly grouped together as social studies.) Ever since the Second World War governments have believed that there exists a shortage of qualified scientists and engineers, and have sought a remedy in the expansion of the appropriate departments of British universities. In Exeter, which had never seriously professed the applied sciences, encouragement of pure science in the 1950s was hindered by the shortage of laboratory space, and until large new buildings for physics and chemistry were completed there was little scope for expanding the intake of science students. Plans for radical new developments were being sketched as early as 1960. The national need for scientists and engineers prompted the University to propose a faculty of applied science. The original scheme envisaged departments of chemical engineering, engineering science and applied biology, but the biological component has never materialised. Since Exeter was not a major industrial city, the new courses were strongly science-oriented, and put more emphasis on scientific principles than on industrial application. The first students arrived in 1965 and in 1968 moved to the large new applied science building designed to receive up to 100 engineers a year. Unhappily a good many years passed before the numbers admitted justified the heavy capital expenditure, but in the past five years, engineering science has prospered and, with some diversification into environmental engineering and computer science, the applied science building has been comfortably full and the faculty* is now well established.

*Renamed the Faculty of Engineering in 1981.

Other schemes for the expansion of science teaching included oceanography and a department of bio-chemistry, a field close to the research interests of Sir James Cook. The establishment of bio-chemistry would have strengthened Exeter's claim to a medical school, but the plans were scrapped during the retrenchment of 1967 that was brought on by national economic difficulties. In any case it was unlikely that the Royal Commission on Medical Education, then sitting, would have accepted Exeter's claim for a pre-clinical medical school. The Royal Commission was anxious to see new medical schools established in large universities in large centres of population with an adequate number of hospital beds. It did not consider the establishment of merely pre-clinical schools, (ie without hospital training), and Exeter was too small a city and at the time had no large modern hospital. The Commission's choice fell on Southampton, Leicester, and Swansea[1] and medical schools were duly established there. It is more than doubtful whether Exeter's claim would have succeeded even if it had previously devoted large resources to bio-chemistry, physiology, and genetics (as Leicester had done). The University having failed to get a medical school when there was a strong demand for more doctors seems to have little chance now, when doctors are no longer in short supply.

The national concern for science expansion did not exclude growth in other faculties. Some expansion in traditional arts subjects was expected and in social studies was positively encouraged, especially in the later sixties and early seventies. The gentle, persistent pressure in favour of science was not intended to make Exeter a technological or scientific university, but to raise the proportion of students reading science or technology from one-third to one-half. There was thus room for expansion all round. Sometimes it took the form of growth within a department, sometimes of growth by splitting a department so that a subsidiary subject formerly taught there might be given a chance to grow in departmental independence. Some already large departments like English, geography, physics, and chemistry have grown and diversified without splitting. The School of English, for example, now offers drama, medieval studies and American and Commonwealth arts as well as the traditional study of English literature. History had included the teaching of archaeology since 1947 when Lady Aileen Fox began her long and fruitful association with Exeter. Archaeology has grown into a flourishing specialism within the department of history, and in 1979 the University appointed Professor Malcolm Todd to the newly-established

Chair of Archaeology. Geography, with a much enlarged staff, has greatly elaborated its range of teaching, particularly in the fields of economic and physical geography. What is true of these departments is true of others also. Growth has allowed the provision of more varied courses reflecting the research interests of teachers and attractive to the student, who now faces a luxuriant array of options. When departments were small the fare had been more austere: outline courses in subjects of major importance always needed to be put on—Shakespeare, cartography, British history in the nineteenth century, the principles of economics, advanced calculus, mechanics, organic chemistry. Large departments allow themselves the luxury of recondite options like Arthurian romance, micro-climatology, medieval books and book production, securities markets and financial analysis, general topology, planetary and space science, advanced heterocyclic chemistry.

In the arts-based subjects new growth often began with the device of the combined honours degree. Thus, the teaching of Spanish and Italian began in the Department of French, and of Russian in the Department of German. When experience had shown that an adequate demand existed for further expansion, new departments offering full honours courses were created by detaching Spanish from French and Russian from German. When Spanish achieved independence in 1964, Italian took its place in the department of French and Italian (as it has since been known). Music and theology, on the other hand, had existed as separate departments from the start. Ever since the days of Principal Hetherington the College had offered a little teaching in music and for many years the cathedral organist of the day acted as director of music; a department was established in 1965 and in 1968 Professor A. J. Hutchings was elected first holder of the chair. This lively department offers not only instruction to its students but also the solace of much music to the University at large. Theology, like music, had close ties with the Cathedral. Dean Carpenter had been for many years Honorary Professor of the History of Christianity before he became in 1946 part-time head of the newly-established Department of Theology. The Chair of Theology dates from 1962 and has been held with distinction by the Old Testament scholar, the Revd Canon J. R. Porter. An enterprising offshoot from the Department of Theology may be noted. In 1971 the university established within the department a lectureship in Arabic and Islamic Studies. Dr (now Professor) M. A. Shaban was appointed to the post and in 1978 became the first head of a separate department of

Arabic and Islamic Studies. In 1979 with support from the Government of Qatar the University set up a Centre for Gulf Arab Studies (the only one of its kind in Western Europe). Dr Shaban as a moving spirit in this development became Director of the Centre.

In the natural sciences there has been as much combination as splitting. The division of the biological sciences into separate departments of botany and zoology was even more arbitrary than most academic divisions. L. A. Harvey, the head of the Department of Zoology, proposed a united department in 1935 when J. L. Sager retired from headship of botany. Sager's successor, John Caldwell, secured the continued independence of botany and it was not until his retirement in 1969 that the union was effected.[2] Mathematics, with a vast literature and rapidly growing specialisms, has, however, felt the need to shed some of its members. A separate Department of Mathematical Statistics and Operational Research was established in 1974, and in 1978 a Department of Computer Science came into existence. Both departments necessarily collaborate closely with the parent Department of Mathematics.

The University acquired its first computer in 1962 — an Elliott 803 costing a mere £25,000. There were only two operators, and users could, if they wished, work the computer for themselves. In 1966 when the word store was doubled to 8k it became possible to use the computer language Algol. Two years later, the Elliott 803 was replaced by the ICL System 4/50, costing ten times as much, but with 16 times the word store of the original 803. Per unit of store, the ICL model was therefore the cheaper of the two. In 1974 the 4/50 was replaced by the ICL 4/72 model — an even more powerful machine that now (1980) has four times the store capacity of the 4/50 and 64 times the capacity of the original 803. The 4/72, by no means the fastest computer in the world, can perform one million operations per second. Research workers and administrative staff in the University have been quick to appreciate the possibilities of so much calculating power at their disposal, and their demands have kept the ever-more-powerful computer busy. The original staff of two (the lecturer in charge of the 'computing laboratory', and an operator) soon needed further assistance and at its height the computer unit had a staff of 37. Economics have since led to some slight reduction. Three-shift working is now the rule, but demand tends to outrun the supply of computing facilities, and recourse to more powerful machines either in London, or in the South-West Network is not uncommon. Scientists and mathematicians are naturally the heaviest users, but departments in the Faculty of Social Studies make considerable claims, and the Faculty of Arts does not despise the help that a computer can afford. It has thrown light on some problems in the poetry of Ovid, and has prepared a concordance and glossary of an early-fifteenth-century Middle English text, *The Pilgrimage of the Life of Man*.

In social studies, growth by splitting has been a common method of encouraging new specialisms. Four of the departments working in the Faculty can trace their origins to a recent separation from a larger department. Psychology separated from education, and sociology from philosophy in 1962, politics from economics in 1963, and economic history from history in 1964. Economics, now a very large department, itself consisted until 1926 of two junior members of the Department of History.

Two further developments may be mentioned; the Postgraduate Medical Institute [PGMI]* and the Institute of Cornish Studies. They have arisen from co-operation between the University and interests other than the UGC. The Postgraduate Medical Institute was initially funded by the Nuffield Provincial Hospitals Trust and the South Western Regional Hospital Board. Its original purpose was to provide in-service training and refresher courses for doctors, many of them from abroad. In 1973 a department of general practice was added, which provided day-release courses in what was until recently a sadly neglected branch of study in the field of medicine.† The Institute is unusual in that it stands alone, unsupported by an undergraduate medical school. The Institute of Cornish Studies, jointly financed by the University of Exeter and Cornwall County Council, was founded in 1970. From its base in Redruth it promotes interest and research in Cornish Studies, and publishes a journal. The Director is Professor of Cornish Studies and a member of Senate. In a period of financial stringency it has led and continues to lead a precarious existence, while fostering much important and interesting work.

The UGC's attempts to promote science teaching and the University's own schemes for diversification represent planned decisions affecting the pattern of university development. Whether these plans have been the major influence on the course of events is by no means clear. Market forces, that is the countless decisions by individual applicants to study

*Renamed in 1980, the Postgraduate Medical School.
†The DHSS finances the Department of General Practice. The University assumed responsibility for funding the other work of the Institute after its first five years, in 1968.

this course rather than that, have also influenced events—and perhaps by at least as much as the plans evolved in Park Crescent and Northcote House. If Exeter had followed the path mapped out by the UGC, it would have attracted more men and fewer women students, because the natural sciences (except biology) and the applied sciences mostly attracted men, whereas the arts subjects, which predominated in Exeter after the war, used mostly to attract women students. In the 1950s men were scarcely more numerous than women in Exeter at a time when in British universities as a whole they outnumbered them by three to one. Over the past 25 years some convergence between Exeter and the national average can be detected. In British universities more than a third of the students are now women; in Exeter the proportion, though still high, (44 per cent in 1977–78) is lower than it was in 1955–56 (47 per cent). Women still choose (though to a lesser extent than in the past) different subjects from men. In 1955, for example, the Faculty of Arts catered predominantly for women, who accounted for three-quarters of its students; in science, these proportions were reversed; social studies, except law, occupied an intermediate position with three men to every two women; in education, the numbers were roughly equal; in law masculine predominance was overwhelming. Over the years tastes have become more catholic: in arts the supremacy of women is under challenge: in law, once almost wholly masculine, women students are as numerous as men. In science, women are now outnumbered by only two to one—but this is owing to the rapid growth of numbers in biology; it is still the case that physics, chemistry, geology and applied science attract few women students. Unhappily for science, men students have declined to behave as predictably as manpower planning requires. Science emerged from the Second World War with high prestige. Its impressive and ominous contribution to victory attracted large numbers of young men. In 1947 and for the next 15 years over half the passes in higher-school certificate and advanced-level examinations were in science subjects, a considerable increase on the pre-war proportion of two-fifths. The planned expansion of science assumed that this popularity would continue indefinitely, but by 1967 the proportion of science passes had returned to the pre-war level and by 1977 was well below it, at 36 per cent. Numbers qualified in science continued to increase because of the much larger total number of candidates presenting themselves for examination, but the growth was too slow to sustain the planned expansion of university science departments. Within the Faculty of Science the growth of numbers has not followed the expected course. The Departments of Physics and Chemistry, traditionally the largest science departments, have at times found it hard to fill the places at their disposal. Mathematics and biology have become the most popular of the science subjects and in recent years have easily had the largest intake of first-degree students. The popularity of biology and mathematics and the introduction of applied science have not entirely offset the relative decline of physics and chemistry; as a result, despite the best efforts of the University and expensive funding by the UGC, science students account for a slightly smaller proportion of the whole than in the 1950s (1955–56 36 per cent; 1977–78 34 per cent).* If the early hopes and plans of the University and the UGC had been realised, more than half the students would now be 'science-based'.

The loss to science has not been the gain of the traditional arts departments. It is true that the numbers reading English, French and history have grown considerably—and could have grown still more if all well-qualified applicants had been admitted. But shortage of accommodation and the desire to encourage the sciences has led the University to limit entry to the over-subscribed arts subjects. The newer departments—Spanish and Russian—and some older ones like classics, German, music, philosophy and theology, have received a more modest number of applications and have therefore contributed only on a small scale to the growth of the Faculty of Arts. The Faculty now has less than one-third of the total number of students, against two-fifths in 1955–56.

Social studies (including psychology and geography) and Law are the two faculties that have grown fastest since Exeter received its charter.† In part this reflects a growing interest in vocational or quasi-vocational courses. The Department of Law is a case in point. Whereas in 1955 only nine students started to read law, in recent years a strict quota of one hundred or less has been imposed and three times that number of students could have been admitted without emptying the pool of qualified applicants. Accountancy (within the Department of Economics) is another vocationally flavoured subject that has proved extremely popular. It is by no means uncommon for students of (say) chemistry, English, or economic history to train as accountants, and the

*On UGC definitions education is an arts subject. The enlargement of the school of education through the absorption of Saint Luke's College in 1978 therefore reduced still further the proportion of science students. However, many BEd students will be studying science subjects as well as education, and to that extent UGC statistics will be a little misleading.
†Law in Exeter has the distinction of being a faculty unto itself. All other faculties encompass more than one department.

profession does not specially favour entrants who already have an accountancy degree. Yet there is no stemming the rush of candidates to read for the degree in accountancy instituted in 1974. In the early 1970s prospective social workers showed a similar eagerness to read social administration, formerly taught as a two-year diploma, and offered as a degree course in 1969. Graduates of these disciplines who afterwards chose not to become lawyers, accountants or social workers could still look forward to prosperous careers in business or the public service. Those who did wish to make use of their qualifications knew that their chosen profession was rapidly expanding, and except in the case of social work, unusually well paid.

Scientists and engineers, on the other hand, had, and have, relatively dismal prospects in industry unless they enter the ranks of general management. Despite the faith shown by government and the UGC in science and technology, the highest rewards in business do not go to engineers and research workers. Marketing, financial, and legal experts earn the highest salaries, and mathematicians, scientists and engineers have to be content with considerably less. These differences have been apparent at least since the mid-1960s when a first degree in science or technology was already worth less in the labour market than a degree in arts, and much less than a degree in social studies.[3] It is possible that the country's industrial and commercial leaders have been following a mistaken and short-sighted policy in undervaluing science, but it is hardly surprising that more and more students have opted for social studies rather than science, for a career in finance rather than in science-teaching or industrial research.* The trend is symptomatic of developments throughout the British economy: manufacturing industry in decline; the service trades expanding. Successive governments pledge themselves to reverse the decline of industry, just as the UGC tries to encourage science; both are baffled by the complexities of the problem and their inability to predict human behaviour.

Sceptics may suggest a less creditable reason for the popularity of social studies—that they are a soft option in comparison with difficult subjects like mathematics and physics. Whether sixth-formers take and act on this arguable view is a matter of guesswork in the absence of

---

*A letter in *The Times*, 16 June 1980, illustrates the problem. A sixth-former taking advanced level mathematics had been offered a post in a bank at £3,700 a year, rising to £4500 after a year's probationary service. His mathematics master after four years of academic training and professional training was earning £3900 a year—with none of the perquisites available to bank employees.

research on the point. Degree results in Exeter do not suggest that there is any substance in the argument. Scientists are much more likely to do really well (gain first-class honours)—and to do rather badly (take a third-class degree) than students in the Faculty of Social Studies. The explanation for the wider spread of marks in science is by no means clear, and the evidence certainly does not suggest that social studies are an easy road to high academic honours. On the other hand, a calculating candidate, unsure of his abilities, would have a better chance of graduating with second-class honours if he chose social studies rather than science.

The one faculty* that enjoyed a steady share of student numbers throughout the years from 1955 to 1978 was education. Every year, between seven and eight per cent of the students of the University were seeking a postgraduate professional qualification (the certificate of education) or a higher degree from the Faculty. Since none of the under-graduates was now financed by the ministry or bonded to teach, the Faculty was no longer the largest and most important part of the University, as it had been for so many years in the days of the University College. A substantial increase in its size could only come from a merger with the local college of education, Saint Luke's. In the first quarter of the century, the airy dreams of a federal university for South-West England had sometimes embraced Saint Luke's College, the diocesan training college for men situated in another part of Exeter. More often, Saint Luke's was left out, and the federal scheme encompassed more distant and wholly secular institutions—Seale-Hayne agricultural college, Plymouth technical college, and the Camborne School of Mines. The UGC and the Board of Education did not encourage the federal idea, and consistently with their long tradition of hostility to a federal university when the future of Saint Luke's College came into question in the 1970s they encouraged the absorption of Sant Luke's College into the University, not a federal link between the two institutions.

Saint Luke's was one of the more flourishing colleges of education. It had a long history, reaching further back into the nineteenth century than that of the University. Until 1964 it had been a men's college, strong in physical education and renowned among the general public for its rugby players, mostly Welsh. When women students were admitted, the

*Until 1969 there was, strictly speaking, no faculty of education, only a Department (in the Faculties of Arts and Science), an Institute of Education, and a Department of Extra-Mural Studies. These three bodies came together in 1969 to form the Faculty of Education. In 1973 the Department and the Institute merged to form the School of Education.

change was part of a policy of expansion, not a response to weakness and falling numbers. The college grew rapidly after 1945 and at the peak of its prosperity in the early 1970s had nearly 1,400 students, all of them taking at least a three-year course, many the four-year course leading to the BEd with honours. Nevertheless, Saint Luke's could not escape the unpleasant consequences of a falling school population and a shrinking demand for teachers. Some contraction was inevitable, and in practice contraction meant loss of independence. The choice lay between a merger with Rolle College, Exmouth, under the aegis of Devon County Council, and absorption into the University's School of Education.

Saint Luke's had had close and sometimes troubled relations with the University College and the University. In the 1920s the Board of Education gave up examining prospective teachers and passed the work to boards representing the local university and training colleges. The South West Board, established in 1929, was one of the smallest. Its three constitute colleges were the University College, Saint Luke's, and the diocesan training college for women at Truro. Most of the students examined by the board came from the two training colleges, but Principal Murray, representing the University College, claimed academic precedence for his institution—to the intense annoyance of Prebendary Collins, Principal of Saint Luke's. Truro closed in 1939, and Saint Luke's seceded to join Bristol's board. A new and happier start was made in 1948 with the establishment of the Institute of Education. Saint Luke's and the University College were again constituent colleges and to them was added Rolle College, Exmouth. The Institute, like the South West Board, recommended successful students for recognition as qualified teachers: it also offered facilities for educational research and for the in-service training of local teachers. By the 1960s the teacher's course had lengthened to three years and the long-cherished ideal of an all-graduate profession was coming closer to fulfilment. The University, in association with Saint Luke's and Rolle College, devised syllabuses and undertook to validate degrees in education to be awarded after four years of study at the College of Education. The first students, who had already completed a preliminary year, enrolled for the course in 1966 and in 1969 took their BEd degrees.[4] The part of the University in this development was to moderate and assess the BEd. The relationship between it and the colleges of education was much closer than that between London University and the colleges that had taught for London external degrees. And when Saint Luke's had to choose between absorption into the University or control by the local authority, there was little hesitation in choosing to approach the University.

For the university the absorption of Saint Luke's had certain attractions. At a time when opportunities for expansion were fast disappearing, it offered some prospect of enlargement, not only by adding Saint Luke's, its staff and buildings, but also by new appointments in other faculties than education. This possibility arose because some of the Saint Luke's staff became redundant with the contraction of teacher training. The Department of Education and Science was prepared to allow the University to make appointments and to expand student numbers in other faculties to the full extent of the reduction effected in the numbers of permanent staff at Saint Luke's. For some years the College had been appointing only temporary lecturers and by 1978 one-quarter of the staff were employed on short-term contracts timed to expire at the moment of merger. These posts were lost when the merger took place, and there was some reduction in the claims that higher education in Exeter made on national resources; but there was also intended to be some redistribution—away from the enlarged School of Education to other parts of the University. Without this douceur it is doubtful if the Department of Education and Science would have secured the University's agreement to absorb Saint Luke's. In the event, in the worsening economic situation, the redistribution did not take place.

The negotiations for the absorption of Saint Luke's were lengthy. The governors of the College approached the University early in 1974. Nearly five years later in October 1978 the process came to completion and Saint Luke's College lost its separate identity and became part, much the larger part, of the School of Education. For many years the University College and the young University had been plagued by the annoyance of a divided site—some departments in Gandy Street, others on the Streatham Estate. These inconveniences gradually disappeared as new buildings rose at Streatham. Gandy Street became empty and forlorn, and what had once been a bustling seat of learning was reduced to the indignity of a reserve book-store for the overcrowded library. The absorption of Saint Luke's reproduced the inconveniences of a divided university once more, made somewhat worse by the greater distance between Saint Luke's and Streatham. But if there was one faculty that was close to being self-contained it was the Faculty of Education, and to concentrate its work on the Saint Luke's site was probably the best that could be done with limited resources in an imperfect world.

Distribution of students (percentages)*

	1955–56	1966–67	1977–78	1979–80
Arts	40	34	32	28
Science (and Applied Science)	36	33	34	32
Social Studies and Law	18	25	28	25
Education	7	7	7	15
Total full-time students	994	2695	4367	5103

*Percentages may not add to 100 because of rounding.

Notes

1 Royal Commission on Medical Education, *Report*, pp.148, 156–60 (Cmnd 3569, BPP 1967–68 XXV).
2 PPC, files 19 and 21.
3 DES, *Survey of earnings of qualified manpower in England and Wales 1966–67* (Statistics of Education, special series, No.3); *Department of Employment Gazette*, October 1979, new earnings survey, table 8 — data relate to April 1979.
4 F. W. T. Fuller, *History of Saint Luke's College, Exeter* (Exeter 1970), I, 48 ff, III, 521 ff, IV, 798–800; PPA, file 27; PPB files 1–3; PPF, files 5 and 9.

XII

BUILDINGS AND FINANCE

In the absence of a medical school and with a low proportion of science students, Exeter has been an inexpensive university to finance and run. Inexpensive is of course a relative term: the sums required to keep a modern university going are so large that only central government can afford them. Throughout its 25 years, the University of Exeter has depended on central government for over half and in most years for three-quarters of its income. Local authority grants* have diminished in money terms and with the growth of the University and the fall in the value of money now represent an expression of good will rather than a substantial contribution to the University's funds. On the other hand, local authorities throughout the country are obliged to pay the tuition fees of undergraduates, however small the student's maintenance grant may be. For many years fees remained at a low, almost nominal level: in the year of the charter, for example, the highest tuition fees were £39-5s-0d [£39.25] for a first degree in science: fees for a higher degree with the use of a laboratory were £25; without a laboratory a mere eight guineas [£8.40]. In 1970, after 15 years of slowly rising prices, all science students paid fees of £75; students reading for other degrees paid only £60. Although 1970 saw the start of a period of rapid inflation, fees remained unchanged until 1975. Since then under strong government pressure, universities have raised fees sharply, and they are now obliged to adjust them upwards every year in line with the rise in the cost of living. The fees of 1974–75 therefore look ridiculously low now that UK students pay £740 for tuition for first degrees and £1,105 for higher degrees[†] The rise in fees has shifted part of the cost of financing

*From Devon, Cornwall and Dorset County Councils and from Exeter, Plymouth and Torbay.
†These are the fees fixed for 1980-81. Overseas students paid substantially more; those registering for the first time in October 1980 were required to pay the full cost of their tuition. The University of Exeter — Council, Senate and Guild of Students alike — has with other universites opposed this inhospitable and short-sighted discrimination, but to no avail.

universities from the Exchequer to the local authorities since fees, which contributed less than a sixteenth of Exeter's income in 1974–75, now supply more than a quarter.

Sources of current income (percentages)

	1955–56	1967–68	1979–80
UGC	74.0	77.9	66.2
Local authority grants	5.9	0.9	0.1
Fees	14.2	10.5	22.0
Other	5.9	10.7	11.7
Income (£000)	327	2081	14996
Income per student (£)	329	698	2978
Income per student (£) at 1955 prices	329	431	421

For capital spending—new halls of residence, laboratories, libraries, teaching buildings, and student amenities—Exeter has relied even more heavily on government. No Vice-Chancellor has shared Principal Murray's taste or talent for raising funds from private or corporate benefactors.* The University did launch an appeal in 1957 with the object of raising £250,000, there being no assurance at the time that the UGC would finance new projects out of public funds. In the event and despite the best efforts of Mr Gerald Whitmarsh, the appeal organiser, the venture proved somewhat disappointing. Some large national firms, notably Imperial Chemical Industries, gave generously, and the City of Exeter raised over £26,000 for the endowment of postgraduate scholarships. But otherwise the response in the South West was less encouraging than had been hoped. When the appeal closed in 1962 it had raised £130,000. In comparison with Murray and others between 1926 and 1939 the new university had done rather badly and could only be thankful that in the event government was willing to shoulder almost the whole responsibility of meeting capital costs.

That responsibility was considerable. When the University came into existence its land, buildings and permanent equipment appeared in the balance sheet at their historic cost, namely £708,000. The corresponding figure at the beginning of the financial year 1978–79 and using the same accounting conventions, was £15,108,000. The net addition—more than £14,000,000—largely represents monies made available by the UGC. The principal exceptions are the sums borrowed privately by the University to finance the Lafrowda flats—about one million pounds. For more than twenty years—from 1956, when work began on Queen's Building, until 1976, when the second stage of the Lafrowda flats was

*But see below, page 173.

completed—hardly a year passed without one major building or another being under construction or newly occupied.

The prospect of an extensive building programme caused the University to take a fresh look at its plans for the development of the Streatham estate. Although the terrain was far from level, land reasonably suitable for building was not scarce. E. Vincent Harris, architect to the university college, revised his pre-war plan for the estate in 1951. The principal change that he then made was a shortening of the proposed grand avenue from the Prince of Wales Road past the Roborough Library to the top of Mardon Hill. In his new proposals the avenue ended where Devonshire House now stands and the vista was closed by an Arts Block occupying three sides of a square. Immediately in front of the Arts Block was to stand the Mary Harris Memorial Chapel. Other buildings—a convocation building, a students' union, an extention to the library— were dispersed symmetrically about the avenue. An extension to the Washington Singer Laboratories was provided for, and two new halls of residence were envisaged to the north of Mardon Hall. Under the pre-war plan the Arts Block would have occupied the site on which the Hatherly Biological Laboratories were built between 1948 and 1952, and biology would have found a home opposite the Roborough Library where the second library was eventually built in 1965. The major buildings would have been dispersed on the edge of the estate to be admired by the spectator standing on the opposite side of the Hoopern Valley. The post-war plan did at least move some of the proposed buildings further back into the estate. But it continued to insist on symmetry despite the hilly and irregular terrain.

In 1953 the University College appointed a new architect and planning consultant—Sir William (later Lord) Holford. Where Vincent Harris sought to impose his will on the natural features of the estate, Holford preferred to accommodate his plans to the lie of the land and the trees that were scattered about the site. In Holford's phrase, not unkindly meant, the Vincent Harris buildings—Mardon Hall, the Washington Singer and Hatherly Laboratories, the Roborough Library—were good examples of 'parade-ground architecture'. Holford proposed to develop the estate along less grandiose and more informal lines, with major buildings sited for ease of communication, rather than to arrest attention and command a view. New roads were necessary for any development of the estate and Holford with his preference for informality favoured indirect approaches rather than a dramatic central avenue: Queen's

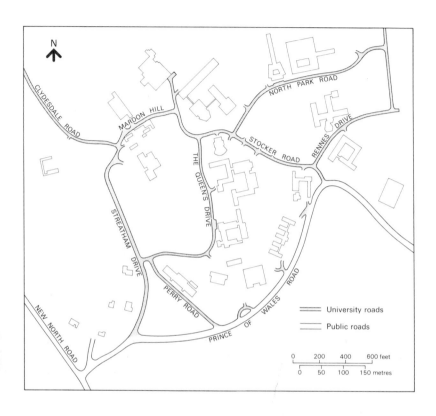

Roads on the Streatham Estate

Drive, Stocker Road (previously a muddy lane), North Park Road and Rennes Drive opened up large areas of the estate for development, and no further roadbuilding seems necessary in the foreseeable future.

Vincent Harris designed one further building for the University— the Mary Harris Memorial Chapel. The architect generously set aside the fees from his several commissions for the University College,* and with the proceeds built a chapel in memory of his mother. Under Holford's plans the grand central avenue came to an abrupt halt at the side of the Roborough Library and there at the head of the avenue on an imposing site rose the Mary Harris Memorial Chapel. The calm beauty of its interior has surprised many visitors misled by its outwardly unpretentious appearance. W. T. Monnington, PRA, designed the delicate painted ceiling. The chapel was consecrated by the Lord Bishop of Exeter in June 1958.

The first buildings designed by Sir William Holford and Partners were Queen's Building, Northcote House and Devonshire House with its adjoining refectory. With the occupation of these buildings in the years 1958 to 1960 the move from city centre to the Streatham estate was largely though not wholly achieved. Queen's Building originally housed the Faculties of Arts and Social Studies together with the Departments of Geology and Mathematics; with the exception of geology, previously housed in the Hatherly Laboratories, all these departments moved up the hill from Gandy Street.† Northcote House, fittingly named after Sir Stafford Northcote, civil-service reformer and one of the founding fathers of higher education in Exeter, at last provided an adequate home for the administration. For many years it had worked in scattered and makeshift accommodation in Gandy Street; the Vice-Chancellor had his office in the main building, and Council and Senate also met in one of the larger rooms there; the Secretary's staff had their quarters in a one-storey building erected after the war to replace the Registry destroyed by enemy action in 1942, and the Academic Registrar and his staff occupied part of the ancient and rickety Argyle House. The further growth of the University necessitated an extention to Northcote House in 1974, but contrary to popular belief the administration has grown more

---

*Besides the buildings on the main estate, Harris designed extensions to Hope and Lopes Halls.

†Although social studies, mathematics and geology have long since departed from Queen's, the Faculty of Arts has grown so much that two extensions have been added to the building. The Faculty also occupies additional accommodation close to the Streatham estate at Thornlea in New North Road, and is still overcrowded.

slowly than the University as a whole. When the University College came into existence the rudimentary administration absorbed a tenth of annual expenditure. In the 1930s administration took as much as an eighth of expenditure, and the proportion was still as high as a tenth in 1958–59. Sir James Cook, cautious to the point of parsimony, reduced it to the unduly low level of 6.7 per cent in 1963–64. Since then a more comfortable ratio of seven or seven and a half per cent of annual expenditure has been devoted to administration, closely in line with the average for British universities. It is satisfactory to know that economies of scale occur in the real world as well as in the textbooks of economics.

The completion of Devonshire House and the refectory in 1960 gave the students — for a time — ample and comfortable quarters for their social activities and for guild affairs. Designed for a student population of 2000, Devonshire House soon became crowded and in 1971 the facilities it offered were supplemented by those of the elegant Cornwall House, sited close to the Lafrowda flats. Residents in the flats who did not wish to cater for themselves could thus buy meals and enjoy common rooms close at hand.

Queen's Building, Northcote House and Devonshire House repre-sented the fruits of planning in the 1950s when a university of modest size was still envisaged. The headlong expansion that continued through the 1960s was accompanied by further extensive building operations. Between 1963 and 1968 no fewer than ten important buildings were completed on the main estate besides halls of residence for about a thousand students elsewhere. Most, like Queen's and Devonshire House, were solidly built to high and in some cases almost lavish standards. Sir Basil Spence was the architect for the Physics and Chemistry Buildings and for the Newman Building, a suite of lecture theatres for those two departments. This group of buildings was expensively appointed in an age when UGC norms were still generous. The one building of poor quality was Streatham Court, built in a hurry and, at the wish of the UGC, in experimental style. As an example of industrialised or prefabricated building, Streatham Court should have demonstrated the virtues of economy and speed of erection. Unhappily for the cause of economy the chosen site was made ground — a low-lying area of the Hoopern Valley filled with spoil from other building operations on the estate. As a result the savings made in the course of erection were offset by expensive pile-driving to stabilise the site. The timber-framed building was flimsy and a fire risk; it was also poorly insulated against cold and noise. The University had acquired an inferior property that cost as much per square foot as other more solid and pleasing structures. The UGC has not since pressed the claims of industrialised building in Exeter.

Other buildings completed in these years included some for academic purposes and some for amenity. The Department of Mathematics, after a period of wandering—from Gandy Street to Queen's Building and thence to Reed Hall—came to rest in a Louis de Soissons building boldly constructed in the side of a hill. This building also houses geology, another much-travelled department. The Applied Science Building, to the designs of the Playne Vallance Partnership, opened in 1968. Of the amenity buildings, the first to be completed was the much-needed Great Hall, inaugurated in 1964 with a concert given by the BBC Symphony Orchestra under Sir Adrian Boult with Moura Lympany as soloist. The Hall has a wide variety of uses—for examinations, degree congregations, concerts both classical and 'pop', conventions, school speech days and mass meetings of the Guild of Students. As an amenity for the whole of east and mid Devon the Great Hall serves a much wider community than the university alone. Similarly with the Northcott Theatre. Built on university land with funds given by the late Mr. G. V. Northcott, supplemented by grants from the Gulbenkian Foundation and the UGC, the theatre is run by a board of management (on which the University is represented) with the aid of grants from the Arts Council and the local authorities. Though situated on the university estate, rather than in the centre of Exeter, the theatre attracts its audience from town and country as well as gown. The Sports Hall, like the Northcott Theatre, opened in 1967, providing students with improved facilities for a wide range of indoor sports—squash, badminton and five-a-side football among others. During vacations it is extensively used by non-university sportsmen and women.

The university library, opened in 1965, served both learning and recreation. The Roborough Library with places for 150 readers and shelves for about 130,000 volumes had provided ample accommodation for a college with 500 students, most of them separated from it by ten minutes of stiff walking. In a university of 2,000 students, most of whom attended lectures and classes within a stone's throw of the library, the Roborough became hopelessly short of space for readers. It was also running out of shelf space for books. Even with accessions at the low rate of 5,000 items a year, the library was rapidly filling up and by the early

1960s books were being stored elsewhere. Planning for a new library began in 1960. John Lloyd, librarian since 1946, had a high conception of the place of the library in a university:

> [It] should aim to be the cultural focus and centre of the whole University, a place in which every reasonable need of the student can be met, whether this be scientific, literary, artistic or — I was going to say practical — since a treatise on spin bowling or the chess tactics of Capablanca would I suppose take their place in any comprehensive provision for the good life.*
> . . . My point is that students should be given the widest possible opportunities of developing whatever interests or talents they may have; and the library can, and should, go a very long way towards their provision. These are vital formative years; and it is our business to see to it that a stimulus is present at every turn.

The new library should therefore have showcases full of manuscripts and specimens of fine printing and binding. Paintings, drawings and prints, sculpture and ceramics should greet the visitor in corners of the building, or at a turn in a staircase. Musical scores and gramophone records should be available — not just to the musicologist, but to all. More technical points were not neglected: a microfilm reading room, a bindery and a photographic department were envisaged as part of the shape of things to come. In accordance with this generous vision, John Lloyd proposed a library capable of holding half a million books and 600 readers, with reading rooms for the fine arts and for postgraduate students, a seminar room, a lecture room equipped with a projector, a sound-proof music room for playing records and tapes, and an exhibition hall. The Roborough Library was virtually one large reading room with stacks below. In reaction from this open-plan scheme, John Lloyd emphasised the importance of ensuring the maximum privacy for individual readers in the new library.[1]

The proposed library would have cost nearly half a million pounds at 1961 prices; the library that the UGC was prepared to finance would have cost no more than £300,000. Nearly all the rooms and equipment that would have made the library the cultural focus and centre of the University disappeared in the slimming process. The exhibiton hall was retained but lost its conspicuous place near the entrance to the building on the ground floor. Accommodation for books and readers was drastically reduced: as built, the library had a capacity of 400,000 books and places for about 400 readers, with the possibility of extension at a

---

*The library does hold some books on games and sports; very properly in view of John Lloyd's devotion to cricket, a few volumes of Wisden are among them.

later date. Not all the weaknesses in the new library can be attributed to the need to adjust to harsh reality. It was too readily assumed that few extra staff would be needed to man the bigger library. This miscalculation has led to the loss of several small rooms to the needs of library administration. Above all, the emphasis on privacy has led to the building of a library which has several small reading rooms and only one large one, and book-stacks with relatively few reader-places close to hand. The modern librarian would prefer large open spaces—like an aircraft hangar—to give him maximum flexibility in the arrangement of books; and for the convenience of the reader he would like reader-places close to the books. In both these respects Exeter's library is less than perfect, though there is no great hardship in walking with a book from the lower stack to a place in the large reading room on the ground floor. At least, the perils of high-technology building styles have been avoided. Philip Larkin, the poet-librarian, was evidently writing from bitter experience when he gave John Lloyd 'a gipsy's warning not to have any truck with electrically operated blinds, or turnstiles; and do not have your issue desk within 15 feet of the open air, however many lines of glass doors and concentrations of heating the architect promises you'.[2]

Modern technology has its place in the university library all the same. It was in 1948 that the Roborough Library acquired its first microfilm reader and its first twenty rolls of microfilm. The library now possesses a battery of machines for reading microfilm, micro-fiche and -card. Mercifully for readers, most accessions still take the traditional form of books and periodicals; microforms make up little more than three per cent of the total number of items. *The Times* has been taken on microfilm since 1956; and much otherwise unobtainable material, printed and manuscript, is being acquired in the same way. Manuscripts from the Vatican Library, the Bibliothèque Nationale, from Leyden and Antwerp, from Lambeth Palace and from the British Library can all be read in microform in the University's library. Enterprising publishers are reproducing on microfilm all the books listed in the Short Title Catalogue of works printed in England before 1640. The library is acquiring copies as they appear, and will eventually have—albeit on film—a virtually complete set of the early books printed in England. The huge mass of British Parliamentary Papers from 1800 to 1950 is available in Exeter on micro-card; unhappily the quality of reproduction is low and users of this invaluable collection look forward to a more legible edition in due course. Modest provincial libraries will in time offer their readers, thanks to modern technology, collections of material almost as rich, though not as convenient or pleasurable to handle, as the oldest and greatest libraries in the country.

The computer is also contributing to a more effective library service. The universities of western and south-western England were establishing a computer network in the 1960s and Will Simpson, an assistant librarian in Exeter at the time, suggested that the computer's powers could be harnessed to the work of running a library. John Lloyd, though neither a professional librarian nor an engineer by training or taste, readily took up the idea and in 1968 chaired the first meeting of the South-West Academic Libraries Co-operative Automation Project [SWALCAP]. The founding members of SWALCAP were the universities of Bath, Bristol and Exeter and the University of Wales Institute of Science and Technology. A feasibility study supported by the Office of Scientific and Technical Information [OSTI] demonstrated by 1972 that co-operative automation could lead to economies. John Stirling, who succeeded Lloyd as University Librarian in 1972, pushed forward enthusiastically with the project. OSTI made a grant towards the purchase of the first computer (now replaced by a larger one) and by 1976 the first fruits of computerisation began to be harvested. Library routines fall into three categories: the ordering of books; cataloguing; the issue and recall of books. The automation of library routines in Exeter reversed this order and it was book issues that were first computerised with some saving in staff and time. In 1978 the computer began to produce micro-fiches of library accessions updated monthly.[3] The existing catalogue also appeared in micro-fiche, but it was not possible to integrate the old catalogue with the new, and readers therefore have to consult two catalogues — one for works acquired before June 1978, the other for works acquired since. An advantage of the new system is that multiple copies of the catalogues are now available, not only in various parts of the library, but also in other buildings. The old card catalogue survives and, being less in demand, is quicker to use than when it was the sole copy; some old-fashioned readers find it more convenient that micro-fiche, and even members of the library staff have been known to consult it. Only the ordering of books now awaits computerisation. The advantages of automation are widely appreciated by librarians: at the latest count ten academic institutions — from Aberystwyth in the north and Reading in the east to Plymouth in the west — had joined SWALCAP.

Readers have benefited from more conventional improvements in the library service. In the days of the University College, the opening hours of the Roborough Library suggested a world of grace and leisure. Until 1953 the library did not open in the evenings. It continued to close for an hour at lunchtime throughout the 1950s.[4] By 1972 the library was opening in term-time from 9 am to 10 pm five days a week, on Saturday mornings and at periods of peak demand for parts of Sunday. Records of attendance show that enough students made use of these extended hours of opening to justify the considerable expense incurred.

Some important specialised Exeter libraries have recently come under the care of the university library. In 1954 the university college assumed responsibility for the Cathedral Library and the archives of the Dean and Chapter, housed in the Bishop's Palace. The Cathedral Library still possesses a few of the books given to it by the founder Leofric in 1072, including the Exeter Book, the largest extant collection of Anglo-Saxon poems. It is fitting that the University should assume administrative responsibilty for these early traces of higher learning in Exeter. In 1972 the University undertook similar responsibilities for the library of the Devon and Exeter Institution housed in the Close and rich in materials for local history. At relatively small cost the University has helped to preserve these important collections.

Small cost has until recently been the keynote of library administration in Exeter, though at no time in the post-war period has the library been run as cheaply as in 1935–36 when it took only 2.6 per cent of college income. The building of the Roborough and then of the second library increased the rate of expenditure but it normally fluctuated between four and five per cent of total outgoings until 1975. Since then the library has accounted for between five and seven per cent of university spending. Accessions to the library averaged less than 6,000 items a year and it took, in the fifties and early sixties, 13 years to double the stock once it had reached 100,000 items in 1955. Books accumulated more rapidly from the later 1960s, and the next doubling of the bookstock (to 400,000 items) took only nine years. The UGC, alarmed at the rapid filling up of university libraries, floated the idea of the 'self-renewing library', a term which could not unfairly be interpreted as the 'self-destroying library'. Naturally the prospect of disposing of old books almost as fast as new ones arrived, was repellent to librarians and readers alike.

In Exeter plans began to be laid for a new library as early as 1972, but the country's economic difficulties prevented a start on construction until 1979. By then the second library was full and many books had been removed for storage in Gandy Street. The site chosen for the third library lies to the west of Stocker Road, which had to be realigned to make enough space for the massive structure. In the first instance, the UGC made available money for the basement only, but a remarkable act of generosity raised hopes that the completion of the whole library would not be long delayed. In July 1980, the Ruler of Dubai, gratified at Exeter's interest in Arabic studies and at the establishment of the Centre for Arab Gulf Studies, gave the University a magnificent benefaction of £750,000 towards the cost of completing the library. From its earliest days the UGC had taken the view that it preferred to help those who helped themselves; the princely gift from Dubai gave the community an opportunity to reaffirm its faith in the old and salutary adage.

Between 1971 and 1976, while the new library seemed less and less likely to be realised, a third set of buildings was completed. Only one of these, Amory Building, was for teaching purposes, but as it was to house two rapidly growing Faculties—Law and Social Studies—it was the largest on the estate even though it ostensibly contained no lecture rooms.* Soundly but not lavishly built and equipped, Amory Building, named after Lord Amory, Chancellor of the University, soon filled up; so too did the space vacated in Queen's Building and Streatham Court. By 1974, when Amory Building opened, the great majority of the teaching staff of the University had satisfactory offices in which to work and conduct small-group teaching. Ever since the great expansion of student numbers after 1918, there has been a shortage of teaching rooms. The end of that shortage was now in sight.† The other major building

*A survey of accommodation in Exeter satisfied the UGC that it would be unnecessary to provide lecture rooms in Amory Building. But the UGC did permit the inclusion of laboratories for the Department of Geography and a Moot Room for the lawyers. These facilities, as it happens, give the university some much-needed large lecture theatres.

†The wanderings of one member of the teaching staff illustrate the changes in the accommodation available. Appointed as a very junior lecturer in 1954, he first occupied a space partitioned off from the landing on the top floor of the main building in Gandy Street. The 'room', which was about five feet square, just held a desk, a radiator, two chairs and a book-case tailor-made by the college carpenters. After a year, our lecturer was promoted to a genuine room in an army hut, heated by gas and with an outlook onto another hut. Jackson Knight, who occupied the next room, enlivened a large part of the day by chanting the *Aeneid* in a high-pitched sing-song voice and a strong Italian accent. From further down the corridor came the sound of a calculating machine as Wallis Taylor, statistician to the Faculty of Social Studies, wrestled with esoteric sums. From the far end of the hut, madrigals and recorder music could be heard as Harold Mason attuned his students to the study of Elizabethan poetry with a gramophone recital. When Queen's Building opened in 1958, our lecturer moved to a spacious room with a view over the still unspoilt valley of the Exe. Even on a quiet afternoon, so good was the sound insulation, he could scarcely hear his next-door neighbour, a Methodist, singing Lutheran hymns in an impressive basso profundo. From Queen's to Streatham Court marked a sad decline. Our lecturer now commanded a room merely ten feet square, as against the 10' × 16' of Queen's, and his neighbour's slightest remark could be overheard. Our lecturer's latest if not final resting place is Amory Building, several architectural grades higher than Streatham Court, but not quite reaching the standards of Queen's Building, with its colonnade and quadrangle, and wallpaper closing the long corridor vistas.

projects of the years 1971-76 were a second students' union (Cornwall House) and the loan-financed Lafrowda flats. On a smaller scale was the modest shopping centre completed in 1974: this provided a self-service shop run by the University, a bookshop, a bank, a newsagent's, and travel and insurance offices. The university shop stocks the range of goods found in a supermarket. But whereas the average purchase at a supermarket is over £7, the average at the university shop is only 46 pence!

The building record and the growth of student numbers might lead the reader to suppose that the University has had a financially trouble-free voyage through its first 25 years. That would be a misleading impression. The periodic crises that have afflicted the British economy since the war have not left the University unscathed. Every attempt to check the growth of public expenditure during the 'stop' phase of the trade cycle has, temporarily at least, diminished the resources available to the university. For example, in 1962 the government's reluctance to speed the process of university expansion led to 'a growing consciousness of increasing burdens, of mounting difficulties and of deepening frustration'. In 1966-67 a 'new cold wind was blowing' and Exeter had to moderate substantially its hopes for expansion in the quinquennium 1967-72; it was then that the University abandoned its proposals for biochemistry and physical planning and put forward applied science as its principal innovation for the quinquennium. In 1969, when universities were expanding rapidly, the Department of Education and Science took fright at the mounting cost and made tentative suggestions for economy. Several of its ideas—encouraging students to attend their nearest university, deferring university entrance for a year after leaving school, the replacement of maintenance grants by student loans—have been revived from time to time, as yet without much success. Indeed the supply of funds to universities remained generous, despite the government's grumbling, until 1973. By then the Vice-Chancellor, Dr F. J. Llewellyn, had emulated some of his distinguished predecessors and moved on to higher things. In the autumn of 1972 he became Director-General of the British Council after six eventful years in Exeter. There followed a short interregnum during which the Deputy Vice-Chancellor, Professor G. D. Mitchell, stood at the head of affairs. The new Vice-Chancellor, Dr Harry Kay, took up his post in the spring of 1973. A long period of growth was coming to an end, financial difficulties were mounting and student troubles, though perhaps past the worst, were by no means over. It was not the happiest of times to take the helm and Dr Kay can consider himself more than a little unlucky in comparison with his two predecessors. Dr Kay went up to Cambridge in 1938 to read English and psychology; he served in the Royal Artillery during the war and resumed his studies in 1946. After graduation he embarked on research into the problems of ageing and in 1949 was psychologist of the Naval Arctic Expedition. In 1951 he moved to a lectureship in Oxford, and in 1960 to the Chair of Psychology in Sheffield. He was President of the British Psychological Society in 1971–72 and, among other official work, served on both the Social Science Research Council and the Medical Research Council. Future events cast their shadow before when from 1967 to 1971 he served as Pro-Vice-Chancellor of the University of Sheffield. Frank, sensitive, far-sighted, and ambitious for his new university, Dr Kay sought, in difficult times, to maintain its position and to strengthen still further its ties with the local community. The absorption of Saint Luke's in 1978 owed much to his patient determination and his vision of the University's future.

He was responsible, too, for substantial changes in the University's administrative structure. Hitherto, strictly academic matters—secretarial services to Senate and faculty boards, advice to students, the conduct of examinations—had fallen to the academic registrar. Services to Council and its committees, finance and buildings were the responsibility of the secretary. When Alan Bartlett, Academic Registrar, and Roderick Ross, Secretary, retired in 1975, after a quarter of a century of unobtrusively efficient and economical administration, the opportunity occurred for reorganisation under unified command. Kenneth Nash, a deputy under secretary in the Ministry of Defence, was accordingly appointed to the joint post of Academic Registrar and Secretary. The administration was reorganised in six divisions under, respectively, the Deputy Registrar, the Secretary of Faculties, the Finance Officer, the Buildings and Estate Officer, the Director of Domestic Services and the Personnel Officer. Unhappily the Academic Registrar and Secretary died after less than six years in office, but not before establishing the value of the new system, which is to continue.

Change was also taking place in the University's machinery for forward planning. The Academic Development Committee was set up, as its name suggests, to guide the further growth of the University. It began work in 1973 and quickly discovered that its functions were to advise on the allocations of resources that were steadily becoming less rather than more plentiful. For the crisis of 1973, much the most serious since the war, pushed government into a tougher stance towards higher education. Ever since the establishment of the UGC in 1919, universities had enjoyed the privilege of knowing their income for five years at a time; shortly before or after the start of each quinquennial period, they were notified of their income for each year of the quinquennium. This agreeable system broke down in 1973, and universities found themselves budgeting from year to year, often not knowing until half or more of the financial year had passed what their income for the whole year was to be! Such a method of finance made planning difficult and extreme timidity the only prudent course.

Until 1973 the University had enjoyed a long period of slowly rising real income. It is possible to calculate the 'unit of resource' (real income per student) for the period since 1962, when the Committee of Vice-Chancellors and Principals first arranged for the production of the Tress-Brown Index, which measures changes in university costs. On the assumption that the same relationship held between retail prices and university prices in the years 1955–62, as in the years for which the Tress-Brown Index is available, it is possible to calculate Exeter's unit of resource for as far back as 1955. The statistical foundations are a little shaky, but the edifice looks like this:

Unit of resource (index of real income per student)
(1955 = 100; financial years beginning 1 August)

1955	100	1972	150
1965	124	1973	143
1967	131	1974	147
1968	135	1975	141
1969	130	1976	133
1970	138	1977	131
1971	136	1978	122
		1979	128

Nearly half the gains achieved in the seventeen years from 1955 to 1972 were lost in the next seven years and by 1980 real income per student had fallen to 85 per cent of what it had been at its peak in 1972–73. New appointments have been deferred, vacancies often left unfilled, equipment grants have been cut, maintenance put off, and levels of heating and lighting reduced. Staff-student ratios have deteriorated from 1:9.9 in 1972–73 to 1:10.9 in 1979–80.[5] This average conceals wide disparities, with some large and growing departments having a ratio of thirteen or more students per teacher. As a result of its fairly drastic measures of economy, the University has just managed to avoid serious budgetary deficits. Whether the seven lean years have much impaired the University's capacity to function as a seat of learning is unclear. What is certain is that Exeter will become a contracting rather than a 'steady-state' university if, as seems likely, there are further cuts in its real income.

Universities are labour-intensive institutions. About 70 per cent of Exeter's expenditure is on wages and salaries, of which the lion's share goes to the salaries of the academic and administrative staff. Had the incomes of these relatively highly paid groups kept pace with the cost of living, the financial predicament of the University would have been even worse. Luckily for the University, if not for its teachers and administrators, national pay policy and low demand for the services of university lecturers have combined to depress real incomes in the profession. While universities were growing fast and inflation remained below ten per cent per year, the rewards of university teaching were not to be despised. After 1972 a sharp fall in living standards occurred, partly because of the preferences for flat-rate pay increases under successive pay policies. By 1976 lecturers at the top of the scale had seen their real incomes drop by almost a sixth since 1972, and for professors the drop was as much as a fifth. Real incomes have recovered slightly from this low point, but remain, except at the bottom of the lecturer scale, more than ten per cent below the levels of 1972.* The declining fortunes of most members of the academic staff severely strained their devotion to the professional ideal of service without much thought of reward. In the spring of 1975, when a high rate of inflation was rapidly eroding the value of money, the members of the Exeter branch of the Association of University Teachers [AUT] rejected a proposal for a one-day strike, but agreed to withhold examination results until a satisfactory pay settlement had been achieved. Even Senate, probably acting *ultra vires*, acquiesced in the threat to withhold examination results.[6]

National arbitration quickly followed and with the prospect of a satisfactory settlement there was in the end no delay in the examination process. However, by a piece of administrative sharp practice, the

*Roughly speaking, in 1980 the lecturer at the bottom of the scale earned the average industrial wage in Britain (in 1972, he earned six per cent less than the average industrial wage); the lecturer at the top of the scale earned less than twice and the average professor less than three times as much. In 1972 the professor earned three and a half times, and the best-paid lecturer 2.3 times as much as the average industrial worker.

Department of Education and Science successfully held up the implementation of part II of the arbitration award until a stiff dose of pay policy had been prepared by the Government. Instead of the substantial sums to which it had a rightful claim, the profession received the national maximum rise of £6 per week. This episode soured relations between university teachers and the DES for several years. The Government blandly confessed that an injustice had been done, but took no adequate remedial steps until the exasperated profession again threatened industrial action in 1978. It then agreed to make belated amends for the injustice of 1975 in two instalments payable in 1978 and 1979, though the payments were not backdated and did not fully compensate for the award withheld in 1975. As a result of recent experience, the profession is suspicious of government, resentful at the erosion of real income and willing to consider taking industrial action — a course that would have provoked shocked surprise in most of its members less than a generation ago. The AUT remains far from militant, but, in common with other teachers' unions, is inclined to abandon the meek and gentlemanly ways of the past. Its Exeter members are, perhaps not unexpectedly, more moderate than their colleagues in some northern and Scottish universities, but even in Exeter respect for the professional ideal has weakened in recent years. Equality with humbler members of the community has come too close for comfort.

Notes

1 From an address given in 1956 [Archives of the University Library, on which this whole section is based]
2 Larkin to Lloyd, 26 January 1960.
3 J. F. Stirling, 'SWALCAP: some political problems of a British Co-operative Library Project' (*Libri*, 1977, vol.27 no.1, pp.84–93)
4 Guide to the Roborough Library, n.d. but between 1955 and 1959.
5 *Annual Reports*; the Tress-Brown Index is not published, but the CVCP sends universities half-yearly reports on movements in the index. The index (July 1966 = 100) stood at 78.6 in October 1962, the first date for which it is available. It reached 148.4 in July 1972, 299.7 in July 1977 and 495.2 in November 1980.
6 Senate, 21 May 1975.

XIII

THE UNIVERSITY OF EXETER
AND THE COMMUNITY

The move from the centre of Exeter to the Streatham estate, north of the city, has not turned the University into an ivory tower. At the personal, the economic, and the cultural level, the University and its members remain inextricably bound up with the local community. They have interested themselves in the life of Exeter and its region in a multitude of ways. They have provided city councillors, magistrates, presidents of the Devonshire Association, governors of local schools and representatives on many other bodies. At a more informal level, members of staff, whether academic, administrative, clerical or manual, play their full part in the range of activities that make up a modern community. They belong to churches, political parties, musical, dramatic and civic societies and follow pursuits extending from rugby football through rifle shooting and industrial archaeology to chess. The list could be lengthened more or less indefinitely. On the evidence available, it would appear that the university's staff is quite as active as the average Englishman in the life of his local community.

In its turn the university attracts as well as gives a good deal of voluntary service. It is natural that former students should band together in the Exeter University Club and through Convocation in order to keep in touch with their alma mater and to promote its welfare. Exeter does not make the elaborate efforts of some universities, especially in the United States, to compile lists of alumni with a view to appeals to generosity. In the days of the University College, when most former students became schoolteachers, an appeal for funds could not have raised a lot of money. Now that there are more former students in a wide range of often well-paid jobs, an appeal might have brighter prospects. It is not only former students who take an interest in the University. Men and women from all over Devon and Cornwall have long been willing to serve it in many ways. The Council of the University, as of the college before it, has a majority of lay members. A few are graduates of the University or were students of the College but most of them, from the late Lord Amory the Chancellor downward, have served, often for many years and in some families for three generations, out of a sense of public duty to a local institution.

The impact of the University on the economy of Exeter and its region is considerable. If a university may be regarded as an army at war with darkness and dedicated to extending the frontiers of knowledge, then the academic staff are its front-line soldiers. They tend also, even after recent setbacks, to be its best-paid employees. But the economic impact of the University by no means ends with the academic staff. As in any modern army, the front-line soldier is kept at his post only with the support of a host of ancillary workers—administrators, librarians, technicians, clerks, secretaries, groundsmen, cooks and cleaners, maintenance staff and porters. The ancillary workers outnumber the academic staff by nearly three to one; some are highly qualified and well paid; others (including large numbers of women) earn small wages. In short, the University gives employment to many grades of service worker in the Exeter district. It has on its pay-roll nearly 2,000 people, over three per cent of the occupied labour force of the Exeter employment exchange area. In common with other large employers, the University has restricted its demand for labour since the early 1970s and the enforced measures of economy and the shift of emphasis from halls of residence to flats have combined to keep down the rate of growth of its labour force. While student numbers have been rising by 47 per cent from 3400 in 1970 to 5000 in 1980, the number of employees has risen by only 13 per cent. In the early 1970s the University was also spending heavily on capital account and gave employment to large numbers of workers in the building trades, most of whom were recruited locally. With large-scale building, except on the new library, now at an end, local building contractors have to look elsewhere for most of their business.[1]

Besides helping Exeter to earn its bread and butter, the University adds a cultural spice to the city's life. The students enliven the town for a week in February with their boisterous Rag which is enjoyable to the often scantily clad participants and it is to be hoped to the citizens of Exeter as well. The Rag has its serious side—large sums of money are raised for local and other charities. The students also have a more regular commitment to welfare work in the city through 'Community Action'. This is an organisation that helps old people, handicapped children, patients in hospital and other good causes; in 1980 it was running, or helping to run, 35 projects in and around Exeter.

On the sports field, students naturally play with other students more than with local sportsmen and in the past decade Exeter's prestige as a sporting university has markedly risen. Successes in cricket, hockey, tennis and basketball are among the most notable of recent years. Success on the rugby field against the old enemy Saint Luke's has been more elusive. One of the benefits that has already accrued from the merger with Saint Luke's has been the emergence of a powerful rugby XV: 'If you can't beat 'em, join 'em.' By contrast with the students, the staff tend to play only against local teams. Two staff cricket clubs have flourished: the Erratics and the Nomads. The Erratics, composed of academic members of staff, have been playing cricket for over 50 years — when they can raise a team. When the college was small, that was not always easy. In 1930 a Cullompton collector for the college appeal found she had an uphill task: 'Many of the families on whom she called are keen cricketers and the name of our team is mud here owing to its unsporting way of scratching at the eleventh hour for no reason.'[2] The Erratics have never taken themselves seriously enough to enter a league; for many years they helped to raise the morale of Devon village cricketers by submitting cheerfully and often to defeat. A scrutiny of the club's scorebooks, carefully preserved in the inmost recesses of the university library, shows that even the Erratics were not without their moments of triumph. In 1939, for example, they scored 77 against Willand and then bowled out the home team for 39 with L. J. Lloyd taking 7 for 21 in 8 overs. The first match played after the Second World War was against the College first XI: the Erratics began promisingly — Lloyd dismissed the College number one (happily named Wisden) for 2, and bowled his partner for a duck; but the college made 95 all out and won by 30 runs. The staff of Saint Luke's proved even more formidable opponents. They scored 106, and then dismissed the Erratics for 29, the highest scorer being 'extras' with 10. In recent years as numbers have grown the quality of the cricket has improved, but it is still played in the same friendly and sporting spirit. The Nomads have a shorter but similar history. Founded in 1965 under the benevolent eye of Roderick Ross, Secretary to the University and himself an occasional cricketer, the Nomads originally intended to complement the Erratics by providing cricket for the non-academic staff. However, they have, in the course of time, ceased to be so exclusive and now welcome players from all ranks of university society. Like the Erratics, they play friendlies and do not enter a league; like them too they are cheerful losers and ambassadors of goodwill, though they are not above winning if opportunity knocks. In 1979, for example, they won ten and lost eleven matches.

Not all of the University's ample grounds are devoted to sports fields. With the acquisition of Reed Hall in 1922, the college became custodian of a valuable arboretum containing many rare and beautiful trees. With the development of the Streatham Estate and the abandonment of market-gardening by the University, more and more of the estate grounds have been laid out as ornamental gardens. Sir William Holford, as planning consultant to the University, was eager to take advantage of the opportunities for landscape gardening that the site offered. He enlisted the services of the distinguished landscape architect Dame Sylvia Crowe, who has advised on much of the tree-planting in the Hoopern Valley and around Lafrowda. The Plantation that lies north of the car park on Stocker Road is now a beautiful little woodland park. Until the end of the war it was a self-sown ticket. Larch and sitka spruce were they planted but little more was done until the harsh winter of 1962–63, when the gardeners, having little else to do, spent their afternoons thinning the trees in the Plantation. A woodland path of pine needles was laid down (more recently it has had to be metalled). When the weather improved, exotics were planted—eucalyptus from Australia, trees from Chile, camellias, rhododendrons and hydrangea. Responsibility for this work lay with Mr A. G. (Alf) Crouch*, who was appointed Superintendent of Grounds (a new post) in 1960. Much of the credit for the imaginative layout of the grounds and for the varied and well-chosen trees, shrubs and flowers that gathered round new buildings almost as soon as the contractors had departed, must go to his learned and enthusiastic practice of the gardener's art. Unhappily, nature has dealt harshly with the gardens in the last few years. Dutch elm disease first appeared on the estate in 1973 and more than 4,000 trees have since been felled, leaving some sad gaps. The drought of 1976, the snow of February 1978 and the severe winter of 1978–79 did much damage particularly among conifers and shallow-rooted and exotic plants.[3] But the labours of the gardeners have gone far to make good the losses and the University gardens are

*HonMSc (Exon), 1981.

widely recognised as one of the great gardens in a country rich in great gardens.[4] These delights the University gladly shares with all—and they are many—who care to visit them.

Another art assiduously cultivated for the general enjoyment is the performance of music. When numbers were much smaller, the University's patronage was limited. In 1954–55, the newly-appointed music committee promoted its first series of chamber concerts. For many years there were only four concerts a year but even so, some outstanding musicians came to Exeter at its invitation—Franz Rostal, the Trio di Trieste, and the Amadeus String Quartet, less well-known then (and less expensive) than it has since become. In addition, in the 1950s the student musical society performed once a year. Twenty years later the musical fare was much more varied. In the Lent Term 1974, for example, the Bournemouth Symphony Orchestra gave three concerts in the Great Hall and the Bournemouth Sinfonietta two; the Dartington String Quartet gave four lunch-time recitals (eight in the academic year, as they did regularly from 1968–1980), Craig Sheppard, the Nash Ensemble, the Ulysses Ensemble and the King's Singers, all gave evening recitals. The university's various musical groups—singers, chamber orchestras and others—put on no fewer than seven concerts, large or small. The Gilbert and Sullivan Society performed *Trial by Jury* and *The Sorcerer*, and the Opera Society *Cosi Fan Tutte*, both in the Northcott Theatre. The concerts by the Bornemouth orchestras, though given in the Great Hall, came under the auspices of the Western Orchestral Concerts Society, not the University, but it is unlikely that so many symphony concerts would have been given in Exeter without the Great Hall or the support of large numbers of students and staff. That Lent Term of 1974 was in no way exceptional.

Extra-mural work is as old as the College itself. It was one of the principal objects of the Exeter Technical and University Extension College from which the University is descended. For more than twenty years, extra-mural teaching had no specialist staff of its own but was carried out by men like Principal Clayden as a normal part of their duties. At the end of the First World War the College began to make deliberate provision for extra-mural work by appointing R. Peers and, when he left in 1920, E. J. Patterson as lecturers primarily for extra-mural teaching. In 1923 Patterson became the first head of the extra-mural department that was then established.[5] Resident tutors were thin on the ground in the early years. From 1924 to 1928 the young Cornish historian Charles Henderson spent the winter months conducting classes in Cornwall, but when he died his post remained vacant until F. L. Harris was appointed in 1936. Other tutors, appointed in the years before the Second World War, taught current affairs, or, in a joint venture with Dartington Hall Trust, undertook extension work in music and drama. None of these ventures proceeded entirely smoothly. The pugnacious principal of the College, John Murray, did not share the Labour sympathies of the Workers' Educational Association with which the College had to co-operate in some of the courses it offered. Nor did he wish to spend more college money than could be helped on the work in music and drama. There were also demarcation disputes with the University of Cambridge, which had a long connection with extra-mural work in Bideford. Murray, while acknowledging Exeter's debt to Cambridge, nevertheless asserted that all Devon fell within Exeter's sphere of influence.[6]

After the Second World War, extra-mural work rapidly expanded. By 1954 there were ten full-time tutors active in the field. H. G. Sellon, formerly Director of the British Institute in Paris, headed the Department and was also Professor of International Politics. Since the mid-1950s, the staff of the department has not expanded, but the number of classes has increased, thanks to the recruitment of occasional lecturers, many of them senior members of the University. It cannot be pretended that the general public is interested in studying the whole range of subjects professed in the University: ecology and geology, philosophy and psychology, local history and archaeology, language, literature and music are the subjects most in demand. The number of three-year tutorial classes, at which subjects may be studied in depth, has never been a large proportion of the whole and most classes last one or two terms. Recent financial stringency has obliged the Department to offer more short courses in order to give the many centres in Devon and Cornwall a fair share of the available money and manpower. The demand remains strong and extra-mural work continues to bear witness to the University's educational ideals and its cultural role in the community.

Not all the paths along which the College and University once promised to move are as well-trodden as that to adult education. The federal idea prominent in the days of Clayden and Hetherington has faded from memory: the absorption of Saint Luke's in 1978 may have unified higher education within the city of Exeter but not on federal terms. And the links with Plymouth, Camborne and Seale-Hayne have long been broken. The ideal of residence so dear to Principal Murray does not command much loyalty today. Over half the students still live in accommodation provided by the University but the style and tone of the large modern hall and of the Lafrowda flats bear little relation to Murray's conception of hall life. Undergraduate scholarships are obsolete in a world of mandatory grants to needy students; in any case there are not many needy students in the present University. It would, however, be wrong to dismiss these past policies as unimportant simply because they matter less today. Federalism, residence, the educational ladder deserve to be remembered for their important and necessary contribution to the past life of the College and University.

Though Exeter now puts less emphasis on some of its traditions, it has been faithful to others. The early theme of the two-faculty college — arts and pure science — has been elaborated somewhat, but is still plainly recognisable. When the Charter was granted, as in the 1930s, Exeter was one of the smallest university institutions, having little more than one per cent of the total student population. Rapid growth since 1955 gives the University a higher ranking today, for Exeter now has 5,000 students out of a total of some 300,000. Nevertheless, Exeter remains somewhat below the mean size for a British university. It has remained smaller than Reading, Nottingham and Southampton, the institutions with which it liked to compare itself in the inter-war years. On the other hand, it has kept ahead of most universities that have sprung up in the last twenty years, whether new creations like York and Warwick, or former colleges of advanced technology like Bradford and Surrey. Ranked by size, Exeter is close to being the median university.

Size and antiquity confer prestige. A former Vice-Chancellor once looked forward in visionary mood to the time when Exeter would have on its staff four or five Nobel Laureates.[7] Such distinction will not come quickly and it would be unrealistic to expect that Exeter can rival in the near future the prestige of older and larger universities like Manchester and Birmingham, still less the ancient universities of Oxford and Cambridge. There will always be a temptation for the most distinguished scholars to gravitate to Oxford, Cambridge or London, or at the very least to compete for provincial chairs once held by a Blackett or a Tout. It is rare for a scholar of the highest distinction to stay in a relatively small provincial university for the whole of his working life. Sir Frank Stenton, the historian of Anglo-Saxon and Norman England was exceptional in spending forty years in Reading as lecturer, professor and vice-chancellor. For a new university, Exeter has had its fair share of men of distinction. Without mentioning the names of those still in post it is possible to compile a list of scholars of considerable eminence who have worked in Exeter within the past thirty years. Walter Hayman FRS published, while he was reader in analysis in Exeter, papers that excited the admiration of the whole mathematical world. Geoffrey Ainsworth, a mycologist of international reputation, taught in Exeter from 1949 to 1957. H. N. Rydon, who succeeded H. T. S. Britton in the chair of chemistry, published many important papers on poly-peptides. In the Faculty of Arts, scholars of distinction have thown light on subjects as diverse as the Norman church (Frank Barlow, FBA) the poetry of Chaucer (John Speirs) and the Enlightenment in France (Robert Niklaus) and in Germany (H. B. Garland).* In Social Studies A. H. Birch, well-known for his work on British government, held the Chair of Political Science from 1970 to 1977. Few members of the academic staff expect their fame to spread far and wide, but many contribute to the literature of their subject. It would be presumptuous in a mere historian to pronounce on the worth of the long list of publications recorded in the university's annual reports. His task is to observe that nearly half the members of the academic staff publish something each year. That does not necessarily mean that in three years everyone will have published a paper or an article or a book; but it is a fair inference that the great majority of the staff are alert and active in the cause of learning.

They also have opportunities to promote research through the supervision of postgraduate students. When Principal Murray took soundings about a charter in 1947, the UGC remarked adversely on the small number of research students in the college. There were only 13 in all, most of them chemists. By 1955, when the application for a charter was successfully renewed, the number had multiplied fourfold and represented six per cent of the full-time students. Since then the proportion of students seeking a higher degree has risen a little further.† In the year 1954–55 such students were still to be found mostly in science —only ten out of 53 research students were in arts or social studies. Since 1955, there has been some change in the nature of higher-degree work.

*The University has conferred honorary degrees on all these scholars except John Speirs, who died early in 1979 before he could receive his DLitt.
† In addition there are similar numbers of postgraduate students who are working for a BPhil (in social work, or education), a diploma (in social work, statistics or education) or for a certificate in education.

Then it invariably took the form of a dissertation for a master's degree, or of a thesis for a doctorate, and required original research. More recently, the University has also offered taught courses leading to a master's degree and nowadays nearly as many students take a higher degree by examination as by thesis or dissertation. In science the number of postgraduates went on rising until the late sixties, when it levelled off. In other faculties growth continued throughout the seventies until postgraduate students were as likely to be found in education or English or politics, as in chemistry or physics. Science following a long tradition, maintained its predominance in research: in the academic year 1978–79, for example, 36 out of 55 doctorates awarded to students were for research in pure or applied science. A master's degree by dissertation, rare in science, was taken by 23 candidates in other faculties.[8] However, as students and their supervisors find all the world over, it is easier to start a piece of research than to finish it. It would therefore be wrong to suppose that the amount of research undertaken by students can be fairly delimited by the number of doctorates and master's degrees awarded in any two- or three-year period—large though that number now is.

Exeter has had some men of distinction and more of solid worth. It has also had not a few characters. Jackson Knight, the classical scholar who did not disdain the help of the supernatural in his quest for Vergil and whose unaffected and good-natured interest in his students and colleagues justly gave him the reputation of a genius for friendship. L. J. (John) Lloyd, University Librarian, connoisseur of many arts— painting, the violin, fine books, cricket, the cinema; he could never bring himself to think ill of a film—at worst it was 'good of its kind'. Julian Hawes, a zoologist who, though he had come up the hard way, was a dandy and a professed but unconvincing snob; on doctor's orders he avoided drink for many years, but heroically kept a generous supply for his friends; his conversation ranged freely from dinosaurs to Dr Johnson and his *Introduction to the Study of Protozoa* was as much a work of art as of science. Professor H. T. S. Britton, whose devotion to chemistry reminded Dean Carpenter of the old sailor who was allowed three wishes by his fairy godmother. Without any hesitation he asked for 'all the beer in the world, all the 'baccy in the world and all the women in the world'. Given a fourth wish, he paused for a moment and asked for 'a little more beer'. Chemistry was to Britton, thought the Dean, as beer to the sailor. There is plenty of character among the living, too. The student of the Enlightenment, a philosophe who dresses like a Jesuit in a huge black opera hat and a black coat and like the popular idea of a Jesuit, appears to be engaged in perpetual conspiracy; however, his generosity is such that he can never keep a secret to himself but always shares it with another. The classical scholar, whose mind is so quick and full of matter that it is hard for the listener to keep up with his darting thoughts; whatever the subject of conversation, he knows something of it, often as much as the supposed expert; to such a man *The Times* crossword is a diversion of some five minutes. The Hispanist, otherwise friendly, who has no front passenger seat in his motor car. The historian, whose library is arranged on no discernible principle, but who, to the exasperation of the methodical, can always find a book when he wants it.

Mild eccentricity has always been an agreeable part of the academic scene. In this respect, as in many others, Exeter represents much that is typical of English universities. And if it is not so very different from its fellows, that may well be matter for congratulation rather than regret. From its earliest years as a day training college, Exeter attached importance to the residential principle; others did so too, although only a few provincial universities and colleges—Durham, Reading, Nottingham and Southampton—succeeded as well as Exeter in carrying the principle into effect. The habit of small-group teaching is much prized in Exeter; that too is a tradition shared with other English universities, which have shunned the large classes and the impersonality of the great continental universities. Nor is Exeter alone in the enjoyment of a spacious university park in which to build its laboratories and libraries, its lecture rooms and halls of residence. It would, however, take modesty too far to liken the Streatham estate to university campuses elsewhere in England and Wales. What other university enjoys such a splendid setting? A silver jubilee, which is conventionally a time for stock-taking, is not long in the prospective life of a university, and the historian is not the man, nor a silver jubilee the time, for final judgements. The future is uncertain, but the University of Exeter can face it with some confidence, knowing that the men of this and earlier generations have built solidly and well and are handing on a valuable inheritance.

Notes

1 For a fuller analysis of the university's place in the economy of Exeter, see F. M. M. Lewes and A. Kirkness, *Exeter — University and City* (University of Exeter 1973).

2 PPE, file 20. Or as Professor L. A. Harvey put it: 'For years there were never enough cricketers on the staff to ensure a regular turnout and we lived up to our name with a vengeance . . .'. (L. A. Harvey to R. B. Behenna, 17 February 1970 on the occasion of the retirement of L. J. [John] Lloyd from the captaincy (University Library MSS).

3 A. G. Crouch 'The Plantation' (*University of Exeter Newsletter* No.78, November–December 1977); 'Twenty years of the estate' (*Staff Forum*, No.7, June 1979).

4 A. G. L. Hellyer, *The Shell Book of Gardens*.

5 Letterbook, December 1918; *Calendar 1920–21*; *Annual Reports* 1922–23, 1923–24. Patterson left in 1938 to become Principal of Ashridge College.

6 PPD, files 2, 3, 5.

7 Dr F. J. [now Sir John] Llewellyn in *The South Westerner*, 28 October 1965.

8 *Annual Reports.*

A NOTE ON SOURCES

This note is not intended as an exhaustive bibliography for the history of the University of Exeter and its precursors, but as a list of the published and unpublished materials that have proved of most value in the preparation of this book.

UNPUBLISHED SOURCES

A Devon Record Office
Archives of the Albert Memorial, later the Royal Albert Memorial
1 Principal records
   (i)   Committee Minutes, 1870–1892 (3 vols).
   (ii) Museum and Technical Education Committee, 1892–1899 (1 vol).
   (iii) Governors of the Royal Albert Memorial, Minutes and Reports, 1900–1931 (4 vols) (including the minutes of the College Committee until 1909).
2 Subsidiary records
   (i)   Finance Sub-Committee, 1878–1886.
   (ii)   Building Committee, 1882–1885.
   (iii) Museum Library and Fine Arts Committee, 1902–1939.
   (iv)   RAM College, letterbook, 1899–1903.
   (v)   UCSW, Library Committee, 1920–1933.
   (vi)   City Librarian, three reports on financial and other relations between the UCSW and Exeter City Library.
   (vii) RAM College, cashbooks, 1904–1923 (3 vols).
   (viii) Hostel accounts, 1906–1922.
   (ix)   Exeter School of Art, Treasurer's account book, 1854–1894.
   (x)   Schools of Art and Science, Sub-Committee minutes, 1870–1894 (3 vols).

B University of Exeter

The University has no archivist and no one place in which its records are kept. Departments keep some records; the Library holds some unpublished material (besides many official university publications); and the archives proper are housed partly in the university strong room and partly in the adjacent storeroom for stationery. These two depositories are referred to below, somewhat flatteringly, as the muniment room. Some pre-1922 records luckily survive because they were being stored in the York wing of the Museum when the Registry was destroyed in the air raids of 1942.

I Muniment Room

1 Records mostly relating to the period 1855–1922.
   (i)   Schools of Art and Science, attendance registers, 1855 onwards.
   (ii)   Albert Memorial, Finance Committee minutes, 1870–1877 (in the same series as A2(i) above in DRO).
   (iii) wages book, 1878–1912.
   (iv)   university extension minute book, 1886–1888.
   (v)   miscellaneous account books, 1893–1905.
   (vi)   letterbooks, 1888–1919 (18 vols).
   (vii) hostel ledgers and other account books.

2 Records mostly relating to the University College and the University.
   (i)   Principals' Papers 1920–1951. Contained in eight cardboard boxes lettered A–G and referred to in this work as PPA etc. When these records came to light, only prompt action by Mr R. A. Erskine, Assistant (now Deputy) Registrar, secured them from destruction. Without the Principals' Papers the sources for the history of the university college would be meagre indeed.
   (ii)   W. H. Lewis papers: a small but important collection, chiefly valuable for the light thrown on the years 1917–20.
   (iii) A. E. Morgan Mss: A. E. Morgan's memories of the University Furtherance Committee, set down in extreme old age in 1970.
   (iv)   Registrar's files: several large boxes containing material for the period 1944–1951.
   (v)   Minutes of Council, Senate and their committees, bound, 1947 to the present. This majestic series of volumes marks the beginning of a systematic archive of the formal records of the college and university. The minutes up to 1942 were destroyed

with the Registry and all that remains is a broken set for the years 1936–1941.

II University Library

1 Rare Books Room
   (i)   Student Representative Council and Guild of Students, minutes, 1909–1969.
   (ii) H. T. S. Britton papers.
   (iii) W. F. Jackson Knight papers.
2 Librarian's room
   (i)   Material relating to the Library.
   (ii) A little material relating to the general history of the University.

C Public Record Office, Kew, London

1 University Grants Committee
   (i)   UGC 1 Minutes of meetings.
   (ii) UGC 2 Agenda and supporting papers.
   (iii) UGC 5 Memoranda by universities prior to visitation.
2 Board of Education
   (i)   Ed 24/1946 has some valuable material for 1914–1927.
   (ii) Ed 119/17 and 18 has material on the years 1917–18 and 1934.

D Cambridge University Library

Board of Extra-Mural Studies
   (i)   BEMS 3 Moulton papers.
   (ii) BEMS 12 (letterbooks).
   (iii) BEMS 22 reports of the local lectures syndicate.
   (iv) BEMS 31 material relating to Exeter.

PUBLISHED SOURCES

1 *Calendar*: first published 1893. Only odd volumes survive in the muniment room, among the librarian's papers and in the Westcountry Studies Library (Devon County Council) for the years before 1950. Complete sets are available in the University Library from 1950.
2 *Prospectus*: a broken set exists 1914–1948 in the muniment room; the Deputy Registrar holds an almost complete set for period since 1922.
3 *Annual Reports*: of the Albert Memorial including the Schools of Art and Science survive for the years 1872–93 in the muniment room; some of reports of the College 1893–1909 are to be found in the papers of the (Royal) Albert Memorial — see above; the Library and the Deputy Registrar have almost complete sets for the University College

and the University. None were published for the years 1939–47.
4 *College and University Lists*: first published in 1928; almost complete sets survive in the muniment room. *The Exeter University Register 1893–1962* lists so far as possible the names of officers, officials, staff and students. The largest gap is that no lists survive of students who took the Board of Education (two-year) teacher's certificate 1901–1929.
5 *Gazette*: the College began to publish a Gazette in 1953. The University of Exeter *Gazette* first appeared in December 1955. There is a set in the University Library.
6 *Newsletter*: first published 1968.
7 Student journalism: the University Library has a fairly complete set of *The Students' Magazine* and its successor *The Ram* (1898–1939). The archives of the University of Cambridge (University Library MSS BEMS 31/10) have eight of the first eleven numbers (1898–1902). *The South Westerner*, published fortnightly since 1937, is represented in the University Library by a broken set from 1949.
8 UGC: since its inception in 1919, the UGC has published valuable quinquennial surveys of university development. Recently the committee has also produced an annual survey.
9 DES, *Statistics of Education*: published annually since 1966. Vol 6 has statistics of universities.

APPENDIX I

SOME OFFICERS AND OFFICIALS OF
THE COLLEGE AND THE UNIVERSITY

President of the University College of the South West of England
HRH The Prince of Wales, 1922–36
Lord Roborough (Sir Henry Lopes), 1936–38
The Marquess of Salisbury (Viscount Cranborne), 1945–55

Chancellor of the University of Exeter
The Dowager Duchess of Devonshire, 1955–71
The Viscount Amory, 1972–81

Deputy President of the University College of the South West of England
Sir Henry Lopes, 1922–36
Sir William Munday, 1939–48
B. G. Lampard-Vachell, 1948–55

Pro-Chancellor of the University of Exeter
B. G. Lampard-Vachell, 1955–65
The Viscount Amory, 1966–72
K. C. H. Rowe, 1972–

Treasurer of the University College of the South West of England
Sir James Owen, 1922–24
J. G. S. Davis, 1924–25
Sir Ian Amory, 1926–31
Sir Francis Acland, 1931–32
Sir Alfred Goodson, 1932–35
V. Thompson, 1935–36

D. H. Amory (Viscount Amory), 1936–43
P. F. Rowsell, 1943–46
B. G. Lampard-Vachell, 1946–55

Treasurer of the University of Exeter
R. W. Turner, 1955–79
P. J. Chalk, 1979–

Principal
A. W. Clayden, 1893–1920
H. J. W. Hetherington, 1920–24
W. H. Moberly, 1925–26
John Murray, 1926–51
Sir Thomas Taylor, 1952–53
J. W. Cook, 1954–55

Vice-Chancellor of the University of Exeter
J. W. Cook, 1955–66
F. J. Llewellyn, 1966–72
H. Kay, 1973–

Registrar
A. K. Woodbridge, 1904–47
Sir Alexander Campbell, 1947–52
R. Ross, 1952–75 (title changed to 'Secretary' in 1954)

Academic Registrar
G. V. M. Heap, 1947–9
A. G. Bartlett, 1950–75 (title changed from 'Academic Secretary' in 1954).

Academic Registrar and Secretary
K. T. Nash, 1975–81

Librarian
H. Tapley-Soper, 1904–33
Miss K. E. Perrin (Mrs Allison) 1933–46 (Assistant Librarian, 1933–5;
    Acting Librarian, 1935–46)
L. J. Lloyd, 1946–72
J. F. Stirling, 1972–

APPENDIX II

NOTES ON THE BUILDINGS OF
THE UNIVERSITY OF EXETER

(The dates given are of aquisition (A) or of completion (C).)

1906A College Hostel. Renamed Bradninch Hall after Bradninch House in Bradninch Place, which served from 1903-6 as an annexe to the hostel.

1911C Main building, Gandy Street.

1915A Hartwell House. Renamed Hope Hall in 1924 after Miss Hope of Bath, whose legacy to Miss C. M. de Reyes was used to extend the hall.

1922A Streatham Hall named after the former home of the Thornton West family. Renamed Reed Hall after Mr W. H. Reed.

1929A Lopes Hall, formerly Highlands. Extension completed in 1933 allowing the sale of Bradninch Hall. Lopes Hall named after Sir Henry Lopes, Deputy President and generous benefactor of the College.

1929A Kilmorie Hall. Named after one of the houses acquired by the College at the time. Renamed Exeter Hall in 1939 as a compliment to the city of Exeter.

1931C Washington Singer Laboratories. Mr Washington Singer gave £25,000 towards the cost of the laboratories.

1933C Mardon Hall, named after E. J. Mardon who gave £25,000 towards the cost of building the hall.

1935A Thomas Hall, formerly Great Duryard. Named after C. V. Thomas whose gift paid for the property.

1940C Roborough Library, named after Lord Roborough (d 1938) formerly Sir Henry Lopes.

1942A   Ibsley House, renamed Montefiore Annexe (to Hope Hall) after Mrs Sebag-Montefiore.

1944A   Crossmead

1945A   Thornlea. Once the home of Mr W. H. Reed.

1946A   Homefield, renamed Lazenby Annexe (to Hope Hall) after Miss K. M. Lazenby, a benefactress of the College.

1946A   Duryard House, from which the Duryard Halls take their name.

1946A   Birks Grange, from which the Birks Halls take their name.

1948A   Barton Place

1949A   St German's House

1949A   Knightley

1952C   Hatherly Laboratories. Built partly with a bequest from Mrs Heath, whose maiden name was Hatherly.

1954C   Taylor (Sports) Pavilion. Named after Sir Thomas Taylor, Principal of the College, 1952–3.

1954C   Clayden. Residence of Sir James Cook. Named after Principal Clayden.

1958C   Queen's Building. HM the Queen unveiled the foundation stone in 1956.

1960C   Northcote House, named after Sir Stafford Northcote, first Earl Iddesleigh.

1960C   Devonshire House and refectory. Devonshire House is so named after Mary, Dowager Duchess of Devonshire, first Chancellor of the University.

1961A   Cumbre. Formerly the house of Sir Arthur, son of W. H. Reed, and like his father a member of Council and a generous benefactor.

1962A   Hoopern House.

1963C   Murray House and Hetherington House

1964C   Jessie Montgomery House

1964C   The Great Hall

1965A   Higher Hoopern Farm

1965C   Chemistry Building

1965C   Newman Building after F. H. Newman, Professor of Physics 1923–52 and Acting Principal, 1951–2.

1965C   The University Library (second library).

1966A   Redcot. The Vice-Chancellor's residence.

1966C   Moberly House

1966C   Brendon, Haldon and Raddon (The Birks Halls), named after Devon hills.

1966–7C Physics Building. The tower was not finished until 1967.

1967C Mathematics-Geology Building. The geology part of the building was finished in 1966.

1967C Ransom Pickard annexe to Lopes Hall after Col. Ransom Pickard, a benefactor.

1967C Northcott Theatre after Mr G. V. Northcott, who gave most of the money for the building of the theatre.

1967C Sports Hall

1967C Streatham Court

1968C Applied Science Building

1971C Cornwall House

1971C Lafrowda flats I. The flats were built in the grounds of Lafrowda, which the University acquired in 1965.

1974C Amory Building, after Lord Amory, Chancellor of the University.

1974C Shopping Centre

1975–6C Lafrowda flats II

1978A Saint Luke's. Formerly Saint Luke's College. The earliest building on the site dates from 1855.

APPENDIX III

SOME UNIVERSITY ROADS

Perry Road and Stocker Road named in 1932 after Mr E. C. Perry and Ald. John Stocker, the longest-serving members of the Council, and of its predecessor College Committee. Stocker Road was not metalled until 1957.

Rennes Drive celebrates the jumelage with the University of Rennes. The agreement for a jumelage was signed in 1955 shortly after Exeter received its charter.

Streatham Drive is the former carriage-way of Streatham Hall.

Prince of Wales Road was built by Exeter City Council and formally opened by the Prince of Wales in 1927.

APPENDIX IV

NUMBERS OF STUDENTS
1922–1980[1]

1922	318	1942	517	1962	1734
1923	309	1943	348[2]	1963	1855
1924	332	1944	355	1964	2138
1925	329	1945	577	1965	2373
1926	326	1946	686	1966	2695
1927	334	1947	830	1967	2953
1928	359	1948	962	1968	3056
1929	437	1949	993	1969	3279
1930	505	1950	942	1970	3387
1931	473	1951	945	1971	3562
1932	444	1952	980	1972	3541
1933	419	1953	932	1973	3656
1934	372	1954	889	1974	3842
1935	395	1955	994	1975	4177
1936	422	1956	1054	1976	4278
1937	421	1957	1189	1977	4367
1938	422	1958	1232	1978	5035[3]
1939	453	1959	1282	1979	5103
1940	590	1960	1410	1980	5173
1941	612	1961	1559		

Notes

1 For the years 1922–37 and for 1947 and after, the figures are taken from the *Annual Reports*. Other figures are from the Principals' Papers and *College Lists*. All refer to full-time students in October each year, except that in the years after 1945, numbers continued to grow throughout the autumn and winter aş ex-servicemen secured release from the forces; for those years the later and higher figures are given. Full-time students are students pursuing a course of at least two terms. For recent years this definition is slightly at variance with that used by the UGC, which regards as full-time only those students who are pursuing courses for a full year of three terms.

2 In July 1943 the London School of Medicine for Women returned to London; in 1942 it accounted for 223 of the 517 students in the college.

3 The 1978 and subsequent figures include students from Saint Luke's College.

INDEX

203

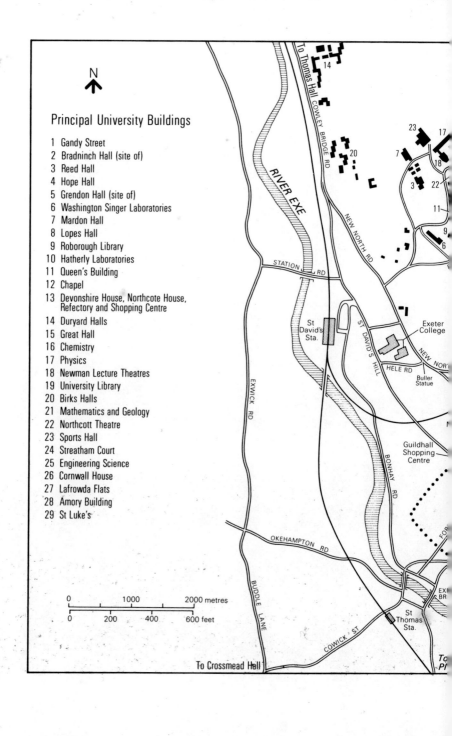

Principal University Buildings

1 Gandy Street
2 Bradninch Hall (site of)
3 Reed Hall
4 Hope Hall
5 Grendon Hall (site of)
6 Washington Singer Laboratories
7 Mardon Hall
8 Lopes Hall
9 Roborough Library
10 Hatherly Laboratories
11 Queen's Building
12 Chapel
13 Devonshire House, Northcote House,
   Refectory and Shopping Centre
14 Duryard Halls
15 Great Hall
16 Chemistry
17 Physics
18 Newman Lecture Theatres
19 University Library
20 Birks Halls
21 Mathematics and Geology
22 Northcott Theatre
23 Sports Hall
24 Streatham Court
25 Engineering Science
26 Cornwall House
27 Lafrowda Flats
28 Amory Building
29 St Luke's